JN
3971
A58
H4
1971

Heidenheimer,
Arnold J.

The governments of
Germany

29284 -2

DATE			
DEC 1 2 1984			
JAN 3 1 1990			

The Governments of
GERMANY

The Governments of
GERMANY

THIRD EDITION

Arnold J. Heidenheimer
WASHINGTON UNIVERSITY

THE CROWELL
COMPARATIVE GOVERNMENT SERIES

THOMAS Y. CROWELL COMPANY · NEW YORK
ESTABLISHED 1834

Acknowledgment is gratefully made to Cornell University Press for per-
mission to reprint the excerpt, on pp. 179–80, from Gerhard Loewenberg,
Parliament in the German Political System. Copyright © 1967 by Cornell
University.

L. C. Card 74-136035
ISBN 0-690-34894-0
3 4 5
MANUFACTURED IN THE UNITED STATES OF AMERICA

TO THE MEMORY OF
OTTO KIRCHHEIMER,
1905–1965

EDITOR'S FOREWORD

In our time the study of comparative government constitutes one of many fields or specialties in political science. But it is worth recalling that the most distinguished political scientists of the ancient world would have had difficulty recognizing the present-day distinction between the study of comparative government and study in other subject areas of the discipline. Think of Plato, for example, whose works abound in references to the political systems of his own and earlier days. Or consider Aristotle, whose *Politics* and related writings were based on an examination of more than one hundred constitutions. Twenty centuries after Aristotle the comparative emphasis continued strong in the work of Montesquieu and Rousseau, among others. In the nineteenth century the comparative tradition entered upon a period of decline, but there are signs that the merits of comparative political analysis are once more gaining recognition. At many colleges and universities, the introductory course in political science is no longer focused exclusively on American government. The comparative approach—in politics, in law, in administration—is becoming increasingly important in the political science curriculum.

This book, one of a series, is designed to reflect that approach without, however, marking a sharp departure from the substance and method of most comparative government courses. Thus most of the books in the series deal with one national government. Several volumes, however, deal with more than one government, and the approach of the entire series is distinctly comparative in at least two senses. In the first place, almost all of the books include material descriptive of other political systems, especially that of the United States. In addition, the books follow a common outline, so far as possible, that is designed to promote comparative treatment. Of course, there is nothing to keep the instructor or student from treating a particular governmental system in isolation, if he chooses to do so. On the other hand, his lectures on political institutions and functions can be as comparative as he wishes.

A further advantage of this series is that each volume has been written by a distinguished scholar and authority in the field; each author is personally and professionally familiar with the political system he treats. Finally, the separate books make it possible for the instructor to design his course in accordance with his own interest or the interests of his students. One book may be substituted for another or any book put aside for one semester without affecting the others. The books, in short, unlike most one-volume texts, give the instructor maximum freedom in organizing his course. This freedom will be virtually unlimited as the forthcoming titles in this series complete a survey of representative governments of the world.

But to return to Aristotle once again, it remains true that the best judges of the feast are not the cooks but the guests. I have tried to indicate why, in my view, the recipe for the series is a good one. Let all those who teach comparative government, and all those who take courses in that field, proceed to judge the books for themselves.

ARNOLD A. ROGOW

PREFACE

This third edition of *The Governments of Germany* is presented to students and colleagues in the expectation that German politics in the 1970's will continue to range high among the interests of students of comparative politics. Where else in Europe is there a party system that has changed as much as the West German one? What other system elected to both the presidency and the chancellorship politicians with the unusual political histories of Gustav Heinemann and Willy Brandt? Where else can the explosive dynamics of expanding educational systems be examined in a frame of reference like that provided by East and West Germany? Where else are the linkages between "domestic" and "interstate" politics as fascinating? For instance, who would care to predict which parts of the audience at the 1972 Olympics in Munich will cheer for the East and West German teams—and why?

Readers of the present edition will find that I have revised and rewritten the text very extensively, even while retaining the basic organization of previous editions. In attempting to keep ahead of developing relations between the two German states, I have reorganized particularly the latter portion of the book in order to maximize the comparative contrast and interrelationships. Several new chapters have been added or substituted for earlier ones, and I would like to draw attention to these.

Thus in Chapter Five, the federal election campaign of 1969 which culminated in Willy Brandt's selection as chancellor is utilized as a framework for examining continuities and changes in West German voting behavior. This election was important because it ended twenty years of Christian Democratic dominance of the federal government. But it also marked the rebuff of challengers such as the National Democrats, the loosening of loyalties within the Catholic urban sector, and a new alliance between the SPD and FPD. Its lessons should help one to anticipate the outcome of the next election, which might come in 1973 or quite possibly before then, if the Brandt government's majority becomes too thin because of splintering within the FDP.

As the West German party system approaches more closely the "two-party" model, political science students in countries such as the United States may become relatively more interested in assessing, say, how West German mechanisms permit relatively effective and uniform administration in a federal system. Hence, the structure of the Federal Republic's tax system, the nature of planning processes, and the problems of urban and regional coordination are scrutinized in Chapters Seven and Eight. Elsewhere, characteristics of the educational systems in both East and West are examined in relation to the policies that helped shape them.

Ralf Dahrendorf's well-known complaint that too many Germans shy away from political conflict has certainly become less generally applicable in recent years. Conflict that used to be externalized along an East-West axis has developed more within society along generational lines. The challenge to established authority has erupted even among backbenchers in the Bundestag, but as elsewhere it has been especially accentuated within universities. These developments and the related socialization phenomena are given special attention in Chapter Ten. Both elements unique in German educational tradition and stratification patterns, as well as the ideological repercussions of the division of Germany, make the relationship between education policy and generational revolt particularly interesting in the German setting.

And, finally, the German Problem! It is not likely to be resolved in the near future, but at least it has come to be structured differently. West and East German heads of government have met, Bonn is establishing new relations with the Soviet Union, and the goal of reunification has been rapidly deflated. The changing relations between the populations and governments of the two German states are traced and explained in Chapters Eleven and Twelve, and documented in the Appendix with reference to the especially important developments of the summer of 1970.

The late Otto Kirchheimer, to whom this volume is dedicated, was a friend and colleague to whom I owe much, and I am happy that his memory has remained alive. For their valuable suggestions and criticisms, which have been taken into account in the preparation of the third edition, I am particularly indebted to Gerard Braunthal, Gerhard Loewenberg, Donald Kommers, Frieder Naschold, Wolf Dieter Narr, Uwe Schleth, and Kurt Shell. And for their patient and valuable assistance with research and editorial preparation, I am grateful to Michael Libal and Martin Baach.

December, 1970   A. J. H.

BIOGRAPHICAL NOTATIONS

At the end of each chapter, except the last, is a short bibliography of items particularly relevant to the subjects covered. There, as well as in the footnotes, frequently cited political science journals have been abbreviated as follows: *APSR–American Political Science Review; FA–Foreign Affairs; JP–Journal of Politics; PSQ–Political Science Quarterly; PVS–Politische Vierteljahresschrift; WP–World Politics; WPQ–Western Political Quarterly.*

In recent years, a convenient tool for following current German affairs has become available in the form of *The German Tribune* (Hamburg, 1962), a weekly English translation of articles from the German press. Its use is recommended.

CONTENTS

PART ONE

GERMANY: ITS HISTORY, PEOPLE, AND SOCIETIES

1

The Molding of
Modern Germany

THE LONG ROAD TO UNIFICATION

An understanding of the tumultous character of much twentieth-century German political experience requires some appreciation of the complex political history of the country and its people. The existence of a German state, characterized by a central government and a uniform splotch of color within definite boundaries on a map, has been, historically speaking, a very short-term phenomenon. When Hitler came to power in 1933 with dreams of subjecting all Europe to German rule, Germany itself had existed in this form for only two generations. For centuries before that, from the Middle Ages right into the nineteenth century, Germany consisted merely of those areas of central Europe whose inhabitants spoke one or another of the German dialects. They had no common flag, no common rulers, and not much in the way of shared history. This situation was in marked contrast to that of most other countries of northern and western Europe, particularly England and France, where a feeling of national identity had been fostered by many centuries of rule by powerful kings who had imposed uniform systems of law and administration.

The common political traditions that Germans could look back upon were remote in time, such as the heritage presumed to have been left by the old Germanic tribes Tacitus had described. In these early German communities there was little in the way of organized government, the settlement of breaches of the law being left to the person injured and his near relatives. There was an emphasis on liberty, but in the peculiar autarchic sense that any man had a right to freedom if he was strong enough to defend his rights by himself. This old Germanic tradition was established in pre-Christian times and continued to be powerful into the Middle

Ages when it was superseded by legal and other institutions based on Roman influences.

A second German political tradition looked back to the unity Germans had enjoyed within the latter-day Roman Empire, particularly under Charlemagne. This tradition emphasized the bonds that—through institutions like Christianity, the inheritance of Roman law, and a common European culture—tied Germany to the Western and the Latin world. Indeed, German princes inherited the nominal leadership of the remnants of the old Roman Empire (First Reich), within which the German areas remained very loosely held together until the time of Napoleon. The emperorship rotated among various German princes and electors until the fifteenth century, when it was finally bequeathed as an empty relic to the Hapsburgs, rulers of Austria.

The decay of the imperial power led to the decentralization of political power and to the complex sets of loyalty typical of the feudal structure, with prelates, free cities, princes, and even minor nobility carving out their own realms. By the thirteenth century there were ninety-three ecclesiastical and fourteen lay princes. A century later there were forty-four lay princes, and their number continued to multiply as partitions took place between heirs. Many parts of the country were converted into tiny fragments of territory incapable of fulfilling the tasks of a state. During this time the free German cities, ruled by a wealthy merchant class, reached the pinnacle of their political and economic power. But changing trade routes, misdirected investments, and war led to their decline in the sixteenth century, thus preventing the further development of a strong German middle class. The weakness of the kings and lay political power allowed the church not only to claim for its clergy exemption from the criminal jurisdiction of the state but also the right to try laymen in its ecclesiastical courts. In England such courts were gradually integrated into the king's courts, where application of the Common Law discouraged localism. In Germany royal courts did not endure, and lay justice was administered by territorial judges applying laws of a strictly local character. When, later in the Middle Ages, lawyers trained in the Roman law entered on the scene, they did so as allies of the princes, rather than as servants of the Emperor.

Administration, too, evolved strictly on the local, or at most regional, level. In the smaller territories the prince often exercised a personal kind of rule, and the evolution of a professional official-dom was slow. Representative institutions contributed little in the way of a centralizing force. Originally the Imperial Reichstag consisted only of those great princes who elected the Emperor. In the fifteenth century the admission of lesser princes and free towns gave this institution a somewhat greater representative character. But the great lords, the lesser princes, and the representatives of the towns met in separate colleges, with the effect that the Reichstag was both less representative and more divided than the English parliament. In this way German particularism manifested itself in a multiplicity of political institutions which for centuries defied effective integration. At the same time, the narrow outlook and lack of awareness of a common bond not only were obstacles to unification, but actually contributed to the formation of deep historical prejudices among the peoples of the different German states and regions.

The great social and economic changes which marked the gradual transition from a predominantly agricultural and feudal to a predominantly capitalist and urban society might yet have generated enough centralizing forces to bring some measure of unity to the German lands. But two factors prevented such a culmination: Germany became the storm center of a European ideological struggle of unprecedented dimensions; and her geographical position, which had allowed her cities to achieve such great prosperity, became more than ever before a great political handicap as her territories became a battleground for rival foreign armies. The Reformation constituted a revolution rending the Christian web that had maintained a European cultural unity, despite feudal particularism. It superimposed on regional and dynastic division schisms based on divergent faiths. The paradox that Luther united Germans as no one before him had—both religiously, in the wake of his movement, and culturally, by establishing a uniform style of written German—while also leaving a heritage of denominational strife which virtually split Germans in two, is characteristic of the contradictory historical development of Germany.

For the cause of German unity and the development of German liberalism, the Reformation had disastrous consequences.

Its effect on the rulers was less significant than on the ruled. Much to Luther's annoyance, his followers were not content with only breaking theological ties to Rome, but in many regions sought to convert the movement into a large-scale social revolution. A peasant rising of unprecedented proportions was initially successful in large sections of southwest Germany, and many princes were forced to accept reforms such as the abolition of serfdom, the lowering of taxes, and the right of the people to elect their own parsons. But, although vastly superior in numbers to the princes, who lacked standing armies, the peasants suffered from a severe lack of discipline. Their cause was already on the decline when they were bitterly attacked by Luther himself, who called them "murderers and robbers who must be stabbed, smashed or strangled, and should be killed as mad dogs." Increasingly, the emphasis of Lutheranism on the freedom of the spirit gave way to new dogmas and rites and a new, bigoted priesthood. Moreover, Luther's interpretation of the Sermon on the Mount— to the effect that every ruling power, whether tyrannical or not, was ordained by God and hence to be obeyed—placed a heavy political mortgage on German Protestantism. It led to the development of separate state churches, each recognizing the suzerainty of the local prince and becoming so identified with the prevailing social and political order that they opposed manifestations of liberalism with misplaced fervor and remained insulated from the misery which plagued the lower classes as a result of war and economic change.

The struggles carried on between princes and Emperor in the aftermath of the Reformation brought Germany to a new low ebb of impoverishment and humiliation, and her once proud cities declined. In the early seventeenth century the Hapsburgs made themselves temporary masters over most of an exhausted Germany. But the wars continued as the more powerful rulers of Sweden and France intervened, and for decades foreign armies ravaged the German lands. When the Thirty Years' War came to a close in 1648 Germany was as divided as ever, with power distributed between weak princes and an impotent Emperor.

However, while foreigners lorded over Germans, at least one German ruling house, the electors of the eastern province of Brandenburg, were expanding their realm at the expense of their Slavic neighbors, whom they ruled with unrestrained absolutism. Building part on the crusading tradition of the Teutonic orders, these rulers gradually shaped the kingdom of Prussia, in which military priorities reigned supreme. In this impoverished and culturally backward area, a succession of brilliant rulers developed a style of politics new to Germany, with an efficient state machinery and an excellent army ruled by kings who knew how to harness their nobles to the task. Frederick the Great turned the Junkers (the East Prussian landed aristocracy) into administrators, spent the bulk of his resources on the army, and, while demanding great sacrifices from his subjects, engaged in a series of limited wars that moved Prussia into the ranks of the great powers, making it a rival to the Hapsburg Emperors for the political leadership of Germany. For a century and a half it was difficult to predict who would become the instrument of unification—the Hapsburgs, who were Catholic, cosmopolitan members of the traditional European "establishment," or the Prussians, who were upstart, disciplined, rough, and, together with their Junker adjutants, oriented much more toward the East than the West.

After the Napoleonic period, developments were greatly influenced by the rise of liberalism and nationalism, the two great political movements of nineteenth-century Germany. The Napoleonic storm swept away most of the decrepit little dynasties, united them into new states, and, most important, gave Germans the first taste of those political rights which the middle classes in the Western countries had established. Feudal privileges of church and nobility were abolished; civil liberties and other Enlightenment ideas found their way into Germany and were warmly welcomed by the hitherto politically apathetic middle classes. But what had been won through revolution in France was imposed on Germany by a foreign administration. Later, when Prussia and Austria joined the Grand Alliance which sealed Napoleon's doom, the middle classes of most countries were ready to hail the Battle of Leipzig as signaling the birth of a new Germany.

However, when the Congress of Vienna returned most of the old rulers to their thrones, they still refused to ally themselves with a national movement they identified with bourgeois radicalism. Some of them granted constitutions, but in Prussia and Austria reaction remained dominant. The German Federation, under Austrian chairmanship, which succeeded the Empire was a sham, and the various customs unions had little impact. Nationalist agitation was left to the urban middle class, particularly to the professional class, who still formed a very small segment of a country whose total town population was not much greater than that of contemporary Paris. Their chance came, again as a consequence of outside initiative, when the Paris Revolution of 1848 touched off popular disturbances in Vienna, Berlin, and elsewhere, which the weak and vacillating regimes could not control. The rulers in most of the states were all but overthrown, and agreed to subordinate themselves to the authority of a national government.

The hour of German liberalism had struck, and several hundred delegates of the educated upper-middle classes met in Frankfurt to draw up a national constitution. But their opportunity slipped away as the delegates became lost in rhetoric, argued whether to offer the position of constitutional monarch to Austria or Prussia, waxed indignant when Czechs, Poles, and Danes sought to claim national rights for themselves as well, and lost contact with the German masses. This allowed the princes to reestablish themselves, so that when the Frankfurt Parliament finally offered the German Emperorship to King Frederick William of Prussia, he turned it down as a "jester's cap lined in red." The few radical members of Parliament who continued to claim power in Frankfurt were chased out by Prussian and Austrian troops. Reactionaries breathed a sigh of relief. In Frankfurt, the great German philosopher Schopenhauer enthusiastically sent his opera glasses to the officer directing the mop-up from a nearby roof and deeded money to the families of Prussian troops who had participated in restoring order.

Twenty years later, a Prussian king did deign to accept the Imperial crown. Speaking in 1871 at the field headquarters for his successful campaign against France, King William agreed to respond to "the unanimous call of the princes and free cities to create the German Reich . . . and to reestablish the Imperial crown." Significantly, he accepted the commission from the princes and not from his subjects. The political happenings of the two previous decades were crucial for this culmination. These included the expansion of Prussian political power in North

Germany, the gradual rapprochment between the nationally oriented middle classes and the ruling forces of militarist-aristo-
cratic Prussia, the deathblow to Austrian ambitions delivered in
the brief Austro-Prussian War of 1866, and the subsequent creation of a North German Confederation. The Franco-German
War merely served to arouse the patriotic sentiment which swept
the reluctant South German states (except Austria) into the
Imperial fold. This development followed exactly the blueprint
of Otto von Bismarck, who had risen from a provincial East
Prussian background to become chief minister of Prussia and,
through immensely skillful use of the forces of diplomacy, military
power, and political blackmail, the real creator of the Second
German Reich.

Bismarck's influence continued to be dominant for another two
decades, during which he firmly established the constitutional
traditions of the Empire and indirectly influenced those of subsequent regimes. His genius synthesized the contradictory elements in the German political tradition. How did it prove possible
to reconcile German regional diversity and the continued existence of most of the smaller kingdoms and principalities with
Prussia's desire for strong unified leadership? Bismarck devised
a federal structure that gave the various states equal standing
but assured Prussian dominance by providing that Prussia's chief
minister would automatically become Imperial Chancellor. How
to reconcile the middle and lower classes' demands for political
equality with the upper classes' insistence on the retention of
their special privileges? Bismarck responded with a clever dual
policy whereby elections to the national legislature, the Reichstag,
were held on the basis of universal suffrage, while the Prussian
state legislature, which shaped the lion's share of domestic legislation affecting most Germans, retained an archaic electoral system
that allowed the reactionaries to remain in control. In like manner,
the Chancellor reconciled demands for constitutionalism with the
autocratic traditions of Prussia by allowing the constitution to give
the illusion of popular influence on the government while in fact
the real decision-making powers remained lodged in the hands
of those tried servants of hierarchical authority, the civil service
and the army.

The Reich Constitution of 1871 combined some political institutions of the "old" Empire with elements of the Constitution of the North German Federation of 1866, parts of which were taken over intact. The Emperor's powers had a dual basis: as Emperor he controlled foreign and military affairs and appointed the Imperial Chancellor; as King of Prussia he ruled over the domestic affairs of his state, as did the other German princes. The integrating function within the federal system was carried out by the *Bundesrat,* composed of delegates from the various states. This body, under dominant Prussian influence, met in secret and had extensive powers both in the legislative and executive areas. (In effect, it combined most of the functions that in the United States are divided among the cabinet, the Senate, and the Governors' Conference.) Its president, the Imperial Chancellor, who held his job by virtue of Imperial confidence, while being at the same time the only minister responsible to the popularly elected Reichstag, was the pivot about which the German constitutional system revolved.

This extremely complex structure functioned with reasonable efficiency as long as the key position was occupied by its architect. But in its relations with parliament the Imperial government was involved in strenuous constitutional conflict from the very start. For in pursuit of his policy of killing parliamentarianism through the parliament, the Iron Chancellor sought both to limit the Reichstag's powers to nonessentials and to harass and discomfit the legislative parties so that they would submit to his wishes. He largely succeeded in depriving the Reichstag of ministers who could be held responsible for policy, and he almost succeeded in depriving the Reichstag of its most basic power, that of approving the budget. Even so, he frequently bullied the legislature into voting military appropriations for as long as seven years at a time. In this way the legislature was placed in a position where it could neither affect the tenure of the Chancellor and his ministers, nor effectively hamper passage of the most important pieces of legislation. Furthermore, the constitution prohibited simultaneous membership in the government and the legislature, thus setting a legal barrier to the introduction of parliamentary government. In contrast to the British system, where ministers sit amongst their parliamentary colleagues on the front bench of the government party, the members of the government in Germany sat on a raised rostrum, looking down on the semicircle of deputies.

Because of his clever and unscrupulous manipulations, Bismarck was never matched against the whole of the Reichstag in his greatest political struggles, but always managed to isolate the parties in an attempt to crush them one at a time. He was ready to cooperate with almost any party in order to achieve his ends, but he usually destroyed them when they gained enough confidence to make strong demands. In turn, he collided with the Zentrum, representing the Catholics of West Germany, the Conservatives, representing the Prussian old guard, the National Liberals, representing the democratic middle class, and the Social Democrats, representing the Marxist-influenced working class. His successive campaigns against the Catholics and the Socialists involved an all-out use of police power, the suppression of meetings and newspapers, and the imprisonment of priests and party leaders. These attempts at suppression backfired. The two parties whom the Chancellor accused of "opposing national development by international methods and fighting against the nation state" were able to resist, not because of aid from the Vatican or the Socialist International but because of the stubborn cohesion of their adherents, who greatly increased their party voting turnout in the face of official repression. But on the whole Bismarck did succeed in intimidating the parties. By limiting them to ineffective debate, he prevented them from forming effective competition to the administrative elite. By blocking their leaders' roads to public office, he prevented them from recruiting the best political talents of their time.

To understand German politics under the Empire it is necessary also to understand the prevailing political goals and the extent to which they were accepted. It might have been expected that nationalist fervor would ebb after the achievement of unification. But Germany's rulers would not have it so. They could not resist the temptation of averting criticism of their policies by keeping the attention of both the educated elite and ordinary folk fixed on the promises implicit in a policy of national expansion. Talk of German colonies, German preparedness, and the superiority of German culture were the order of the day. New generations were inculcated with memories of the Franco-German War, and under Emperor William II a vigorous start was made on the creation of a navy which would eventually rival Britain's. The virtue of war was the subject of sustained glorification. Whereas earlier philosophers like Kant had written of the hope of achieving a state of perpetual peace, now generals like Moltke attested that "perpetual peace is a dream and an unlovely one at that, while war is a link in the divine order of the world. In it are developed man's purest virtues, courage, faithfulness to duty and the willingness to make sacrifices. Without war the world would sink in the swamp of materialism." Such sentiments were expressed outside of Germany as well, but nowhere else were they so well received as in a country permeated with militaristic influences through institutions like the reserve officer corps and the martial figure of the Emperor himself.

Consensus on national goals was, however, far from complete. Sentiment in South and West Germany remained skeptical of the military ambitions of the Prussian rulers. Catholics found it difficult to identify with a dynasty which had allowed their persecution. Radicals poked fun at the self-conscious posturing of members of the official establishment. Historians like Mommsen bemoaned a "miscarriage of national feeling." Marxists resisted demands for the strengthening of national power by calling for international solidarity of the workers. Each of these groups, as well as the various factions supporting the government, developed complex philosophical systems to buttress their political positions. These ideologies or *Weltanschauungen* did much to shape political movements and at the same time to lend intellectual reinforcement to the divisions that still existed among the German people despite the cloak of unity their rulers imposed. The ideologies of the more extreme left and right promoted militancy, but at the center the middle-class liberals reacted in the main by retreating from active participation in politics. Writing at the turn of the century, Friedrich Naumann noted that forty years earlier a bond had still tied the educated classes to liberalism. "But this tradition was lost as Bismarck's greatness crushed liberalism. The majority of the educated . . . believed in the greatness and power of the single great man. . . . The disdain with which Bismarck treated the parliamentarians was taken over as though it was a permanently valid value judgment. And as Bismarck was forced aside and then died . . . a great vacuum remained in the intellectual conscious-ness of the educated German. He fell back into the apolitical attitudes of the eighteenth century."

Thus, by the time that socio-economic developments came in-creasingly to favor the German middle classes in terms of wealth and numbers, their political ideas were adulterated and they had lost their self-confidence. In England, where the difficult stages of industrial "takeoff" had been completed in the early nineteenth century, the self-confident middle classes could press gradually toward a political victory over the aristocracy. In Germany, on the other hand, the middle classes looked back on a string of political defeats and became increasingly worried about a work-ing class that was only then being exposed to the hardships and strains through which the British workers had passed earlier. By playing the middle classes off against the Marxist-led workers, Bismarck's regime managed to retain absolute political control.

Though it arrived belatedly, German industrialization assumed tremendous momentum in the decades after unification. Backed by a dynamic banking system, built on the fruit of intense scien-tific and technical research, and developed within tight cartel structures, German industry grew phenomenally on all fronts. In the four decades after 1870 German iron production increased tenfold, surpassing Britain's output along the way. In the course of this period Germany was transformed from a land where two out of three people lived in villages and hamlets to one where three out of five lived in urban, predominantly industrialized centers. The Ruhr developed into a mighty arsenal of cartelized heavy industry, ready to forge the Emperor's weapons. The new industries demanded and got high tariff protection, while the small tradesmen were pushed increasingly to the side. These changes did place the hierarchical order under great strain, but buttressed by a phalanx of bureaucratic, academic, and military supporters, it held fast without having to make too many concessions, except to the new captains of industry, who were granted places within the ruling class. Kaiser Wilhelm II, who assumed personal con-trol after Bismarck was eased out of office in 1890, was still basi-cally ruling a great industrial nation much as his forefathers had imposed discipline on the ignorant peasants of a frontier province.

Outwardly, German society presented a picture of sobriety and orderliness. Its members knew their place according to their titles and ranks, whether as reserve officers, commercial counselors, or assistant deputy street cleaners. But in the twilight zones new forces were generating strength. The Socialist-led working class, embittered by its exclusion from decision-making, sought to beat the state at its own game by developing a supremely disciplined political organization, drawing on those same qualities of sacrifice and courage which the militarists had idealized. Growing stronger with every election, until they received almost one-third of the vote in 1912, the Socialists represented a vast unintegrated political element, which was divided between its commitment to revolution and its eagerness to display its political responsibility, if only given the chance. Among the artisans and shopkeepers a movement based on political anti-Semitism found considerable response. Despite the Emperor's friendship with leading Jewish capitalists, many of his subjects and even his court chaplain participated in the movement, though it was not nearly as strong as in Austria and some other countries. Elsewhere, too, dissatisfaction was rife. In East Prussia the great landowners were alarmed at their worsening economic position and sought to compensate by retaining political power on the basis of the reactionary Prussian election law. There was strong pressure to extend the vast welfare program, including health insurance and social security which Bismarck had introduced. But efforts to introduce reforms from above, even through an incorruptible civil service, lost much of their value, because the masses were not allowed to feel that they had won victories for themselves.

The acid test of the political system which Emperor William II developed on Bismarck's foundations came in World War I, unleashed in good part by hazardous German diplomacy. At first the system and the German population lived up to the Emperor's highest expectations. Regional jealousies disappeared as the nation dedicated itself to the national cause. The Reichstag voted huge military credits with barely a murmur. Even most of the Socialists gave wholehearted support to the war effort, rationalizing their disavowal of previous commitments to international workers' solidarity with the assertion that they were aiding the cause of progress by helping a conservative regime to defeat an even more reactionary one, that of the Russian tsar. But as the

German victory failed to eventuate, the tensions which the Bismarckian system had sought to submerge came to the surface. Liberal and Catholic politicians asked themselves why they were supporting an autocratic regime against countries whose governments had granted their citizens the privileges of parliamentary government and ministerial responsibility. The workers, tired of providing cannon fodder and bearing the brunt of economic sacrifices, were encouraged by their leaders to ask why they were dying for an Emperor who did not deem them worthy of an equal vote in the Prussian legislature. Awkwardly, the Emperor made promises of reform, but they came too late. Under the impact of unceasing Allied pressure, morale on the home front sagged noticeably. Then, in November, 1918, inevitable defeat was hastened by the political unrest in German cities, which quickly developed into demonstrations demanding bread, an end to hostilities, and the overthrow of the regime. As the revolutionary spirit spread to units of the army and navy, German leaders saw the ground slip beneath their feet. The army high command, which had indirectly ruled Germany since the outbreak of war, advised the Emperor that further resistance was useless and suggested that he seek refuge in neutral Holland. Thus did the German Empire crumble.

THE WEIMAR REPUBLIC, 1918–33

After the downfall of the Emperor's regime, Germans were suddenly presented with the opportunity to follow the dominant political tradition of the West by establishing democratic political institutions. Surprisingly, the opportunity caught most German political parties unprepared. Even the progressive groups had prepared only piecemeal reform plans looking at most toward a constitutional monarchy. There were virtually no republicans. Earlier liberal democratic sentiment had atrophied or been stunted. Of all the German parties only one carried the word "democratic" in its name, and this by its program was pledged to achieve a socialist revolution. To most Germans domestic democrats seemed like political animals out of the dim pre-Bismarckian past. They thought of great-grandfathers who in the early nineteenth century had cursed into their beer at the arrogance of the local prince or had climbed grandiloquently onto make-shift barricades in the picture-book revolutions of 1848.

In the interval, most educated German opinion had drawn broad philosophical conclusions from limited historical experience, so that they saw in the decay of liberal movements proof that democratic forms were not suited to German politics. The experiences of the Western countries were dismissed as inapplicable. The German upper-middle class tended to share the snobbish ethos of the old ruling classes, who looked askance at Britain as a country of traders where even the nobility had accepted mercantile values. Parliamentary institutions were viewed as suitable for the compromise of sordid economic interests, but not adequate for a nation of poets and philosophers. As Thomas Mann wrote in 1918: "Away with the foreign and repulsive slogan 'democratic.' The mechanical democratic political institutions of the West will never take root here."

The dominant influence of the tradition of philosophical idealism that derived from Hegel, depreciating the significance of objective phenomena, was instrumental in causing Germans to reject Western political values. Western concepts of liberty, which stressed the absence of checks on the visible exercise of freedom of speech and assembly, were dismissed as vulgar and superficial. *German* freedom was conceived as the freedom of the inner man to engage in poetic flights of the imagination and daring metaphysical speculation. Its exercise depended little on the will of the official legislator, except that the passions aroused under a popular form of government were likely to disturb the tranquillity required by the creative mind. Moreover, the sharp class cleavages in German society had perpetrated exaggerated notions of the intellectual and moral weakness of the average voter, whose voice would be decisive under a democratic system. Although Germany had achieved a higher degree of literacy than any country, much educated opinion—the crucial elite who controlled German administration, culture, and education—expected that "the masses" would give free rein to their low instincts and install a political system which would smash the proud achievements of German culture. Conservative German constitutional lawyers argued that if a people sought to exercise sovereign rights through a legislature, power would inevitably fall into the hands of parties and factions which would corrupt the national will by tearing it into little pieces.

It was a tradition molded by such concepts that had to be overcome by the politicians entrusted with the task of drafting Germany's first republican constitution. Their meeting place, Weimar, the city of Goethe and Schiller, was symbolic of the democrats' attempt to identify themselves with an earlier, pre-Bismarckian tradition which, if not democratic, was at least humanistic. Significantly, they did not meet in Hamburg, Berlin, or one of the other large cities where revolutionary skirmishes had actually taken place and where radical sections of the working-class movement were strongly in favor of emulating the Bolshevik precedent set in Russia. Actually the Socialist government which took over responsibility for maintaining order did set up workers' soviets, but, though Marxist in programmatic commitment, the majority of the Socialist leaders had come to accept gradualist aims. They opposed the radicals' suggestion that they establish a proletarian dictatorship and initiate a sweeping revision of the social and economic systems, which could only have been achieved through the use of force. In any case, when the radicals sought to enact their plans, they were suppressed by fellow Socialists with the aid of regular troops and reactionary volunteers. This led to a division within the German working-class movement and the beginning of that tradition of hostility between German Socialists and Communists which was to contribute to the downfall of the Weimar Republic.

Having split with their own left wing, the majority of the Socialists cooperated in drafting the constitution with the two other parties which by 1919 had accepted the republic—the progressive German Democratic party (DDP) and the Catholic Center party (Zentrum). That the constitution was to bear a primarily liberal democratic, rather than Socialist, character was borne out by the fact that the drafting work was entrusted to a Democratic party constitutional law professor. There was wide agreement that the constitution should establish a parliamentary system, but little in the way of German traditions to build on. Looking abroad, the drafters were attracted by the relative stability of British governments, but mistakenly attributed this to a constitutional balance of power between the king and Parliament. Thus they concentrated on creating a constitutional figure, the President, who would take the place of the British monarch as the authoritative balancing force and help shape order out of the diversity of opinions represented in the powerful and popularly elected legislature.

The difference between the Weimar Constitution and its predecessor is reflected in the changed sequence of sections in the two documents. In the 1871 document the section dealing with the princes' organ, the Bundesrat, was followed by those dealing with the executive and the popularly elected Reichstag. In the Weimar Constitution, the section dealing with the popularly elected legislature was placed first. The Reichstag was given the predominant share of legislative power and, in contrast to earlier practice, the power of approving and dismissing the Chancellor and his ministers. Second place, but potentially equal power, was given to the President as head of state, who was elected directly by the people so that his mandate would be as strong as that of the Reichstag. He was also given the power to nominate the Chancellor, dissolve the Reichstag, and rule through emergency decree. Closely linked to the sections dealing with the presidency came those dealing with the political executive, the Chancellor and the cabinet. The cabinet was viewed as a link between President and parliament and thus made dependent on both institutions. Finally, in last place, were the sections dealing with the considerably weakened federal element within the constitution. As befitted a constitution with a strong centralist bias, the second chamber, the *Reichsrat,* which included representatives of the *Land* (state) governments, was endowed with extremely limited powers, mainly of an administrative nature.

Structurally, the experiment with the creation of a dual authority, Reichstag and President, neither of which carried executive responsibility, was a dubious one. The two Weimar Presidents were distrusted by large segments of the population. Friedrich Ebert (1919–25), because he was a Socialist ex-saddler, Otto von Hindenburg (1925–34), because he was a conservative ex-general. Most precarious of all was the constitutional position of the cabinet, the most important organ in shaping the political prestige of the regime. For the cabinet was given little power to maintain itself against a demanding legislature, and successive ministries found themselves at the mercy of either the President's

pleasure, or shifting legislative majorities, or both. The weakness
of the cabinet, moreover, was directly related to the functioning
of the party system, which the constitution's drafters did not
adequately take into account. To stay in power, cabinets had to
retain the confidence of a legislative majority, in other words,
the confidence of parties. Parties were thus the supremely important institutions, but the constitution neither recognized nor regulated their position. The stability of the larger democratic parties
was threatened by the ease with which splinter groups could sap
their strength through the prevailing system of proportional representation that allowed even minute parties to gain parliamentary
representation. Finally, the ease with which anticonstitutional
parties could contribute to the overthrow of successive governments made the position of the parties supporting the regime
increasingly difficult.

In many respects the Weimar Constitution was a very progressive document. But its drafters lacked sufficient understanding of
practical political relationships, and too often—as in their treatment of civil rights—they tried to face in two directions at once.
Compared to the Constitution of the Second Reich, which had
left civil rights entirely to the Land constitutions, the Weimar
charter pledged the national government to protect the liberties
of the citizen. Then, after enumerating civil rights admirably,
they added another article (Article 48) giving the President
power to cancel the same guarantees if the public security was
threatened. The same sweeping article also provided the President
with power to suspend large parts of the constitution, by allowing
him to direct the Chancellor to enact legislation during crises
without even the support of the Reichstag.

The Weimar Constitution might nevertheless have served as
the basis for a stable democratic state if subsequent political
conditions had been more favorable. As it was, the antidemocratic groups were given an initial advantage by the fact that
the democratic parties, who acted as midwives to the constitution, also had to take responsibility for accepting what practically
all Germans regarded as a humiliating and ruthless peace treaty.
"Versailles" became a club for the extreme nationalist groups
which soon organized amidst the chaos caused by civil strife and
economic hardship, followed by ruinous inflation. By arguing

that "traitors" on the home front had caused defeat by stabbing the army in the back, the extremists won the cooperation of many reactionary officers, who had lost economic position and social status as a result of the virtual disbanding of the German army. (The peace treaty provided for a *Reichswehr* or regular army of only 100,000.) The nationalist fanatics showed their determination by assassinating some of the most prominent of the new republic's statesmen, including the ministers Erzberger and Rathenau, who belonged respectively to the Center and Democratic parties. Further difficulties for the regime were caused by the French occupation of the Rhineland and the need to pay large reparations to the victor nations, in addition to having to renounce claims to all German colonies.

By the mid-twenties, however, the regime was beginning to gain stability amid worldwide prosperity. The working class reaffirmed its support of the moderate constitutional policies of the Social Democrats, who remained the most solid backbone of the regime. The SPD (Sozialdemokratische Partei Deutschlands) discarded much of its semirevolutionary ideology and, together with the dominant trade union movement with which it was affiliated, supplied the bulk of the mass electorate, local officials, and grass-roots support that sustained the regime among the people. From its ranks also came most of the volunteers who joined the pro-republican organizations which kept the Nazi and Communist street gangs in check. The other of the two original "Weimar" or pro-republican parties proved less stable. Most of the German Democratic party's middle-class voters deserted it in the course of the twenties, mainly in favor of two more conservative parties—the moderate right-wing German Peoples' party (DVP) and the nationalist-Protestant German National Peoples' party (DNVP), whose attitude toward the republic was much more critical. Gradually these two parties shared in assuming governmental responsibility, and the DVP even produced the single outstanding parliamentary figure of the Weimar Republic, Gustav Stresemann, who as foreign minister went furthest in seeking to strengthen German ties to the Western world, particularly to France. Cabinets including representatives of these parties alternated throughout the twenties. Even the victory in the 1925 election of Hindenburg, the right-wing parties' candidate for the presidency, caused no grave concern, for the venerable ex-general pledged himself to support the republican constitution.

But the regime proved unable to radiate the political magnetism necessary to convert either its grudging supporters or its open enemies, or to solve through political means the social and economic problems which served to keep Germans deeply divided among themselves. Some of its most serious weaknesses lay within the governmental structure. Large numbers of the civil servants and judges carried over from the preceding regime served the republic with questionable loyalty. Relying on the sacrosanct German tradition of civil service tenure and on the lack of qualified candidates for high office from outside the old ruling classes, these officials felt free to flaunt their reactionary commitments. Right-wing agitators, libelers of republican politicians, and virulent anti-Semites could pursue their aims with relative impunity, for the republic's courts were rarely severe with their kind. Even those clearly guilty of assisting Adolf Hitler in his attempt to initiate an overthrow of the government in Munich in 1923 were sentenced to only a few years' imprisonment. In the Reichswehr, which became an increasingly important political factor during the last years of the republic, officers with democratic sentiments were a distinct rarity. Outside these official circles, a considerable portion of the intellectuals allied themselves with a movement that called for a "conservative revolution" to end the party quarreling of Weimar and sought to replace the parliamentary system with some form of authoritarianism based on national solidarity.

But while considerable portions of the educated elite served as the republic's gravediggers, the most direct threats came from political movements that attracted large segments of the masses. Leading the groups which sought to destroy democracy through the use of democratic elections were the National Socialists and the Communists. Both recruited strong cores of members dedicated to the establishment, respectively, of Fascist and proletarian dictatorships. But, though well organized and able to agitate with relative impunity, these movements proved no serious threat during the period of prosperity. In 1928, the total anticonstitutional vote of these and similar movements was less than 15 per cent. (The Nazis polled only 2.6 per cent.) But the repercussions of the world depression aggravated the underlying economic and social tensions. The failure of the market mechanism seemed to lend support to those prophets of doom who had long predicted that both liberal democracy and capitalism were on their last legs. Large social groups became disaffected because of very severe grievances. Small businessmen felt themselves driven to ruin by the bankers and the cartels. Farmers rallied to use force to prevent foreclosures. Skilled artisans rebelled against the pressure to join the industrial proletariat or even the long line of the unemployed. Workers of all kinds lent a ready ear to radical exhortation, as the cutbacks in production cost them their jobs and the government's attempt to maintain balanced budgets cut into their meager unemployment benefits. University-trained intellectuals and technicians, unable to find responsible jobs, joined the antidemocratic forces in droves, and the universities became hotbeds of radicalism, mainly of the rightist kind. Finally, the disgruntled among the insecure lower-middle classes rallied in large numbers to the siren songs of the splinter groups and the totalitarian movements.

Under the resulting pressures, the party alliances which had supported the regime began to crumble. Interest groups within the larger parties made irreconcilable demands and frequently split off into special interest parties. On election day the voter was wooed by as many as twenty parties. The air was full of party strife as policies based on economic interest calculations were superimposed on older programs based on ideological traditions. If there was little agreement on substantive questions, there was even less on procedural ones. Extremist groups espoused a variety of radical solutions. Among the larger parties, the DNVP and the DVP began to edge away from their earlier, partial commitment to the constitution and called for the creation of a presidential regime and other strong-man solutions. The workers shifted their strength from the Socialists to the Communists. But the biggest gains were made by the Nazis.

The real political crisis of the republic began with the 1930 elections, brought about by the inability of the democratic parties to agree on basic economic policies. Public support for both the right-wing and Nazi parties (the latter jumped from 12 to 107 seats) increased sharply, and these parties began to coalesce into a powerful anticonstitutional force. Viewed with suspicion by the moderate left and denied the cooperation of the right, Center party Chancellor Heinrich Bruening sustained his government even without the support of a parliamentary majority, as a result of President Hindenburg's delegation of powers to rule by emergency decree. From that point on, government on the basis of democratic legitimation ceased, and administration based on a negative impasse began. The decrees issued by the Bruening government remained in force, not because they were accepted by the legislature, but because the Social Democrats dared not vote to annul them for fear that the Chancellor's resignation would lead to new elections in which the antidemocratic parties would make still greater gains.

On the other hand, this possibility did not frighten some of Hindenburg's more conservative advisers, who hoped to "tame" the Nazis and to make use of them for their own purposes. The goal of this "kitchen cabinet," supported by many groups among the industrial, agrarian, and military elites, was to replace parliamentary democracy by an authoritarian government and to embark on a more active foreign policy, including a policy of rearmament. Since Bruening's relations with the extreme right had steadily worsened, he was forced out of office by Hindenburg at the end of May, 1932. His successor, von Papen, tried to win the support of the Nazis by dissolving the Reichstag and holding new elections. Nothing could have helped the Nazis more. In the elections of July, 1932, they became by far the strongest party, capturing 230 seats. However, they did not keep their part of the bargain and, forming a negative majority with the Communists, were able to prevent the creation of any government based on a stable parliamentary majority.

The prodemocratic parties ceased to be influential forces altogether. Widespread rioting, unceasing economic crisis, and virulent agitation by nationalist, Nazi, and Communist forces made the state's continued existence dependent on the limited power of the Reichswehr and the fading willpower of the aging President. Three possibilities were now open to the military-conservative groups around Hindenburg: they could form an alliance with the old democratic parties against the Nazi movement; they could create an openly dictatorial but basically conservative government which would suppress both the Nazis and democracy; or, lastly, they could form an alliance with Hitler in the hope of controlling him. The conservatives did not want to return to parliamentary democracy, on the one hand, or to risk a civil war against both extreme right and left, on the other. Ultimately, they chose the third solution. In the meantime, Hitler had realized that only a coalition with the conservative right would provide him with the chance to seize power.

Hitler proved extremely adept at playing up to the image which both the right-wing parties and the President wanted to form of him, that of a leader who would forget his more excessive commitments once entrusted with the mantle of authority. The DNVP supported his claim to the chancellorship and so did many of the President's military and civilian advisers, as well as many agrarian and industrial leaders. On January 30, 1933, Hitler was duly invested as the last Chancellor of the Weimar regime, which he had sworn to replace with a one-party dictatorship.

With the wisdom of hindsight, we can easily deduce that the German democratic system of the interwar period was not adequately prepared to sustain itself against the threat of totalitarian movements seeking to capture it from within. But can we pinpoint the faults? Was the constitutional system badly designed, or was distortion caused by the political forces which operated it? Were the electoral machinery and party leaders at fault, or were the Germans so hopelessly divided that neither leadership nor constitutional devices could save them? Was the republic doomed because of the Germans' lack of experience with self-government and lack of commitment to democratic values, or because powerful minority groups unscrupulously encouraged a demagogic leader's mad ambitions? Experts are still very much divided on the questions, but a number of statements can be made about the lessons of Weimar, especially as perceived by those Germans who sought to reinstate democracy after the Nazi regime had collapsed:

(1) The Germans' first national experiment with self-government occurred both under extraordinarily unfavorable circumstances and at a time when too many Germans were still too divided on too many basic political ends, and on how to achieve them. A basic prerequisite of parliamentary democracy is a wide consensus on national goals, or at least on acceptable alternatives.

This did not exist in Germany for most of the period of the republic.

(2) German political and interest-group organizations, and especially the leaders who guided them, were not well adapted to functioning within a democratic system. Unduly influenced by outdated ideological systems and/or narrow concern for special interests, they were unable to grow beyond their earlier subordinate positions and to produce leaders who could define, shape, and confront the larger issues. Even parties which were intellectually committed to democracy proved unable to redirect their energies from the effective criticism of an authoritarian state to the effective strengthening of a democratic state. On the other hand, the traditional affinity of the elites for an authoritarian form of government was reinforced by the sharpening of the social conflicts, especially between the industrialists and the workers. While the social democrats accepted parliamentary democracy as a starting point for further social reforms, the elites accepted it only as long as their own economic and social position would not be in danger.

(3) The Weimar Constitution was not well adapted to regulating the political system and, in part, contained the seeds of its own destruction. The ease with which methods contrary to the spirit of the constitution were legally invoked through use of emergency powers weakened the respect for rules and procedures. The creation of a strong presidency encouraged the legislature to act irresponsibly, while the cabinet's lack of political power led to executive instability and administrative irresponsibility. The legislature failed to evolve basic rules which would lead to meaningful decision-making within the parliamentary system. The liberal spirit of the constitution also led its defenders to display misguided tolerance toward the regime's open enemies.

(4) While the Nazi movement built its large popular support essentially on the chauvinism, gullibility, and short-sightedness of the German middle classes, it also found fertile ground among the frustrated and embittered German masses at large. It could not have developed momentum without the tolerance of large sections of the intellectual elite and the active support of influential power-holders, particularly among the industrial leaders. Unable to distinguish their distaste for democracy from the fear

of Communism, many in high economic and social positions in Germany gave the Nazis both the financial means and the cover of respectability needed for their swift rise from the gutter to the Chancellery.

NAZI TOTALITARIANISM

With Hitler's assumption of the chancellorship, Germany was rapidly coordinated into a totalitarian state and society and, eventually, into an armed camp for the subordination of other peoples. To emphasize the theme of national revival, the regime was called the Third Reich. In guiding its course, Hitler, as Fuehrer and dictator, aroused intensities of blind loyalty and immeasurable hatred matched by no other modern politician. He amazed the world and delighted most Germans by rapidly turning an economically listless, politically divided, and dispirited country into a prosperous, self-confident, and aggressive world power.

The economy was turned on essentially by a program of rapid rearmament and a few conspicuous public works programs. In contrast to similar attempts in other countries to stimulate the economy by government action, the overriding concern of the Nazis was not to raise the living standard of the masses but to enable Germany to wage wars of conquest. The masses were deceived by the extension of welfare programs and by an elaborate system of propaganda and symbolic gratifications that provided them with a sense of status and belonging. On the other hand, the regime produced such a staggering display of deliberate violations of basic human, individual rights that it overshadowed the dismal records of other totalitarian regimes.

Nazi Germany produced many variants of the characteristics usually associated with totalitarian dictatorships. Ideologically, the Nazi movement created initial appeal by exciting popular resentments and jealousies. It promised to protect a "downtrodden" Germany from the evil machinations of "international" Jewry, the "decadent" rapaciousness of Western democracies, and "subhuman" Marxists. The center of its crude philosophical basis was a melodramatically developed concept of race, proclaiming the Aryans (i.e., Germans) the master race and all other peoples destined to either subservience or extermination. History was seen as an unending struggle of races for survival. The German nation could avoid extinction only by fostering "racial purity" at home, and by becoming a world power and securing "living space" through wars of conquest in the East. This would also be the only way to solve Germany's economic problems and thereby to stabilize the new political system for "a thousand years." Thus, war and extermination of "racial enemies" lay at the heart of the Nazi doctrine, although this was not too openly advertised since most Germans would not have been willing to draw such extreme conclusions from the Nazi ideology. For the most part, the Nazis played on a more conventional nationalism.

The Nazi party was organized on a hierarchical principle and completely intertwined with the state machinery. It recognized neither constitution nor law, only the will of the leader. Leader and party in turn felt free to employ a system of police terror to achieve those ends which enticement and threats could not attain. Under the Fuehrer, the Nazi party and its allied organizations finally assumed complete control not only over the machinery of the state but also over communications and most social organizations, and they gained indirect control over the armed forces and all branches of the economy.

Adolf Hitler, the son of a minor Austrian official, had imbibed his violent racialism in the occult intellectual underworld of pre-war Vienna. After serving voluntarily in the wartime German armies, he joined a radical rightist group in Munich and soon took over its leadership. He displayed extraordinary speaking ability and was able to organize a mass movement that drew together the most diverse elements. The only common denominator in the movement was a violent hatred of liberalism, democracy, and socialism and a dissatisfaction with the existing social order. This dissatisfaction, expressed with unbridled militancy and violence, distinguished the movement from the older and more respectable groups of the extreme right. Nevertheless, "respectable" representatives of society and big business soon welcomed Hitler as another ally against the left in general and the labor movement in particular. For these people Hitler possessed one enormous attraction: he was the leader of a so-called workers' movement (the

National Socialist Workers' party), yet he did not threaten the existing economic and social privileges of the German elites; instead, he directed the energies of his movement toward a "national revolution" against the Weimar democracy and the settlement of Versailles.

In November, 1923, however, Hitler made a serious miscalculation. Despite their sympathy, the conservative elites were not yet ready to hand power over to the Nazi movement. The *coup d'etat* that sought to overthrow the Bavarian government in Munich as a prelude to a march on Berlin failed. But because of friends in high places (the Bavarian justice minister entered Hitler's cabinet a decade later), Hitler was given a prison sentence just long enough to permit him to write *Mein Kampf,* which was to become the movement's bible. During the mid-twenties the movement was reorganized and established roots all over Germany, building up an organization of several hundred thousand devoted members and activists in its tough fighting formations, the brown-shirted SA (*Sturmabteilung*) and the black-shirted SS (*Schutzstaffel*), the latter sworn to personal loyalty to the Fuehrer.

The defeat of the Munich putsch persuaded the Nazi leaders to abandon attempts at violent overthrow of the state and to concentrate instead on courting the military establishment and winning strength in electoral contests. As early as 1928, Joseph Goebbels, whose name later became a byword for propaganda lies, openly stated the party's intent: "We are going into the Reichstag in order to seize our supply of weapons in the very arsenal of democracy. We are becoming deputies only in order to use its own institutions to undermine the values of the system. If the democrats are so stupid as to reward us for this . . . with legislators' pay and free railroad tickets, that is their affair."

CONSOLIDATION

When he assumed the chancellorship, many conservative Germans believed that Hitler, under pressure from Hindenburg and other parties, would forget his extreme statements and settle down to rule together with the Nazi and conservative ministers who made up his cabinet. They failed to understand how fanatically he was committed to his program and underestimated his ruthless acumen. Confident that he could force the divided opposition to yield him complete power legally if he played his cards right, Hitler exploited Nazi control of the pressure and communications channels of the Reich and Prussian governments in an attempt to win an outright majority in the elections scheduled for March, 1933. Events played into his hands. In late February, a heroically demented Dutch anarchist, whom the Nazis used as an unwitting tool, set fire to the Reichstag building. The Nazis blamed this sensational act on the Communists, and demanded and received an emergency decree from the dazed President Hindenburg that allowed the Chancellor to suspend civil liberties and to take over police control in *Laender* (states) where "threats to public security were not being adequately met." This allowed the Nazis to imprison political opponents under the guise of legality, seize police power where it was held by non-Nazi Land ministers, and use this power to get out an immense Nazi vote. For the record, the election results demonstrated the stubbornness of non-Nazis; despite terrorism and propaganda, the Nazis did not quite succeed in winning the desired majority. But the 17 million votes cast for their ticket constituted 44 per cent of the total vote; together with his German National allies, Hitler had a majority.

After outlawing the Communist party and arresting most of its deputies, Hitler wanted the Reichstag to pass an Enabling Act yielding its powers to the Chancellor, in effect liquidating itself without formal constitutional amendment. By means of threats, promises, and pledges of good behavior, the Nazis succeeded in inducing the Center party and the remaining Liberal and Conservative deputies to vote for the ignominious act that marked the formal end of the Weimar system. Only the remaining Socialists stood firm against Hitler. A few months later all non-Nazi parties were declared illegal and dissolved.

In the following year the Nazis laid the basis of their dictatorship, even though the senile Hindenburg remained President. Large numbers of Socialists, intellectuals, and other potential opponents were arrested, and the concentration camps were organized. Jews began to be weeded out of the civil service and the professions. Editors unfriendly to the regime were forced to resign and were replaced by Nazis. Free trade unions were taken over and converted into a state-controlled Labor Front. Nazi-oriented clergy were encouraged to take over the Protestant churches, and Catholic opposition was cleverly diminished by Hitler's promise to respect church rights in a Concordat with the Vatican. Leaders of all mass organizations were pressured to give evidence of their loyalty to the new regime, and the ranks of the party expanded greatly as they and many others sought to climb onto the bandwagon. The use of terror became widespread as the dread secret political police (Gestapo) expanded its network. Although the scales fell from the eyes of many Germans who had previously evaded the dark side of Nazism, there was little active resistance. Just as the democratic mass organizations, such as the trade unions, had surrendered without struggle, so most of the moderate officials, officers, and professors lacked the courage to make a show of protest. Some even took heart from the fact that in June, 1934, Hitler purged that part of the Nazi leadership which had advocated radical anticapitalist action. But the bloodbath which annihilated some of his oldest party comrades also claimed many conservative opponents and should have served notice of things to come. Opposition, however, occurred only underground, mainly among Socialist and Communist groups in contact with their exiled colleagues abroad. In August, 1934, the death of Hindenburg finally allowed Hitler to do away with the last shred of constitutionalism. He declared himself both head of state and Chancellor, and as Fuehrer demanded and received a personal oath of loyalty from all servants of the state.

Like the masters of all totalitarian systems, the Nazis were not content with seizing control of the state and merely expanding its functions; they sought to control all phases of economic, social, and even personal life. Gradually, satellite organizations were developed to carry the Nazi ideology and the Fuehrer principle into the most remote sectors of the social structure. But complete control could not be brought about at once by the party alone, even in highly organized Germany, with its rapidly swelling party apparatus. Instead, the party infiltrated and took over the most crucial organizations, taking some into partnership and making concessions to others (such as the Catholic church) to buy a benevolent neutrality until the regime was stronger.

During the first five years, something of a division of authority was worked out between the Nazi hierarchy and its allies in the army and business. The latter groups were usually left alone as long as they followed government policy. They were allowed to continue as a general second force, not politically, but in the sense of commanding executive positions parallel to those of the government and party. Thus the expanding army organization, based on its corps of professional officers, and the business-controlled sector of the economy, were both allowed for a time to resist open nazification. This same lenience also applied in part to the state bureaucracy, another institution with a tightly organized group life which the Nazis did not want to disturb since they depended on it to carry out their orders.

But all other economic, professional, and labor organizations were taken over directly by the placement of tried Nazis at their helm. The Labor Front became an important subsidiary organization of the state, as the Nazis tried to lure the workers over to their cause. Welfare benefits were expanded, the unemployed were guided to new jobs created by the armaments industry and the vastly expanded public works program, and recreation and vacation programs were set up in which amusement and propaganda were cleverly mixed. Enlisting the support of peasant and artisan groups was simpler. These groups had been strongly pro-Nazi even before the take-over; their loyalty was won by the party's glorification of romantic pre-industrial ideals. Their anti-democratic sentiments were redirected and brought into line with the party's political and economic programs. Some trouble occurred when the artisans found that the Nazis were not going to carry out their earlier promises of carving up or taking over their hated big-business rivals. But the Nazis succeeded in persuading these lower-middle-class groups to see their enemy only in Jewish-controlled big business, and to regard the German capitalists as fellow workers in the Fuehrer's vineyard.

"National solidarity" was the slogan employed to bring the uncommitted into line, and it was reinforced by the success of the Fuehrer's policies that led to the return of the Saar by a referendum of its population, Western acceptance of the illegal German militarization of the Rhineland, prestigious German intervention in the Spanish Civil War, and the "bringing home" of Austria in 1938. But as the Nazis' domestic strength grew and plans for military aggression were developed, it was found advisable to extend party control over sectors previously left with a certain independence. Thus the army was "nazified," at least at the top, by the retirement of its traditional leaders and their replacement by generals loyal to the regime. Civil servants were no longer allowed to remain aloof but were expected to join the party. Business also was drawn more completely under state influence, though it remained in private ownership until the end.

The Nazi state was based solidly on the cult of one individual, a charismatic leader who recognized no other legal or personal authority. Hitler's leadership was essential to the movement, since only his demagogic talent and the almost religious faith of many Germans in his abilities could hold the highly heterogeneous Nazi movement together. Without him the party would have disintegrated, and institutions like the bureaucracy, the army, and certain interest groups would have regained the primary loyalty of their members. Hitler's leadership was also an institutional necessity, since the Nazis were both unwilling and unable to provide the country with a coherent, well-organized system of government. After the seizure of power, the government quickly degenerated into a bewildering system of partly overlapping individual "empires" run by the Nazi paladins in an atmosphere of mutual distrust and competition. Only the misplaced zeal of the average German official and the possibility of an appeal for arbitration and overall direction by Hitler saved the system from early breakdown.

In the resulting competition among the Nazi chieftains, Heinrich Himmler, the head of the SS, gained a dominant position soon after the take-over, which he solidified by gaining effective control over the entire German police system. Vital areas of administration were taken away from regular government agencies and placed under his indirect control. The SS quickly overshadowed the party bureaucracy itself, which was preoccupied with integrating its vast membership and exercising indirect control on the local level. The party organization in fact was relegated to the status of a control organ over the masses, making sure that non-

Nazi groups and individuals were deprived of any opportunity to make effective decisions.

It was not by accident that the SS gained the crucial position in the Nazi system. Hitler needed an instrument of terror which was not bound by any legal or moral restrictions but would efficiently and discreetly carry out his basic ideas. The absorption of the police system into the SS successfully blurred the line between actions at least formally covered by legal norms and measures that, even according to existing German law, were unquestionably of criminal character, such as executions without trial and the wholesale extermination of specific groups and peoples. The SS was furthermore destined to become the new racial and political elite of the empire that was to be created in Eastern Europe. It even developed its own army, the Waffen-SS, which, recruited all over Europe, grew to almost a million and was beyond the jurisdiction of the army high command. After the war the SS expected to carve out its own model state, to be made up of sections of France and Belgium with the capital at either Ghent or Dijon. The official language was to be German, but at the beginning the people would be allowed to continue to speak French.

While the Nazi leaders fought each other for control over the vast conquered areas of Europe, the rest of the German administrative and military elite worked with customary efficiency to keep the vastly swollen state machinery functioning relatively smoothly. This elite worked out the difficulties arising from the erratic policies and battle commands which emerged from the Fuehrer's headquarters in an endless stream, and it prevented the contradictory pressures from the various Nazi cliques from causing fatal internal conflicts. Though largely excluded from the inner councils, members of the elite maintained an extraordinarily high discipline, which allowed Hitler to make even greater demands. Many secretly rejected the Nazi regime or even belonged to the "inner immigration," but they followed the dictates of obedience and duty to the Fatherland which generations of forebears had shaped. The idea of measuring orders and official policies by the moral yardstick of personal values was alien to the German bureaucratic outlook. It took even the bravest among them years of soul-searching before they could bring themselves to attempt the only possible solution—over-throwing Hitler and ending the Nazi regime. The attempt on Hitler's life in his East Prussian command headquarters on July 20, 1944, was the culmination of years of planning in a number of highly secret resistance groups which consisted mainly of the most courageous members of conservative German social groups. But the handful of aristocrats, generals, high civil servants, and labor leaders failed in their endeavor to end the regime that was leading Germany to the abyss. Their attempt did have symbolic value for postwar Germans seeking to restore some measure of national self-respect.

The horrors inflicted on European populations during World War II finally convinced the world of Hitler's earnest determination to carry out the program first outlined in *Mein Kampf,* and subsequently elaborated in his tirades before the Nazi party meetings and in private discussions, since published in his *Secret Conversations.* Developments bore out his declaration of November, 1933, that he had not become Chancellor in order to turn away from what he had preached for the past fourteen years. His phenomenal success in realizing seemingly fantastic plans, first of internal, then of world revolution, can be attributed in large part to his extraordinary readiness to gamble all previous achievements on higher stakes. Because of his unchallengeable position he was able to use first the party as an instrument to capture Germany, and then Germany as an instrument to capture control of Europe. When by 1942 German armies had overrun almost the entire continent of Europe and also penetrated into North Africa, his promise of turning the Germans into a master race seemed well on the way toward realization. Hitler took personal command of operations on the waterfront, and the success of operations based on his intuition impressed not only the generals, but his people and the world as well.

However Hitler was not content with fulfilling the positive promises of greater "Lebensraum." Confident of victory almost to the end, he ordered an energetic start on the "reforms" that were necessary in establishing the new order. High priority was given to the elimination of the "Jewish problem." First in Germany and then in the occupied countries Jews were deprived of all civil rights, herded together into ghettos, and eventually transported to areas in Poland and Czechoslovakia. Ostensibly they were to be resettled in isolated "pales," but in reality this was the road to the awful "final solution" that led to the mass murder of millions of human beings in the gas chambers and ovens of the extermination camps. Carried through with terrifying efficiency by special SS and other units under the direction of genocide engineers like Adolf Eichmann, this operation was duplicated on a smaller scale by many other programs designed to eliminate groups considered undesirable under Nazi racial theories. Thus gypsies and the mentally retarded were methodically dispatched, as were hundreds of thousands of political opponents, resistance fighters, and civilian hostages. Never had absolute power corrupted so absolutely what had initially been accepted by many as an idealistic program for national regeneration.

The extermination programs were kept relatively secret, and after the war most Germans declared that they had known nothing of these and other abominations. Indeed, only a small number of selected party fanatics had been so completely shaped by the totalitarian mold that they were able to suppress their consciences altogether. But large numbers of "average" Germans who held positions in the party and its affiliated organizations had come to adapt themselves to the regime's excesses, rationalizing acceptance with the argument that they were inevitable or that they were more than balanced by the regime's positive achievements. Even the majority of Germans who conformed only outwardly could not help but be carried along by an unceasing propaganda campaign. The exposure to years of uninterrupted nationalist frenzy, exhortations to discipline, acceptance of party orders, and self-submersion in racialist mystique made such a deep impression on Germans of all backgrounds that those few thinking of re-creating a democratic order after the inevitable defeat frequently had to ask themselves whether Hitler's handiwork might not require several generations to undo.

THE AFTERMATH

With the collapse of the Nazi regime and Hitler's suicide in Berlin in April, 1945, as the Soviet and Western armies swept their way deep into German territory, German political development had come full cycle. What had begun a century earlier as an attempt to unify diverse states culminated, after sporadic attempts at domestic integration and external expansion, in the complete disintegration of the German Reich and the assumption of German sovereignty by the victorious occupying powers. As a result of inter-Allied agreements reached at Yalta and Potsdam, the central European map was completely recast. Territories that Germany had annexed from Poland and Czechoslovakia in 1939 were returned, and Austria was re-created. In addition, very large sections of Germany east of the Oder and Neisse rivers, which were German even before 1933, were turned over to Poland and the Soviet Union "for administration." Although their final status was to be determined in the peace treaty, they were in fact annexed, and their indigenous German population of about 10 million was driven out. Finally, the rump of German territory was divided into zones of occupation, administered respectively by American, British, Soviet, and French military governments, while Berlin was divided into sectors occupied by the same powers.

The Allied agreements had left open the question of what final political status Germany was to be granted. East-West tensions soon began to hamper the operation of the Inter-Allied Control Council, which never succeeded in coming to grips with the problem of reconciling the contradictory policies of the occupying powers; the council ceased to function in 1947. For a time Germany was divided into what were in effect four zonal states. The three Western powers gradually moved toward the economic and then the political merger of their zones. This process culminated in 1949 in the creation of the Federal Republic (West Germany), to which the Soviets responded by quickly establishing a rival German Democratic Republic (East Germany) in their zone.

BIBLIOGRAPHY

GERMANY TO 1918

Alexander, Edgar, "Church and Society in Germany," in J. Moody, ed., *Church and Society* (New York, 1953).
Clapham, J. H., *Economic Development of France and Germany, 1815–1914* (Cambridge, 1936).

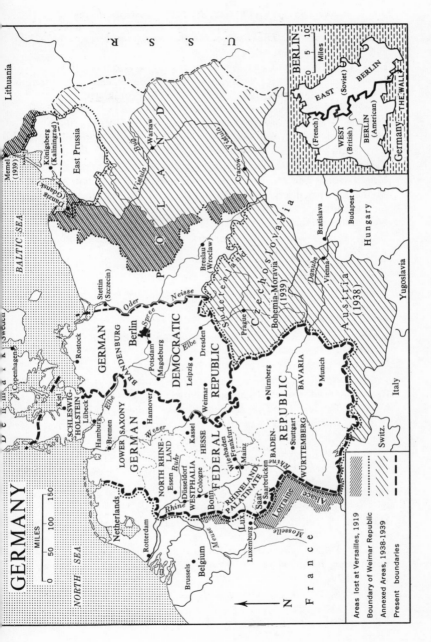

GERMANY

MILES

0   50   100   150

N

Legend
- Areas lost at Versailles, 1919
- Boundary of Weimar Republic
- Annexed Areas, 1938-1939
- Present boundaries

BERLIN inset

0   5   10

Miles

EAST (Soviet)

WEST (British)

BERLIN (French)

BERLIN (American)

Germany — THE WALL

Map labels

NORTH SEA

BALTIC SEA

U.S.S.R.

Lithuania

Memel (1939)

Königsberg (Kaliningrad)

East Prussia

Danzig (Gdansk)

POLAND

Warsaw

Bug

Vistula

Cracow

Vistula

Copenhagen

D e n m a r k

Sweden

Kiel

SCHLESWIG-HOLSTEIN

Lübeck

Rostock

Stettin (Szczecin)

Hamburg

Bremen

Elbe

LOWER SAXONY

Hannover

Weser

BRANDENBURG

Berlin

Spree

Potsdam

Magdeburg

GERMAN DEMOCRATIC REPUBLIC

Leipzig

Elbe

Dresden

Weimar

Breslau (Wrocław)

Neisse

Oder

Prague

Bohemia-Moravia (1939)

C z e c h o s l o v a k i a

S u d e t e n l a n d

Bratislava

Budapest

Hungary

Vienna

Danube

AUSTRIA (1938)

Yugoslavia

Italy

Munich

BAVARIA

Nürnberg

Stuttgart

WÜRTTEMBERG

BADEN-

GERMAN FEDERAL REPUBLIC

Kassel

HESSE

Wiesbaden

Frankfurt

Mainz

RHINELAND-PALATINATE

Saar

Saarbrücken

NORTH RHINE LAND

Essen

Ruhr

Düsseldorf

Cologne

Bonn

WESTPHALIA

Rhine

Netherlands

Rotterdam

Belgium

Brussels

Meuse

Luxembourg

Lux.

Rhine

Moselle

Mosselle

Lorraine

Alsace

F r a n c e

Switz.

Swz.

37

Craig, Gordon A., *The Politics of the Prussian Army, 1640–1945* (Oxford, 1955).

Eyck, Erich, *Bismarck and the German Empire* (London, 1950).

Hamerow, Theodore S., *Restoration, Revolution, Reaction: Economics and Politics in Germany, 1815–1871* (Princeton, 1958).

Hertz, Friedrich, *The German Public Mind* (London, 1957).

Holborn, Hajo, *History of Modern Germany* (New York, 1959).

Kohn, Hans, ed., *German History: Some New German Views* (Boston, 1954).

Krieger, Leonard, *The German Idea of Freedom* (Boston, 1957).

Mann, Golo, *The History of Germany Since 1789* (London, 1968).

Meinecke, Friedrich, *Weltbuergertum und Nationalstaat*, 4th ed. (Munich, 1917).

Naumann, Friedrich, *Die politische Parteien* (Berlin, 1913).

Pross, Harry, *Die Zerstoerung der deutschen Politik: Dokumente 1871–1933* (Frankfurt, 1959).

Taylor, A. J. P., *The Course of German History* (London, 1948).

Valentin, Veit, *The German People* (New York, 1953).

Vermeil, Edmund, *Germany in the 20th Century* (New York, 1956).

THE WEIMAR REPUBLIC

Blachley, F. F., and M. R. Oatman, *The Government and Administration of Germany* (Baltimore, 1928).

Bracher, K. D., *Die Aufloesung der Weimarer Republik*, 2d ed. (Stuttgart, 1957).

Brecht, Arnold, *Prelude to Silence* (New York, 1944).

Carsten, Francis L., *The Reichwehr and Politics, 1918–1933* (Oxford, 1966).

Eschenburg, Theodor, *Die improvisierte Demokratie der Weimarer Republik* (Laupheim, 1954).

Eyck, Erich, *Geschichte der Weimarer Republik*, 2 vols. (Munich, 1956–57).

Flechtheim, Ossip K., *Die kommunistische Partei Leutschlands in der Weimarer Republik* (Offenbach, 1948).

Halpern, S. William, *Germany Tried Political Democracy* (New York, 1946).

Heberle, Rudolf, *From Democracy to Nazism* (Baton Rouge, 1945).

Klemperer, Klemens von, *Germany's New Conservatism* (Princeton, 1957).

Rosenberg, Arthur, *A History of the German Republic* (London, 1936).

Ryder, A. J., *The German Revolution of 1918* (Cambridge, 1967).

Schulz, Gerhard, *Zwischen Demokratie und Diktatur* (Berlin, 1963).

Sontheimer, Kurt, *Antidemokratisches Denken in der Weimarer Republik* (Munich, 1962).

Watkins, Frederick M., *The Failure of Constitutional Emergency Powers Under the German Republic* (Cambridge, Mass., 1939).

Wheeler-Bennett, John W., *The Nemesis of Power* (New York, 1954).

THE NAZI PERIOD

Allen, William S., *The Nazi Seizure of Power: The Experiences of a Single German Town, 1930–1935* (Chicago, 1965).

Baumont, Maurice, et al., eds., *The Third Reich* (Praeger, 1955).

Bracher, Karl Dietrich, *Die deutsche Diktatur* **(Cologne, 1969).**

————, Wolfgang Sauer, and Gerhard Schulz, *Die nationalsozialistische Machtergreifung* (Cologne, 1960).

Bullock, Alan L. C., *Hitler: A Study in Tyranny* (New York, 1952).

Friedrich, Carl, and Zbigniew Brzezinski, *Totalitarian Dictatorship and Autocracy* (Cambridge, Mass., 1956).

Hale, Oron J., *The Captive Press in the Third Reich* (Princeton, 1964).

Heiden, Konrad, *Der Fuehrer* (Boston, 1944).

Hitler, Adolf, *Mein Kampf* (Boston, 1943).

Jarman, T. J., *The Rise and Fall of Nazi Germany* (New York, 1956).

Kogon, Eugene, *The Theory and Practice of Hell* (New York, 1950).

Lewy, Guenther, *The Catholic Church and Nazi Germany* (New York, 1964).

Meinecke, Friedrich, *The German Catastrophe* (Cambridge, Mass., 1950).

Neumann, Franz, *Behemoth* (New York, 1942).

Neumann, Sigmund, *Permanent Revolution* (New York, 1942).

Peterson, Edward N., *The Limits of Hitler's Power* (Princeton, 1969).

Prittie, Terence, *Germans against Hitler* (London, 1964).

Reitlinger, Gerald, *The Final Solution: The Attempt to Exterminate the Jews of Europe, 1938–1945* (New York, 1953).

Schoenbaum, David, *Hitler's Social Revolution* (New York, 1966).

Shirer, William L., *The Third Reich* (New York, 1960).

Taylor, Telford, *Sword and Swastika* (New York, 1952).

Trevor-Roper, H. R., ed., *Hitler's Secret Conversations, 1941–44* (New York, 1953).

Vogelsand, Thilo, *Reichswehr, Staat und NSDAP* (Stuttgart, 1962).

2

Society and Economy in West and East Germany

POPULATION STRUCTURE

It is important to remember that the Germans constitute the largest national group in all of Europe west of the Soviet Union. It was this fact which led the French to build the Maginot Line and which today makes unification so much more difficult. There are many on both sides of the Iron Curtain who do not relish the idea of a powerful state made up of some 75 million Germans. As things stand, war and its aftermath brought considerable dislocation of large population groups, particularly expulsion of the bulk of the German population from East Prussia, Silesia, and the other "Oder-Neisse" territories, as well as from the Sudetenland in Czechoslovakia and German-populated areas in the Balkans. The figures in Table 2–1 suggest the magnitude of these changes.

It is noticeable that the overall effect of the redistribution has been to increase greatly the population of West Germany. This is because the bulk of the expellees did not care to remain

TABLE 2–1: GERMAN POPULATION CHANGES, 1939–68 (IN MILLIONS)

	1939	1968	Gain or loss
West Germany (Federal Republic)	40.2	58.3	+18.1
East Germany (Democratic Republic)	15.1	16.1	+ 1.0
West Berlin	2.7	2.1	− 0.5
East Berlin	1.6	1.1	− 0.5
"Oder-Neisse" territories	9.6	1.1	− 8.5
TOTAL	69.2	78.7	+ 9.6

in the Soviet zone but headed for the western parts of the country. In addition, the GDR suffered an exodus of some 2 to 3 million, mostly younger, productive inhabitants who crossed into West Berlin and the Federal Republic between 1949 and 1961. In those years the GDR's population remained almost static, since the number of those leaving about balanced the natural population increase. By contrast, the population of the Federal Republic increased by some 8 million between 1947 and 1958. The overall increase in the German population is explained by the fact that the influx of ethnic Germans who had previously lived outside the Reich (i.e., in Poland, Yugoslavia, Rumania) plus the natural population increase has more than made up for the 6 to 7 million military and civilian casualties of World War II.

The population in both East and West Germany is predominantly urban. In West Germany (including West Berlin) about one-fifth of the population lives in eleven large cities with more than 500,000 inhabitants each; about 45 per cent lives in small and medium-sized towns and cities with populations of over 5,000; while slightly over one-third lives in smaller, rural communities. In the GDR there is a somewhat greater population concentration in rural communities and medium-sized towns, but there too population tends to be concentrated in heavily industrialized areas. Thus the heavily industrialized Land Northrhine-Westphalia and the Dresden-Leipzig-Karl-Marx-Stadt district each contain one-third of the population of the two states.

Only the minutest portion of the German population still inhabits those picturesque old cities whose panoramas grace tourist posters. Although the old city of Rothenburg annually attracts 600,000 tourists, the area within its walls is becoming depopulated. Two-thirds of the rather static town population lives in modern outlying areas, and many others have left for the large, industrial cities which produce the cars and buses that bring the visitors.

In both German states, farmers have been diminishing in significance as a demographic and social factor. In the GDR, collectivization has undercut individual ownership of the land and has eliminated the small farm. The latter process has proceeded at a much slower pace in West Germany. Between 1960 and 1966, 200,000 of the 1.2 million farms of less than twenty-five acres were eliminated. Whereas in 1950 the agricultural sector still accounted for 25 per cent of West German employment, by 1961 this figure was down to 12.9 per cent, and by 1970 it was further reduced to about 9 per cent. In both states the proportion of the work force engaged in manufacturing continued to increase throughout the 1950–70 period. But in West Germany the rate of increase slowed down considerably during the 1960's. The largest gains were made by the tertiary sector—composed of commerce, transportation, and service industries—which employed two out of five people in the West German work force in 1965.

There is considerable political significance in the religious structure of the population, not only in the proportions between Protestants and Catholics but also in their regional distribution. Since the formation of the Second Reich, Catholics, though predominant in certain sections, were outnumbered about two to one in Germany as a whole. They were always influential in predominantly Catholic areas like Bavaria, the Rhineland, and Silesia, but they were a minority nationally. The division of Germany has changed this situation radically. Within the Federal Republic they now claim almost half (45 per cent) of the population, a fact which has been of much greater advantage to the West German Christian Democrats than to the Social Democrats. The religious affiliation of East Germans is by contrast predominantly Protestant; only 11 per cent are Catholics. The Catholic church has been both better organized and more successful in maintaining touch with its following than the Protestant churches. This is because the Protestant churches were organized predominantly on a Land and regional level, and only loosely unified within several national church organizations. In addition, the Protestant churches almost completely lost contact with the working-class population, while the Catholics were much more successful in sponsoring a whole network of working-class organizations to help maintain this important link.

In West Germany the decreasing relevance of religion in everyday life is illustrated by information about the influence of religious denomination on choice of marriage partners. In 1921 only 12 per cent of marriages were between Protestants and Catholics; by 1964, Protestant-Catholic marriages accounted for 23 per cent of the total. The propensity to marry within or outside one's religion varied greatly according to size of community and its denominational makeup. In rural areas where the population was about equally split between the two religions, interfaith marriages amounted to about 40 per cent of what might have been statistically expected if "religion made no difference." In large cities, on the other hand, the actual intermarriage rate was quite close to the "secular" expectation. In most of the cities the increase in interfaith marriages was much greater in the 1960's than in the 1930's. (However, in the capital city of Bonn, interfaith marriages actually decreased.)

TABLE 2–2:   GERMAN INTERFAITH MARRIAGES

City	ACTUAL INTERFAITH MARRIAGES AS A PROPORTION OF STATISTICAL EXPECTATION IF RELIGION PLAYED NO ROLE IN CHOICE OF PARTNER (IN PER CENT)		
	In the 1920's	*In the 1930's*	*In the 1960's*
Bochum	47	47	71
Bonn	64	65	47
Essen	54	55	76
Frankfurt	76	74	81
Mannheim	77	76	84
All cities			62
All nonurban counties			49
Federal Republic			55

SOURCE: *Wirtschaft und Statistik,* June, 1967, p. 359.

THE WEST GERMAN ECONOMY

The differences in economic policy between West and East Germany were not so stark initially as they were to become later. This was because in both West and East the crisis conditions of the immediate postwar years made it necessary to continue the system of rationing and tight economic control introduced under the Nazis. The critical parting of the ways occurred in June,

1948. By then, it had become evident that attempts to achieve unified Allied policy were futile, and the United States and Britain introduced a new currency in their zones and allowed the German economic administration to initiate a policy of radical decontrol of the economy. This policy was carried through under the direction of future federal Minister of Economics Ludwig Erhard, who, with the support of the non-Socialist parties, gambled that the incentives of a free market economy would liberate long dormant productive capacities. His policy proved phenomenally successful; Germans eagerly sought to earn more of the new hard currency in order to buy goods that shopkeepers had previously withheld, while manufacturers rapidly expanded production facilities in order to keep up with the swelling demand for goods which became available on a nonrationed basis for the first time in almost a decade.[1]

It took the East Germans far longer to reach prewar levels of production and even longer to supply the average citizen with something like his prewar standard of living. The Russians carried through the dismantling program much more thoroughly than the Western Allies, thus depriving the East of a far larger share of its productive capacity. Moreover though possessing only one-third of total German resources, the Soviet zone was forced to supply over three-quarters of all German reparations, to the value of perhaps 10 billion dollars. These factors, plus a continued labor shortage, due in good part to the flight to the West of skilled workers and technicians, handicapped East German reconstruction. It was only in 1954 that the regime achieved the equivalent of prewar levels.

In West Germany, the subsequent increases in production were impressive. In many industries production doubled within six months. Total industrial production, which had stood at barely half the prewar (1936) figure in mid-1948, surpassed this mark by the end of 1949. With characteristic vigor Germans of all classes—managers, workers, and foremen—worked longer hours than anybody else in Europe in order to expand productive capacities, modernize communication facilities, and rebuild

[1] Henry C. Wallich, *Mainsprings of German Revival* (New Haven, 1955), chap. 4.

housing. Differences between labor and management were sub-
ordinated to the common task. Trade union leaders showed great
restraint in making wage demands in order not to impede the
German drive to recapture overseas markets, thus setting the

TABLE 2–3:   WEST GERMANY'S POSTWAR ECONOMIC RECOVERY

	1948	1950	1957	1960	1968
Crude steel production (million tons)	5.6	12.1	24.5	34.1	41.2
Employment (millions)	13.5	14.3	19.0	20.4	26.5
Unemployment (millions)	.8	1.3	.4	.1	.3
Standard of living (private per capita consumption compared to prewar standard; 1936 = 100)	—	92	151	171	225

SOURCES: UN Statistical Yearbooks; Wolfgang Stolper, *Germany between East
and West* (Washington, 1960); unofficial estimates for 1960 and 1968.

stage for a low wage, high profit growth. German technical in-
genuity met the challenge of improving production methods and
product design in order to catch up with competitors in the United
States and elsewhere. Primarily, however, industry sought to fill
the demands of the domestic market, shaped by the great acquisi-
tive fervor that gripped the German population once it saw the
opportunities for satisfying material wants.

Production continued to increase without any significant recession or leveling off. Steel production in West Germany climbed
from 5 million tons in 1945 to 30 million tons in 1960, surpassing
Britain to become the world's third largest producer (but it was
overtaken by Japan in 1964). Total industrial production doubled
once again between 1950 and 1957 as the West Germans marked
up annual growth rates averaging 10 per cent, roughly four times
the American figure. The Federal Republic's gross national product had already surpassed the 1936 level in 1950, and this figure
was doubled by 1957. Records like these were made possible
through extremely high investment figures, which continued at a
rate of from 20 to 25 per cent of the national income. Though
encouraged by tax legislation, the high investment rate indicated

that Germans were working not merely to satisfy current demand, but because they possessed confidence in the future potential of their economy.

In the period following the Korean crisis, German industry was able to supply at low prices goods that had become scarce as a result of the shift to military production in other countries. Success in this endeavor led to a strong interlacing among the economies of West Germany and those of other Western countries.[2] The great increase in trade between Germany and the Western countries not only made up for lost traditional markets in areas like the Balkans but also provided a substitute for trade with East Germany, which declined to one-tenth of its prewar significance. Thus, whereas in 1936 West Germany had spent 8.6 per cent of its gross national product on imports from East Europe, in 1958 it spent less than 1 per cent. However, imports from other countries (mainly in the West) increased from 5.6 per cent to about 13 per cent of gross national product during the same period.[3]

American Marshall Plan aid supplied a considerable part of the crucial initial capital required for expansion, but further investment was made possible by the large profits that manufacturers and businessmen were able to plough back into their firms. The attempt to restore private business as a dynamic economic factor in the reconstruction of Germany was supported by extremely generous tax policies, which favored the creation of new wealth and brought economically powerful groups to identify their fortunes with those of the state whose economic basis they were helping to shape. The question of ownership and control of industry was settled in their favor. Originally there had been much sentiment for nationalizing heavy industry, especially among Socialists and the trade unions, but this impulse was pushed aside by the newly found enthusiasm for private enterprise. Instead, the Co-determination Law of 1951 gave the trade unions the opportunity to help influence company policies by sending representatives to the board of directors of the large steel and coal

---

[2] Ludwig Erhard, *Germany's Comeback in the World Market* (New York, 1954), chap. 1.

[3] Wolfgang Stolper, *Germany between East and West* (Washington, 1960), pp. 10–11.

companies.[4] Since then, the "basic industry" character of mining, employment in which is scarcely half what it was, has been radically reduced. As a consequence, the unions have been pressing for legislation that would extend the worker-management participation principle to all large firms in important industries. Opponents argue that the average worker is scarcely affected by the system and that it would give too much power to union leaders. But the proponents argue that the councils provide a platform for discussion outside the usual wage and salary negotiations, and that over the years the mutual interchange has helped to keep German industrial conflicts at a very low level. (In 1968, strike incidence was lower than in any other major industrial country.)

The owners and managers of the very large industrial and commercial firms, organized in tightly knit industrial and trade associations, demonstrated their power by undoing many of the deconcentration measures introduced under the Occupation. Firms like Krupp, which had been ordered to divest themselves of parts of their industrial empires, were able to avoid the implementation of these orders and even to acquire other large firms to increase their dominance. A similar development occurred in banking. The Allies had broken up the "Big Three" banks that had dominated German banking into thirty independent units. By 1952, however, these had been reconsolidated into nine banks, and by 1957 the "Big Three" were reestablished.

Thus postwar West German economic development has been marked not only by large production increases but also by a return to earlier patterns under which a relatively small number of managers and bankers hold control over large sectors of the economy. In view of continued prosperity and full employment, this fact has not caused any serious conflicts affecting large parts of the population, but it worries many critics of German big business as well as adherents of the free market economy. Obviously, if concentration of ownership and interlocking directorates continue unabated, the doctrine of free competition will become less and less meaningful. Though official policy sought to deal with these problems, it was long handicapped by the fact that the

[4] Wallich, *op. cit.,* pp. 307 ff.

CDU government's political backers in industry opposed the necessary stringent regulations. However, while not making much progress in the area of concentration of ownership, the government did pass Germany's first anticartel law in 1957,[5] and such formerly typical German business practices as price-fixing and market-sharing have been somewhat curtailed. But the organizations representing industry and big business remain the most powerful of economic groups. Where they have led, other economic groups have followed. Labor, farmers, white collar workers, artisans, and civil servants are all highly organized and seek to achieve their ends through the political process as well as through economic bargaining. As in other advanced industrial countries, the government has become the embattled regulatory mechanism of a complex system.

SOCIETY IN THE WEST

A politically significant aspect of the West German recovery program is that it absorbed the millions of exiles from former German areas in Eastern Europe, who had for years been forced to remain in makeshift refugee camps or had been quartered with resentful local families. As new production and service facilities were created, more jobs opened up. By 1954 the demand for labor began to increase much more rapidly than the supply, even though the work force continued to be augmented not only by youths reaching working age but also by refugees from East Germany and those returning late from Russian prison camps. By 1959, unemployment was almost nil (1.3 per cent). Employment had increased by more than 50 per cent in the course of a decade, prosperous housewives were leaving the labor market, and German businessmen were forced to import workers from Italy and even Spain. In 1965, more than one million foreign workers were employed in West Germany, and personnel chiefs were sending agents all over Europe to recruit factory hands willing to work for the German mark.

---

[5] E. Guenther, "Das Gesetz gegen Wettbewerbsbeschraenkungen im Rahmen der deutschen Wirtschaftspolitik," *Wirtschaft und Wettbewerb*, X (November, 1960), 747 ff.

While the economic miracle doubled the number of West German millionaires in four years (1936: 1,957; 1953: 1,566; 1957: 3,502), benefits deriving from economic expansion were fairly widespread. Industrial wages rose gradually. In 1950 the average industrial worker received the equivalent of about thirty cents an hour, much to the annoyance of British and other competitors whose labor was more expensive and who felt that German union leaders were not militant enough. By 1965, however, German unions had succeeded in raising the average hourly rate to more than a dollar an hour[6] without delaying economic expansion by more than a minimum of work stoppages. Throughout the 1950's the average German worked close to fifty hours a week, but by the end of the decade the unions were pressing for a reduction with posters showing a little girl saying, "I want my daddy at home on weekends." Tax returns also showed the general increase in prosperity. In 1950, 54 per cent of all wage and salary earners made less than $900; in 1957 only 16 per cent were in this category while 53 per cent were earning from $900 to $1,800 a year.[7]

Between 1954 and 1960, the number of privately owned cars quadrupled to 4 million, and their number tripled once again in the following eight years to almost 12 million in 1968. The 1970 car-ownership rate of 200 per 1,000 population is expected to increase to 280 by 1975 and to touch the expected saturation point of 300 about 1980. Further increases will require enormous road-building expenditures, possibly as much as DM 380 billion over a twenty-year period. The diffusion of automobile ownership became widespread as Germany entered the age of high mass consumption. In 1965, one-third of the country's private automobiles were owned by working-class families. Their rate of car-ownership (about 35 per cent) was still below that of white collar employees (51 per cent) and businessmen and professionals (70 per cent), but the gap is narrowing quickly. The rapid increase

[6] The official exchange rate for the Deutschmark (DM) has been close to DM 4 to the U.S. dollar during most of the postwar period. Before 1960, the exchange was DM 4.20 = $1, from 1960 to 1969 the exchange was DM 4 = $1, and since 1969 the rate has been DM 3.68 = $1.

[7] Gerhard Zeitel, "Einkommenstatistik," *Handwoerterbuch der Sozialwissenschaften,* sec. 28, p. 65.

in new drivers led to an equal increase in traffic fatalities—almost twice as numerous as in Britain. During the 1960's the number of accidents per 1,000 cars had gradually decreased, but as car ownership has become more widespread, the number of accidents in personal automobile injuries has remained constant at a high annual rate of about 800 traffic casualties per 100,000 population.

What have been the social consequences of this economic revival? For some years observers of German society detected a so-called restorationist trend which led Germans to seek to regain social position by competing for material and status symbols. This appears to have been an essentially short-term phenomenon, associated with the surprisingly rapid ascent from rags to riches of many social groups. A more fundamental trend may be a development toward the kind of society based on personal achievement typical of the United States. Traditional external signs of status are becoming outdated. Rank in the governmental hierarchy has lost significance as the civil service bureaucracy has become only one among many. Cosmopolitan experience no longer suffices, as millions of workers stream across the Alps to vacation by the shores of the Adriatic. Domestic servants are becoming museum pieces as country girls find that they can earn twice as much in the factory as in the nursery. Family background has declined in importance as vast numbers now leave their native towns in search of new homes or job possibilities. Many signs indicate that Germany's social structure is becoming very much like that of other industrial countries, where feudal traditions were eclipsed earlier or were nonexistent. If there is still somewhat less social mobility than, for instance, in the United States, this is partly because of the higher percentage of stable groups like professionals (2.9 per cent versus 1.4 per cent in the United States), small entrepreneurs (10.7 per cent versus 6 per cent), and farmers (10.6 per cent versus 5.9 per cent), who tend to pass on positions and status to their children, and the lesser significance of mobile groups like technical and other employees (18.8 per cent versus 30.8 per cent).[8] But basic socio-economic trends tend to bring West Germany closer to the American pattern.

[8] Morris Janowitz, "Social Stratification and Mobility in West Germany," *American Journal of Sociology,* LXIV (1958), 8.

One institution that does not contribute as much to increasing social mobility as it might—or as its equivalents do in countries as different as the United States and the Democratic Republic—is the educational system. The quality of the German educational system is rightfully held in worldwide esteem both for its success in bringing literacy to the masses and for its traditional ability to produce outstanding scholars and scientists. But as in most continental countries there tends to be a strong class bias in determining who gets advanced education, for many the only route to higher social status. Four-fifths of the pupils leave school at the age of fourteen, and those who do go on proceed to the *Gymnasien*, the academic high schools that prepare for university entrance. Gymnasien students, however, have always been drawn disproportionately from middle-class families which supply both the incentive and the financial means. In Britain, a concerted effort has been made to remove at least the financial barriers for working-class children by providing aid to families that keep their children in secondary school; there is also a generous public scholarship program for university students. West Germany has not followed this example, and consequently only 5 to 10 per cent of university students come from working-class families, even though all universities in Germany are public, their tuition rates are quite low, and the state does provide other marginal subsidies and a limited scholarship program.

It is the living standards of most West Germans that have benefited most from the distribution of goods and services in this age of mass consumption. In the two prosperous decades since 1950, most West Germans have acquired goods and other benefits which their parents never had or which were previously the privilege of upper strata. Thus, only about one-third of the apartments built before 1930 contained bathtubs, and about one-third did not have their own toilets. Of those built in the 1950's, 85 per cent included both bath and toilets, and about one-fifth also had central heating. Almost all apartments constructed in the 1960's had both baths and toilets, and some two-thirds also had central heating. As housing has become both better and more abundant, the number of occupants per apartment has dropped steadily from about three and one-half per apartment in 1960 to less than three in 1970. In the mid-1960's, the curve of per capita beer consumption, which had risen steadily with increased prosperity, reached a peak and began to decline as the comforts of the home came to outmatch those of the pub.

TABLE 2–4: CONSUMER GOODS IN WEST GERMAN HOUSEHOLDS*

	PER CENT OF FAMILIES OWNING		
Article	In Low-Income (DM 500/mo) Homes, Mainly Pensioners	In Working-Class Families (DM 1,000/mo)	In Middle-Class Families (DM 2,000/mo)
Radio	87.2	87.8	91.9
Television	53.4	77.4	68.7
Vacuum cleaner	71.6	89.1	97.0
Refrigerator	48.0	90.4	98.7
Record player	16.9	39.1	60.1
Automobile	2.0	41.5	76.5
Telephone	4.7	10.9	72.0

*Data pertains to December, 1967.
SOURCE: *Wirtschaft und Statistik* (May, 1968), p. 275.

The range of consumer goods found in West German homes still varies to some extent with class and income, but not nearly so much as before. Goods like vacuum cleaners and refrigerators became the proud new acquisitions of most lower-income homes, as well as middle-class ones. As elsewhere in Europe, television became even more characteristic of the homes of well-paid workers than of middle-class and professional homes. Except for low-income elderly people on retirement or welfare incomes, the consumer goods are distributed widely across class lines. There are very few instances where the ratio of goods ownership in middle-class over working-class homes is greater than two to one. An exception is the telephone, which only about one out of ten working-class homes possesses. This is probably because the state monopoly has not utilized advertising to overcome an inherited class resistance, as private sellers of other goods and services have.

The drive for the acquisition of consumer goods has produced a notable disproportion in the accumulation of wealth and non-consumable property. Thus, in 1959, manual workers who constituted close to half of the population and received some 31 per cent of all personal income accumulated only 15 per cent of all personal savings. Their savings quotient was a mere 4.3 per cent of their disposable income, compared to 10.8 per cent for white-collar employees and 16.1 per cent for the self-employed. In 1967 over 70 per cent of West German private property was in the hands of 17 per cent of all families. The share of workers and employees in the total personal wealth actually declined during the years of prosperity, and on a per capita basis amounted to only about DM 7,200 ($2,000).

Until the 1960's, even most members of the middle class invested their savings conservatively in bonds, real estate, or mortgages. Playing the stock market was not a widespread habit, and the banks, who handled most stock sales, did not actively solicit new entrants. Then aggressive representatives of American-organized mutual funds began a highly successful campaign to induce middle-class investments. By soliciting German capital for American companies, they provided much of the capital with which American companies bought larger and larger shares in many European industries.

COLLECTIVIZATION IN THE GERMAN DEMOCRATIC REPUBLIC (GDR)

About the same time that the West moved to decentralize economic control through adoption of the "social market policy," the East began to move energetically in the other direction. In 1945 only the larger industrial and business enterprises had been socialized, and even these remained under control of communal and Land authorities. The changeover to centralized control and planning began in 1948 and found expression in the Two-Year Plan adopted for 1949 and 1950. Subsequently a state planning commission was created on the Soviet model, and this commission developed two additional Five-Year Plans which concentrated on building from almost nothing a heavy industrial base. Despite lack of adequate coal and iron resources, steel production was increased tenfold in the period from 1948 to 1958. At the time, however, West Germany was still outproducing the East by a ratio of 26 to 3 million tons annually.

Within the framework of a Seven-Year Plan (1958 to 1965) paralleling that of the Soviet Union, the East German economy became integrated with the economies of the entire East European bloc. Thus, East Germany concentrated on expanding its chemical, heavy mechanical, and electro-technical industries in order to serve as a specialized supplier to the other "peoples' democracies" and to the Soviet Union, for whom it has become the most important foreign source of investment goods. In little more than a decade, East Germany not only has set up a planned economy in sharp contrast to the West German system but also has extended the framework of the planning from the local, to the national, to the supranational level.

Although experimenting with planning formulas caused considerable waste and privation, the East German regime was not deterred from gradually eliminating the remaining private sectors of the economy in accord with its ideological goals. Small private factory owners found it increasingly difficult to secure the materials necessary for achieving assigned production targets. Frequently the authorities would find minor infringements of planning or tax regulations and, while the owners were thus under pressure, offer to provide public capital to help modernize the plant.[9] In this way the state became the dominant partner even of enterprises that it did not directly run, and the private sector, which in 1950 accounted for almost a quarter of East German industry, was gradually reduced to the vanishing point (in 1959, 5 per cent). A similar development occurred in areas like the construction industry and wholesale trade, where the "socialist" sector became predominant in the course of the 1950's. Private farmers, artisans, and retail store owners continued to be tolerated as long as they were useful to the state, which was anxious not to overload its economic agencies to the point of organizational breakdown. Ingenious types of "socialist" organization— such as producers' collectives and state-controlled trading coop-

[9] John Herz, "East Germany: Progress and Prospects," *Social Research* (1960), p. 147.

eratives—were set up to encourage the smaller owners to place themselves voluntarily in dependent positions, thus allowing the state to carry out complete socialization at a later date with a minimum of struggle or interruption of economic activity.

The process that was used to virtually eliminate private property in agriculture by 1960 illustrates how East German collectivization was carried through and its similarity to the earlier Soviet model. The first stage, the land reform program of 1945, actually increased the number of private farmers by distributing nearly 7,000 large estates among approximately 300,000 ex-pellees, land-poor farmers, and farm laborers, most of whom received less than ten acres. After a period of consolidation comparable to the "New Economic Policy" period in the Soviet Union, middle-sized farmers owning between twenty and one hundred acres came under pressure. In 1952, still only about one-quarter of the total land area was in the "socialist" sector—half in collectives and half under direct state operation.[10]

When pressure caused the large-scale flight of peasants to the West, the regime substituted a propaganda campaign urging small-scale farmers to deed their land voluntarily to collectives in order to benefit from the preferred position in terms of better machine tractor service and lower production quotas. The pressure was maintained with varying degreees of intensity; it was relaxed during crisis periods—like those following the June 17, 1953, uprising and the Polish and Hungarian revolts of 1956—and intensified when conditions stabilized. Between 1953 and 1958, the proportion of land in collective ownership increased from 13.8 per cent to 29.4 per cent, climbing to 45 per cent by 1959. Then in the spring of 1960, the regime decided to stage an intensive drive to complete collectivization. Thousands of Communist activists descended on the villages to undertake a personalized pressure campaign on the peasants who were still holding out. It was made clear that jail or flight was the only real alternative to "voluntary entry" into at least a "class-one" collective, an arrangement in which the peasants gave up their land but kept title to their animals and implements. As news-

[10] Frieda Wunderlich, *Farmer and Farm Labor in the Soviet Zone of Germany* (New York, 1958).

papers reported district after district achieving 100 per cent collectivization, the peasants realized their position was hopeless
and surrendered title to their land.

The elimination of entire social groups, such as the independent peasants and industrial and commercial entrepreneurs, has
been part of the huge social revolution engineered in East Germany. Social mobility has been tremendous as elements of the old
middle and lower-middle classes have been forced down the social
scale while large masses of workers have been carried upward.

TABLE 2–5:   WEST AND EAST GERMAN AGRICULTURAL PRO-
DUCTIVITY (WITH COMPARISONS)

Country	Wheat (a)	Rye (a)	Barley (a)	Meat (b)	Milk (b)
East Germany	3.67	2.32	3.32	+41	+27
Hungary	2.17	1.17	2.02	+ 3	− 2
Poland	2.06	1.84	2.08	+ 5	+ 5
West Germany	3.26	2.50	3.00	+ 4	+ 7
France	2.80	1.75	3.03	− 2	+14
Italy	2.28	1.77	1.53	− 5	− 2

(a) = Yield in tons per acre, 1965.
(b) = Per cent production increase, 1962–66.
SOURCE: U.S. Agriculture Department Report cited in Jean Edward Smith,
Germany Beyond the Wall (Boston, 1969), pp. 122–27.

In the years following 1960, lowered productivity reflected
the low morale of many East German farmers. As the situation
stabilized, however, the greater rationalization made possible by
the enlarged farm collectives was reflected in the production results. Thus, by the mid-1960's, the GDR led all the East European countries in almost all categories of crop productivity. Not
only did it surpass the farm productivity of Poland and Hungary
in crops like rye and barley, it also exceeded West German productivity for some of these same crops. And the GDR's meat and
milk production increases were higher than those of any other West
or East European country. "By 1967," wrote one American author,
"East Germany had reversed years of agricultural retardation

and was moving ahead rapidly. . . . The GDR may well be the first Communist nation to make collectivized agriculture a success."[11] In 1968, a West German author agreed that the GDR had achieved what "four years ago appeared almost impossible," the matching of productivity levels of the Federal Republic with regard to most farm crops and products. This means: Food supplies have become regularized, the trust of the people in the government is strengthened, and valuable foreign currencies which previously had to be expended for imports have been partially made available for investment goods and cultural imports.[12]

SOCIAL CHANGE IN THE EAST

The capacity of various levels of the educational system, and rules determining who could go on to higher education and what was to be studied there, have been powerful factors shaping the character of the generation that has inherited the jobs of the older generation. In part these rules have worked negatively. For a time in the 1950's, the children of middle-class parents were discriminated against in admission to secondary and university education, but this policy has since been largely dropped. Within the universities the number of places in the liberal arts faculties has been reduced, while enrollment in technical and education faculties has grown considerably. Thus, in 1966, there were less than half as many students studying philosophy and art at GDR universities as in 1953, but enrollment in the education faculties more than tripled.

The training of teachers was stressed so heavily because the GDR planned to upgrade the median level of education for the present generation. By the mid-1960's statistics already showed very considerable differences in this area between West and East Germany. Whereas the median school-leaving age was still the eighth grade in the Federal Republic, it had moved up to the tenth grade in the Democratic Republic. The distribution of school-leaving groups shown in the Table 2–6 points up the great emphasis in East Germany on polytechnical middle schools, where

[11] Jean Edward Smith, *Germany Beyond the Wall* (Boston, 1969), p. 136.
[12] Ernst Richert, *Die DDR Elite* (Hamburg, 1968), p. 66.

students receive both more theoretical and more practical training for their vocations. The curricula in these schools has a strong bias toward technological and economic models, which seems to have benefited the middle echelon of East German managers.

TABLE 2–6: PRIMARY AND SECONDARY SCHOOL ATTENDANCE IN WEST AND EAST GERMANY (1964)

Of 100 Eighth-Grade Pupils	*GDR*	*FRG*
Education was completed in eighth grade	29	55
Education was due to be completed in ninth grade	—	14
Attended a secondary school which led through tenth grade	58	14
Attended a secondary school which led through twelfth grade	13	17
	100	100

SOURCE: Georg Polikeit, *Die sogenannte DDR* (Jugenheim, 1966), p. 163.

The proportion of students in an age group who received this type of training was four times as high as in the Federal Republic. The proportion of an age group completing study at a university is also higher in East Germany, and many more students in the GDR receive technical or university degrees than in the FRG.

It is from this group of relatively highly educated young men that the new elite of the GDR has been drawn; its members have moved up into top positions much faster than their age-group peers in the FRG. Moreover, with the relative depoliticalization of the 1960's, ideological emphasis gave way to pragmatic orientations. In various practical and scientific fields—including increasingly the social sciences—East German specialists showed that they could innovate and produce as effectively as their counterparts in the West. Most of these younger members of the elite have won their positions through individual achievements rather than political conformity. They have played a key role in the GDR's considerable economic and technological achievements in the 1960's.

INDUSTRIAL PRODUCTIVITY

By the 1960's, jubilant announcements issued from the East German Statistical Office concerning industrial production. In 1967, a recession period in West Germany, it could trumpet that industrial production had risen by 6 per cent in East Germany but had remained stagnant in the Federal Republic. And, in most other years since the early 1960's, GDR production increases reached or slightly exceeded the West German figures. These achievements may be attributed, in part, to the East German economy's finally hitting its stride; until "the Wall" was built in 1961, it suffered from the loss of vitally needed skilled labor. But probably a more important factor was the adoption in 1963 of the New Economic System, a decentralized planning system which paralleled the proposals of the Soviet economist Liberman. After the Liberman ideas won Kremlin approval, the GDR was the first Socialist country to put them into full-scale operation. As an East German economist stated to an American: "We are far ahead of our socialist neighbors. Our New Economic System borrows some from Liberman, but we have really been working along these lines for a long time."[13]

The New Economic System aimed at adjusting the overcentralized, top-heavy planning mechanism to a complex economy by giving greater authority to those who were in closer touch with what the consumers wanted and needed. Then the central planning authority was stripped of its detailed managerial functions, and authority was delegated to some ninety industrial associations that acted as clearinghouses for the recommendations from individual factories. At the same time, a great preoccupation with new models and techniques developed. Cybernetics and econometrics were eagerly studied by the young technocrats, and a vast variety of management courses was introduced at trade and evening schools.

The decentralization of planning and management was accompanied by reforms eliminating state subsidies and by the introduction of more accurate cost-accounting systems. The main purpose

[13] Smith, *op. cit.,* p. 95.

of the reforms was to bring domestic prices of raw materials and finished goods more in line with those on the world market. By 1968 the price at which East German factories bought metal products was some 10 per cent above the going rate on the world market —quite an improvement over previous periods when the variation was much greater. But to pure market economists in the West a miss was as good as a mile and they derided the East German effort as the "eunuch system": "Everyone knows how to mesh market and plan in theory, but no one can actually do it."

Throughout the 1960's, the East Germans debated how close to self-regulation the economic system could or should be brought. The cybernetics enthusiasts projected their self-regulation thesis as far as the top party press, only to be disavowed in subsequent party announcements. In the late 1960's, party leaders began to shift course again and to accuse economic functionaries of overrating individual achievement and of "acting too much like capitalistic managers." In 1968, new guidelines reduced the decision-making powers of the industrial associations, once again strengthening the central authorities. This appeared to be in line with a gradual transition to a new Economic System of Socialism.

Because, in relation to population and resources, they are both among the world's most advanced industrial societies, the two Germanys remain more alike than their radically different routes of postwar recovery would suggest. In some ways, as is suggested by the indicators in Table 2–7, the societies and economies of West and East Germany are more similar to each other than to countries within their respective ideological blocs. Thus the relative significance of agricultural and industrial employment differentiates both states about equally from Britain on the one hand, and the Soviet Union on the other. In holding down private consumption so as to increase investment, both societies have shown a large measure of restraint which, while not as great as that imposed on the Soviet population, surpasses a country like Britain. Data on facilities such as hospitals indicate that both states have maintained a tradition of extensive public services in this area. And even in as politically relevant an area as mass communication systems, as measured in terms of the diffusion of radio and television receivers, East and West Germany remain remarkably similar.

TABLE 2–7:   SOME WEST AND EAST GERMAN SOCIO-ECONOMIC
INDICATORS, WITH BRITISH AND SOVIET COMPARISONS

Indicator	West Germany	East Germany	United Kingdom	Soviet Union
Per cent of labor force in agriculture	14	19	5	48
Industrial employment as per cent of working-age population	32	30	35	24
Military as per cent of population aged 15–64	.90	.95	1.86	3.02
Private consumption as per cent of gross national product	58.7	60	66.7	55.8
Inhabitants per hospital bed	100	90	110	140
Radios per 1,000 population	319	348	289	205
Television sets per 1,000 population	109	91	220	28

NOTE: The base periods for most of the statistics cited lie in years 1959–61. Only the East German figure for industrial employment dates from a period considerably earlier than those used for the other countries.
SOURCE: Bruce M. Russett et al., *World Handbook of Political and Social Indicators* (New Haven, 1964).

BIBLIOGRAPHY

ECONOMIC STRUCTURE

Arnold, Felix, *Die sozialistische Planwirtschaft und der demokratische Zentralismus in der Volkswirtschaft der DDR* (Berlin, 1959).

Erhard, Ludwig, *Germany's Comeback in the World Market* (New York, 1954).

Koenig, H., ed., *Wandlungen der Wirtschaftsstruktur der Bundesrepublik* (Berlin, 1962).

Mueller, Hans, and Karl Reissig, eds., *Wirtschaftswunder DDR* (East Berlin, 1968).

Ortlieb, H. D., "Unsere Konsumgesellschaft," *Hamburger Jahrbuch fuer Wirtschafts und Gesellschaftspolitik*, IV (1959), 225–45.

Stolper, Gustav, et al., *The German Economy: 1870 to the Present* (New York, 1967).

———, and Karl Roskamp, *The Structure of the East German Economy* (Cambridge, Mass., 1960).

Wallich, Henry C., *Mainsprings of German Revival* (New Haven, 1955).

Bilanz unserer Erfolge: 20 Jahre DDR in Zahlen und Fakten, published by Staatlichen Zentralverwaltung fuer Statistik (East Berlin, 1969).

SOCIAL SYSTEMS

Abendroth, W., "Die Soziale Struktur der Bundesrepublik und ihre politischen Entwicklungstendenzen," *PVS*, IV (1963), 150–67.

Childs, David, *East Germany* (London, 1969).

Claessens, Dieter, Arno Klonne, and Armin Tschoepe, *Sozialkunde der Bundesrepublik Deutschland* (Duesseldorf, 1965).

Dahrendorf, Rolf, "The New Germanies," *Encounter*, XXII (1964), 50–59. The entire issue of this number is devoted to evaluation of German cultural, political, and social developments.

Friedl, Gerhard, *Gesellschaftspolitik in Deutschland* (Munich, 1967).

Fuerstenberg, Friedrich, *Die Sozialstruktur der Bundesrepublik Deutschland: Ein soziologischer Ueberblick* (Cologne, 1967).

Greinacher, H., and H. T. Risse, eds., *Bilanz des deutschen Katholizismus* (Mainz, 1966).

Gross, Johannes, *Die Deutschen* (Frankfurt, 1967).

Holm, Hans Axel, *Bericht aus einer Stadt in der DDR* (Munich, 1969).

Hornstein, Erika von, *Die deutsche Not* (Cologne, 1960).

Huffschmid, Joerg, *Die Politik des Kapitals* (Frankfurt, 1970).

Janowitz, Morris, "Social Stratification and Mobility in West Germany," *American Journal of Sociology*, LXIV (1958), 6–24.

Jolles, Hiddo M., *Zur Soziologie der Heimatvertriebenen und Fluechtlinge* (Cologne, 1965).

Nell-Breuning, Oswald V., *Mitbestimmung* (Frankfurt, 1968).

Richert, Ernst, *Das zweite Deutschland* (Guetersloh, 1964).

———, *Sozialistische Universitaet: Die Hochschulpolitik der SED* (Berlin, 1967).

Stern, Carola, et al., "Ulbricht's Germany: Studies in Intellectual Gleichschaltung," *Soviet Survey*, No. 34 (1960), 30–73.

PART TWO

Politics in the Federal Republic

3

Rules, Parties, and Publics

The dominant patterns of continuity and stability in the Federal Republic present a sharp contrast to previous German regimes and also to the patterns in most other countries in the contemporary world. Thus the first Chancellor, Konrad Adenauer, held office continuously for a longer period of time than did all his twelve predecessors of the Weimar period combined. Unlike other rump states in divided nations, such as South Korea, the maintenance of constitutional government has not been threatened by military putsches or the like. For a long while West Germany seemed similar to Japan, the other country that underwent extensive post-1945 "Occupation surgery"; both were continuously ruled by a single conservative party. But in 1969, after two decades, the Federal Republic accomplished its first complete transition in government.

Certainly there have been different problems and decision-making styles during various phases of the institutionalization process. The physical changes in West Germany between 1950, when many marks of wartime destruction were still evident, and 1965, a time of general prosperity, were paralleled to an extent by changes in political goals and styles. While the earlier period was dominated by questions about equitably sharing the burdens and dislocations inherited from the Nazi regime, the latter period was increasingly concerned with distributing benefits and subsidies from the well-filled coffers of the federal treasury. Whereas earlier West German politicians were still seeking full sovereignty, later they pondered how to use greatly increased political power to restore the balance of power among their former occupiers. But at no time were there any sharp breaks in the system. Discontinuities between successive phases were bridged either by institutions or by personal leadership, often by both.

OCCUPATION THERAPY

Allied policies to uproot Nazism and to punish those who had assisted the Hitler regime brought the impact of defeat home to many Germans. The highest ranking survivors of the Nazi hierarchy, as well as its military and civilian appendices, were of course held to account in the Nuremberg War Trials (in which the Soviet Union also participated). But, in addition, millions of Germans were subjected to denazification proceedings in which the attempt was made to investigate the degree of assistance they had given the Nazi regime and to punish them accordingly. Sentences ranged from prolonged imprisonment, through dismissal from office (418,000 in the United States zone) and the payment of heavy fines, to the obligation to spend stipulated periods of time working as ordinary laborers helping to clear up the rubble or repair desecrated Jewish gravestones. But the difficulty was that obvious criteria—such as membership in the Nazi party and its numerous affiliates—did not provide a reliable means of identifying the worst offenders. The British and French placed relatively little emphasis on punishing the small-time party member, and so they could concentrate their efforts on prosecuting the more active agents of the regime. The Americans, however, decided to have denazification boards review the cases of no fewer than 3.6 million out of 16 million adults in the United States zone, thus creating a staggering task for the relatively few Americans and proven anti-Nazis who had to carry it out. Consequently, denazification proceedings deteriorated; the boards became less thorough and more lenient just when they began to deal with the more serious cases.[1] The Germans, among whom the collective guilt doctrine had created a kind of negative solidarity, were quick to develop theories of self-justification that minimized their role in Nazi excesses and maximized the weaknesses of the denazification process. Gradually the program was

---

[1] John D. Montgomery, *Forced to Be Free: The Artificial Revolution in Germany and Japan* (Chicago, 1957), pp. 10 ff.

replaced by wholly German proceedings against individuals guilty of criminal acts under German law.

The Allies were sufficiently wise to recognize that they could not uproot one elite without replacing it with another. Their policy manuals prescribed that denazification steps were to be matched by democratization actions, not only through the appointment of demonstrated anti-Nazis to public positions but also through the creation of new institutions which would help Germans with impressive democratic credentials assume positions of influence. In this manner, the leaders of the pre-Hitler trade unions were reinstalled in office long before similar invitations were extended to business and professional leaders, whose overall record was far more ambiguous. Similarly, the Occupation authorities began to divest themselves of their monopoly in the communications field by issuing licenses allowing certain anti-Nazis to publish newspapers and by replacing the personnel of the state-run radio. But the most important political instruments of democratization were the political parties, which were licensed only after their programs and membership lists had been screened.

At first, the Western Allies pursued rather disparate aims. The French sought to bring about the dismemberment of Germany, while the British espoused a centralized political system based on the nationalization of industry, and the Americans advocated a federal system based on the maintenance of maximal private property rights. The impasse was resolved, however, by a combination of economic necessity and Soviet intransigence. The Americans and the British were the first to plan the merger of the economic administrations of their economically complementary zones. When the Russians and French refused to join, they gradually began to build up interzonal agencies, which culminated in the creation of the bizonal Economic Council. The French, recognizing the futility of attempts to hold out for a loose confederation of German states, eventually joined forces with the British and Americans, thus turning the bizone into the trizone. This expansion of German government allowed the German politicians to look beyond the horizons of their Laender and to think concretely of vying for national power. The two strongest parties—the Social Democrats (SPD) and the Christian Democrats (CDU)—staked out their positions in the Economic Council, where the

CDU joined the smaller parties in supporting Erhard's free market policy. The Socialists, still loyal to the idea of a planned economy, were confident that Erhard would fail and that the support of the impoverished masses would then bring them to power.

Meanwhile, the widening rift between the Western powers and Soviet Russia in effect reduced the number of alternatives. West Germans could either continue to hope that despite the failure of successive foreign ministers' conferences the Allies would come to an agreement paving the way to an all-German government; or else they could support the immediate efforts to create a German rump state based on the territory of the three Western zones. By the summer of 1948, the mass of West German political opinion was moving toward acceptance of the "Western" solution. All the major party groups were now organizationally cut off from their counterparts in the Soviet zone, while Soviet rejection of the Marshall Plan, followed soon after by the launching of the Berlin Blockade, tended to undercut the arguments of the minority that Germans should accept no constitutional arrangements that were not based on the unification of all four zones. With varying degrees of reluctance, the West German politicians thus accepted the Western Allies' proposal that a constituent assembly be called to draw up a constitution for a West German state, to which the Occupation powers would yield the bulk of German political authority. Although the politicians gave legalistic expression to their reservations by refusing to talk of either a "constituent assembly" or a "constitution," the "Parliamentary Council," which started meeting in September, 1948, to draft the "Basic Law," constructed more than the transitional instrument described in its preamble.

BASIC RULES OF THE BASIC LAW

The members of the Parliamentary Council could not ignore evidence that the traditional operating concepts of the European nation-state were archaic, that the most beautifully drafted constitutions could easily be converted into useless scraps of paper, and that they had little cause to base grandiose plans on an optimistic evaluation of man's political potential. The political complexion of the Council—composed of equally large groups of

CDU and SPD delegates, with minor parties holding a balance of power—also discouraged attempts to incorporate basic economic and social policy goals within the framework of the constitution. But, the name notwithstanding, the delegates did produce a complete constitution, which sought to draw realistic consequences from specific historical experiences.[2]

Contributing to the failure of the Weimar Republic, as the delegates recognized, was the inability of the legislature to surmount internal party strife, the consequent weaknesses of cabinets and the political executive, and, finally, the disappointing function of the President as a guardian of the constitution. There was some talk of forgoing the parliamentary system altogether, in favor of a presidential system based on the separation of powers. But the lack of European experience with this type of government, the unwillingness of all groups—in view of recent experiences— to concentrate as much power in one person as the American system calls for, and a decided distrust of the voters' reliability led them to discard this idea. Instead, the delegates sought to create a "rationalized" variant of the parliamentary system which would meet the traditional problems of German politics.

As a result, the two institutions that had held greatest power under the Weimar Constitution—the popular branch of the legislature and the presidency—were both retained, but their power was greatly reduced. The lower house, whose name was changed from Reichstag to *Bundestag,* lost much of its power to overthrow cabinets. The presidency was shorn of most independent political power and almost reduced to the figurehead position of the British monarch. But the people were also deprived, through the abolition of the initiative and referendum, of those direct political powers which the optimistic drafters of Weimar had provided. By contrast, two traditional institutions gained in influence. One was the federal upper house called the Bundesrat, which, with Allied encouragement, was made much stronger than the Reichsrat had been. But most important, it was the executive, especially the Chancellor's position, that was markedly strength-

.

[2] John F. Golay, *The Founding of the Federal Republic of Germany* (Chicago, 1958); and U.S. Military Government, *Documents on the Creation of the German Federal Constitution* (Washington, 1949).

ened. The constitutional basis on which Adenauer was later able to develop what many people have called a "Chancellor democracy" was in good part due to the drafters' conviction that the Weimar democracy might have been saved if some of its Chancellors had had greater power to impose their policies both on a divided legislature and on fellow cabinet members. The specific constitutional provisions will be examined in greater detail in succeeding chapters, but it is important to become aware at this point of the redistribution of powers which the Basic Law used to make the politics of Bonn so different from those of Weimar.

The dominant characteristic of the Basic Law is the grafting of multiple check and balance mechanisms onto a parliamentary structure. German parliamentarianism had always been heavily adulterated and it became more so. The delegates particularly liked the idea of the American Supreme Court, and they set about creating a Constitutional Court of their own which would assume the role of an arbiter of the constitution. It was empowered to decide not only the constitutionality of legislation and administrative acts but also basic questions of constitutional interpretation, which were expected to develop both among the various parts of the federal government and between it and the Laender. By endowing a novel Constitutional Court with powers to discourage unconstitutional action and to adapt the constitution to changing circumstances, the drafters were confident they had gone far toward eliminating the internal contradictions that had plagued the Weimar system. And they allowed very little room for "emergency powers" which could be used to hollow out the constitution.

The challenge posed by the need to come to terms with the problems associated with the rise of Nazism and the abolition of democratic rights was met by the Parliamentary Council in a piecemeal, but by no means ineffectual, manner. The prominence given civil rights is indicated by the conspicuous place accorded the Bill of Rights at the very beginning of the Basic Law, and also by the fact that its provisions are declared to be directly binding on all courts and authorities. Thus the rights of free speech, press, and assembly are strongly anchored; censorship is prohibited; and equality before the law and the equivalent of habeas corpus are guaranteed. German citizens have the right

FROM THE BASIC LAW

Article 20

(1) The Federal Republic of Germany is a democratic and social Federal state.

(2) All state authority emanates from the people. It shall be exercised by the people by means of elections and voting and by separate legislative, executive and judicial organs.

(3) Legislation shall be limited by the constitution, the executive and the administration of justice by legislation and the law.

Article 79

(1) The Basic Law may be amended only by a law which expressly alters or adds to the text of the Basic Law. [*Note: Special conditions are applicable for the implementation of certain kinds of treaties.*]

(2) Such a law shall require the affirmative vote of two-thirds of the members of the Bundestag and two-thirds of the votes of the Bundesrat.

(3) An amendment to this Basic Law affecting the division of the Federation into Laender, the participation in principle of the Laender in legislation, or the basic principles laid down in Articles 1 and 20 is inadmissible.

Article 73

The Federation shall have exclusive legislation on:

1. foreign affairs as well as defense, including both military service for males over 18 years and the protection of the civilian population.

2. citizenship of the Federation . . .

11. statistics for Federal purposes.

Article 74

Concurrent legislative powers extend to the following matters:

1. civil law, criminal law and execution of sentences, the system of judicature, the procedure of the courts, the legal profession, notaries and legal advice;

2. registration of births, deaths and marriages. . . .

23. railroads, other than Federal railroads, except mountain railroads.

to carry a constitutional plaint directly to the Constitutional Court. Guarantees of civil rights are reinforced with significant provisions for the general maintenance of the democratic order, particularly through provisions which permit the suppression of antidemocratic movements. Thus, "parties, which, according to their aims and the behavior of their members, seek to impair or abolish the free and democratic basic order" may be declared unconstitutional by the Constitutional Court.

LAENDER AND FEDERALISM

Like the American institutions of 1789, the national political institutions created for West Germany were imposed upon an existing structure of state governments. The traditional German states or Laender, which had been abolished by the Nazis, were resuscitated and reorganized by the Allies, who abolished the previously dominant state of Prussia. In setting up the Laender two basic problems were encountered. In south and southwest Germany, loyalty to the Laender was still very much alive, but the zonal boundaries imposed by the Occupation cut across traditional Land boundaries. In northwest Germany, on the other hand, a century of Prussian hegemony had largely destroyed regional loyalties, so that after Prussia, the British had to set up Laender without much regard to local traditions. Apart from the two city-states of Hamburg and Bremen, the only revived Land with both historical traditions and prewar boundaries was Bavaria, a fact which has helped the Bavarians gain influence in national politics. With the hope of preventing the re-creation of a strong central government, the French, and to some extent also the Americans, encouraged the small Laender in their zones to set up elaborate governmental machinery, and they encouraged a largely artificial Land patriotism. The British on the other hand exercised centralized control through zonal authorities, and though they too set up such new Laender as Lower Saxony, Northrhine-Westphalia, and Schleswig-Holstein, they did not attempt to revive archaic boundaries or to encourage Land governments to exaggerate their political significance.[3]

[3] Roger H. Wells, "State Government," in E. H. Litchfield, ed., *Governing Postwar Germany* (Ithaca, 1953), pp. 84–117.

The proper role of the Laender and the federal principles to be incorporated in the Basic Law caused great controversy among the Germans and the Allies. Regarding the division of legislative powers between the Laender and the federal government, German traditions and preferences for a maximum degree of uniformity favored giving the lion's share of authority to the federal government. Among the exclusive legislative powers of the federal government are those relating to the areas of foreign affairs, citizenship, and so on; the list of federal powers is very similar to that in Article 1, Section 8, of the United States Constitution. But the provisions concerning concurrent powers are a more significant index to the greater legislative predominance of the German federal government. Here too both constitutional provisions and German practice leave the federal legislature the lion's share of power in relation to such subjects as civil and criminal law, legislation relating to economic affairs, agriculture, forests and fisheries, housing, and many other areas usually left to state or provincial legislation in other countries. The Laender's reserved powers are kept rather limited, but do include the power to legislate in important areas like education, the police, radio and television, and on other subjects not listed as either exclusive or concurrent powers of the federal government.[4]

Though the "federalist" forces influencing the drafting of the Basic Law realized that the bulk of legislative power would remain with the central government, they were concerned nonetheless about reversing the long-term trend in which the Land governments had gradually become subsidiary and dependent units. To strengthen the position of the Laender in the area of administration, they successfully reintroduced the earlier German practice of confining the federal bureaucracy largely to policy-making, leaving the execution of federal legislation on the lower echelons to the Laender. In this and in their efforts to assure the Laender independent tax sources, they were largely successful. But they also wanted to assure the Laender an effective voice in the federal legislative process, so the type of second chamber to be established was important. The "centralists" were

[4] Carl J. Friedrich and H. J. Spiro, "The Constitution of the German Federal Republic," in Litchfield, *Governing Postwar Germany,* pp. 117–51.

in favor of a Senate-type chamber; its members would be directly elected by the populations of the various Laender and would, presumably, come to represent their parties more than their states. The "federalists," on the other hand, advocated a second chamber composed exclusively of the Land ministers themselves; this Bundesrat solution was the one that was finally adopted.

EMERGENCY PROVISIONS

In June, 1968, many amending articles and paragraphs—the long-debated set of Emergency Laws—were added to the Basic Law, making it 50 per cent longer. The amendments were much more complex than the infamous antecedent, the emergency article (48) of the Weimar Constitution; the vast web of the 1968 amendments altered nearly 30 of the 160 articles of the Basic Law. Together with related legislation, the amendments (a) created a new organ with both peacetime and emergency responsibilities; (b) permit peacetime surveillance of written and oral telecommunications for security purposes under nonjudicial control; (c) in emergency situations reinforce police powers, provide for extensive command of the economy and its labor force, and greatly centralize the distribution of powers.

No legislative proposal in the history of the Federal Republic was so bitterly contested for so long a time. In one form or another Emergency Law drafts had been considered in the legislature for more than a decade. For a long time the trade unions and the SPD opposed their passage, but when the Social Democrats entered the coalition under Kurt Kiesinger in 1966, they agreed to negotiate for passage of an acceptable version. The negotiations, of course, made the texts even more complex. But this did not lessen a very vocal opposition which organized many highly publicized, nationwide demonstrations throughout 1967–68. Its leaders argued that the limitations of civic freedoms contained in the amendments could be misused by reactionary and militarist elements. They asked why the Federal Republic needed a set of constitutional emergency laws when many countries, such as the United States and Britain, managed to do without them. The supporters answered that, for instance, the rights of the Japanese-Americans interned by executive fiat during World War II might have been better safeguarded if the United States laws had been more explicit about powers and rights during national emergency.

Many limitations on civil rights can be imposed only in specifically defined "internal" or "external" emergencies. Thus, even prior to the determination of a defense emergency, individuals may, if the Bundestag approves, be required to attend training courses that would prepare them for emergency service (ART. 12). Similarly, the privacy of mail and telecommunications messages may be infringed in peacetime without recourse to the courts "if it serves to protect the free democratic order" (ART. 10). Proponents of these changes argued that such infringements had been occurring right along anyway under the umbrella of Allied "reserve powers" carried over from the Occupation period. If, henceforth, German police want to tap the phone of a Communist or anarchist, they at least don't any longer have to work through the CIA. To counter arguments that they were tilting the constitution too much in favor of the state and its police power, the government inserted a balancing clause which provides: "All Germans shall have the right to resist any person or persons seeking to abolish the constitutional order, should no other remedy be possible" (ART. 20). However, critics argued that this did not really add to existing rights, and in fact subjected the right to resist to control by the main body of emergency legislation.[5]

Some of the emergency powers are intended to apply to situations of civil unrest. These do not allow broad suspensions of civil liberties, but they strengthen police power and its coordination by the federal executive. These provisions were criticized in an American law journal because "the vague standard for invoking the powers, the absence of a prior procedural check, and the weaknesses of *post hoc* check leave the federal executive considerable discretion to suppress even legitimate dissent."[6] Upon the declaration of a defense emergency, following a threat from outside, many more civil rights may be infringed, including the rights to travel and to choose one's occupation. Rules against the expropriation of property and pre-arraignment detention are re-

---

[5] Otto Ernst, "Widerstandsrecht," in Dieter Sterzel, ed., *Kritik der Not-standsgesetze* (Frankfurt, 1968), p. 85.

[6] "Recent Emergency Legislation in West Germany," *Harvard Law Review*, LXXXII, 2 (June, 1969), 1724.

laxed. The federal government may take over the Laender's legislative powers and issue instructions to Land governments. The application of emergency powers requires Bundestag and Bundesrat approval, but in a situation of defense emergency the legislative power of the two houses is transferred to an "emergency parliament," consisting of a joint committee of twenty-two Bundestag and eleven Bundesrat members. This committee has the power to amend all legislation with the exception of the Basic Law itself. But what happens if the joint committee itself is unable to function in a war situation? The otherwise meticulous rules do not answer that question.

PARTIES AS ORGANS OF GOVERNMENT

The political party system has contributed much to the achievement of political stability in the Federal Republic. Contrary to pessimistic expectations, the original parties licensed by the Allies managed to build and maintain independent followings. Moreover, their number did not expand to the point of inhibiting the functioning of parliamentary government, but shrank in the course of the 1950's and 1960's; as a result, Germany moved closer to a two-party system than any other continental country. Unlike their predecessors in Weimar Germany or many contemporary parties in other European countries, the major German parties have avoided significant splits and have maintained a remarkably stable following. For the first time in German history, the Federal Rupublic produced a party which could win the votes of an absolute majority, and together the democratic parties have attracted the support of all but a small minority of the German electorate. In sharp contrast to the Weimar period, extremist parties have had minimal influence, and small, special interest parties have had little success in drawing support away from the major parties.

Taking advantage of the recognition granted them by Article 21 of the Basic Law, the major parties progressed toward institutionalization as components of the governmental apparatus. Just how far this process should go—was it legitimate, for instance, for political parties to allocate public funds to themselves—became a subject of controversy both legalistically, in cases brought to the Constitutional Court, and among publicists and laymen.

The decrease in the number of parties and in the degree of partisan polarization of opinion has also meant that the public has fewer alternative policy solutions. To an extent, this has caused nonparty and even nonpolitical organs to become more important forums of deliberation and has made the established parties appear hostile to nonconformist ideas. Cumulatively, all these factors have caused "input" processes in general and party politics in particular to appear decreasingly interesting from the perspective of the "only-voter" spectator. But they have of course not lessened the activities of the professional lobbyists and other representatives of organized interests vying for the support of the party politicians.

In time, especially after 1965, a reaction against what was viewed as the oligopolistic sharing of power by the major parties —the Christian Democrats (CDU/CSU), the Social Democrats (SPD), and the Free Democrats (FDP)—brought about a slow-down in the process of party system concentration that had been going on for twenty years. The fissiparous tendencies emerged in four related ways. First, the trend toward a two-party system came to a halt, in part because the third party, the smaller FDP, did not wither away. The attempt to relegate the FDP to a status comparable to the British Liberal party failed when politicians were unsuccessful in their efforts in 1967–68 to introduce a majority electoral system. Second, the CDU/CSU itself showed fissiparous tendencies, especially after its Bavarian wing (the CSU) decided to call itself a distinct party for public subsidy and other purposes. Third, and perhaps most important, third parties now have a much better chance of success, in part because of the growth of radical and nationalist antisystem sentiment of various ideological colorations. This anti-establishment feeling helped the hypernationalist National Democratic party (NPD), which, after 1966, succeeded in electing numerous *Landtag* deputies, but was not able to enter the Bundestag in 1969. Other small parties, including a rather docile German Communist party founded in 1969, were encouraged to run candidates by court rulings that even small parties which won as little as one-half of one per cent of the vote were entitled to public party subsidies. Finally, though the student-based Extra-Parliamentary Opposition represents only a small minority that specifically disavows channeling its opposition through structured organizations like parties, it too has had complex impact on the way the party system is perceived and supported by the population at large.

THE CHRISTIAN DEMOCRATIC UNION (CDU)

To understand the changed structure of the German party system one must look at the character and growth of the Christian Democratic Union. This party was established in 1945 by Catholics who wanted to overcome the limitations of the all-Catholic Center party of the pre-1933 era and by Protestants, conservatives, and liberals who had previously belonged to half a dozen right-of-center or center parties. They now rallied to unite, partly because of common values, but mainly from fear that they would be overwhelmed by the anticipated strength of the left-wing parties. They never attempted to work out fundamentals or details of their political program, and the party retained quite different complexions in different parts of the country. Many, including the Socialist leaders, expected that this alliance would soon fall apart, but they were proved wrong. What held the party together was neither its loose organization nor its largely negative

---

POLITICAL PARTIES

Article 21

(1) The political parties shall participate in forming the political will of the people. They can be freely formed. Their internal organization must conform to democratic principles. They must publicly account for the sources of their funds.

(2) Parties which, by reason of their aims or the behavior of their adherents, seek to impair or abolish the free and democratic basic order or to endanger the existence of the Federal Republic of Germany, are unconstitutional. The Federal Constitutional Court shall decide on the question of unconstitutionality.

(3) Details will be regulated by Federal legislation.

anti-Socialist ideology, but strong personal leadership which turned the party's weaknesses into virtues. Konrad Adenauer, a pre-1933 mayor of Cologne who had never played a significant role in national politics, quickly emerged as the leader of the Christian Democrats, first in the British, and finally in all three Western zones. He proved himself an extremely skilled tactician, utilizing the party's lack of attachment to organization, program, or ideology to seize the opportunities which opened up in the rapidly shifting political situation. In contrast to his great rival Kurt Schumacher, Adenauer never "fought City Hall" but accepted the consequences of the East-West split as inevitable and goaded his party to accept the facts, to get behind successful programs like Erhard's Social Market Policy, and to assume the responsibility of government.[7]

So adeptly did Adenauer play his cards that he was installed as Chancellor before the CDU had even formally elected a leader or set up a national organization. He succeeded in identifying himself with Germany's reacceptance into the Western family of nations and with achievements in the area of German reconstruction. By appealing to the German tendency to support established authority, he succeeded in developing a powerful popular following, both for himself as Chancellor and for the CDU as the party favoring constructive policies. This appeal allowed the CDU, together with its Bavarian branch, the Christian Social Union (CSU), to win the smashing electoral victories of 1953 and 1957 which resulted in successively larger majorities in the Bundestag. Thus Adenauer did not have to rely so much on minor party support. In the early 1960's, Adenauer's power was on the decline, and he finally acceded to widespread pressure to yield the office to Ludwig Erhard in 1963. But Erhard never won control of the party as Adenauer had. In fact, he was not allowed to become Adenauer's successor as party chairman until March, 1966; then, six months later, he had to pay the price of weak government leadership by resigning as Chancellor. The CDU survived the unhappy Erhard interlude, but only barely, and to carry on the government it had to form a coalition with the SPD.

[7] Arnold J. Heidenheimer, *Adenauer and the CDU: The Rise of the Leader and the Integration of the Party* (The Hague, 1960), pp. 92–178.

Because of its continuing domination of the federal government, and for other reasons as well, the CDU became identified as *the* government party of the Federal Republic. As the Social Democrat Herbert Wehner put it, "The CDU has too much of that quality of which the SPD has too little: a sense for how to handle political power."[8] The disparate CDU leadership developed into an *ersatz* ruling class; for a long time, no other party gave it effective competition. But CDU leaders also exuded self-confidence because of their close contact with the elites in all spheres of German society. Thus, most of the power wielders in German industry and business, agriculture, the churches, and the civil service were either members or adherents of the CDU. It is a middle-class party, but it is also much more than that. It is or has been a party of the Chancellor's loyal followers, of those who put economic stability first, of those who have accepted the NATO alliance as their guiding light. When Kurt Georg Kiesinger inherited the leadership in 1966, he had to share government power with the SPD, and he had considerable difficulty persuading some CDU/CSU circles that they could no longer have as much power as before. At numerous party congresses Kiesinger was subjected to personal criticism, and even discourtesies.

During its Grand Coalition with the SPD (1966–69) the CDU gradually became the most conservative of the three major parties. As the Free Democrats turned to the left, many of its more conservative followers joined the CDU. At the same time, the "Euronationalist" CSU wing, led by Franz Josef Strauss, sought to compete with the NDP for the nationalist-authoritarian vote. The party's left-wing is based on Catholic trade unionists, and there are numerous progressives among its parliamentary and middle-echelon leadership groups. In recent years, as it has moved away from its role as a vehicle for economic interest groups, the CDU has sought to develop integrated programs. Aware that the bulk of its voting support comes from rural and small-town areas, the party has also been trying to attract urban voters, whose proportion in the total population is increasing all the time.

The CDU reelected Kiesinger party chairman at its post-elec-

---

[8] Herbert Wehner, "Die programmierte CDU," *Neue Gesellschaft* (February, 1969).

tion convention in November, 1969, and he proclaimed that he intended to lead the party again into the 1973 elections. For him as well as for the party, this was the first exercise in playing the opposition role. In the Bundestag, Kiesinger shares leadership of the CDU with Rainer Barzel, chairman of the parliamentary party. The unclear division of responsibility between the two leaders could cause friction, especially in view of continuing problems with the Bavarian sister party, the CSU, and its ebullient leader, Franz Josef Strauss. Skeptics, whose prediction of a split in the ranks of the CDU/CSU remained unfulfilled for two decades, believe that the strains of the opposition role may wear down the bonds that have held the party together. In recent years, a younger generation of men born in the late 1920's have moved into the top rungs of the party leadership. Besides Barzel, these include Gerhard Stoltenberg and Helmut Kohl, who were newly elected to party vice-chairmanships in 1969. Another vice-chairman is Hans Katzer, a leader of the party's left wing that draws its strength from Catholic workers.

The Social Democratic Party (SPD)

When Konrad Adenauer, as a septuagenarian, helped found the CDU in Cologne in 1945, he was seeking to check the SPD, a party which was already well established when he himself was a youth in the Bismarckian era. Founded in the 1860's, the SPD was avowedly a working-class party pledged to the eradication of private ownership of the means of production and the abolition of capitalist society. Though relegated under the Empire to the minor role of an "opposition of principle" that found no common ground between itself and the regime, it rallied increasing majorities of the working class to its banner. In the decade before 1914, it had become the largest party in the Reichstag. Though the war and the subsequent split-off of its left wing into the Communist party halted a further increase in its growth, the SPD remained throughout the Weimar period a strongly disciplined organization committed to evolutionary social change and the defense of democratic parliamentary institutions. During the Nazi period its leaders went into exile and concentration camps because of their democratic convictions.

After 1945, the Socialists were supremely confident that as

the party with the strongest anti-Nazi record, a long history of support of democracy, and a strong party organization they would lead Germany's reconstruction. Their expectations were frustrated. The shotgun marriage between Communists and Socialists in the Soviet zone, which resulted in the formation of the Socialist Unity party (SED), and the subsequent division of Germany separated the Socialist leadership under the forceful Kurt Schumacher from those areas where it had traditionally enjoyed the strongest support. Next, the success of the CDU created a formidable rival for middle-class and even working-class support. But worst of all, the Socialists found the very strength of their organization and program an embarrassment. The loyalty of the workers maintained the class party image, and none of Schumacher's policies—championing German national interests against Allied policies, opposing economic liberalism and German rearmament, and finally even coming out against German participation in organizations like the Council of Europe and the European Coal and Steel Community—won the party any significant new share of middle-class votes. Thus, while the CDU succeeded in breaking out of the prewar Center party's traditional "Catholic ghetto," until 1961 the SPD was unable to expand much beyond the industrial working-class districts.

The SPD's failure to win significant new followers among the voters or potential allies among other parties can be attributed to the dysfunctional tactics of Schumacher. As Lewis Edinger's biography forcefully shows,[9] the psychological forces driving this domineering personality led him to foreclose to the party all chances of achieving national power. After his death it took almost a decade for the party to establish a viable new position.

The groundwork for the SPD's new self-image and role orientation was laid in a Basic Program adopted in 1959. Named the Bad Godesberg program after the city where the special party congress met that year, it replaced the previous basic program adopted by the party in 1925. The new program jettisoned most of the Marxist theoretical constructs that had been its heritage

[9] Lewis J. Edinger, *Kurt Schumacher* (Stanford, 1965).

for generations. Largely dropping its commitment to economic policies based on a planned economy and socialization, the SPD embraced the free market economy and conceded that private ownership of the means of production had "a claim to protection and support insofar as it does not hinder the building of a just social order." Philosophically, the party also abandoned many concepts based on class categories and economic determinism and showed a desire to embrace new supra-class symbols and more effective styles of communication. The party also sought to end its traditional hostility toward established religion and, as a result, changed its role definition: "A party is no longer regarded as a church or a counter-church. It is not a school of philosophers. It does not feel obliged to explain the history of mankind. This has to be left to the universities and individual thinkers and searchers." In its new image as an efficient instrument for implementing reforms and modernization in an industrial society, the SPD appeared more attractive to some middle-class voters, although the CDU claimed that it had merely taken over many CDU programs.

The turn toward pragmatism was particularly noticeable in the West Berlin SPD, which had control of the Land government there and was under considerable pressure to react against the ideology-laden messages from the GDR. An American political scientist who interviewed both SPD and CDU party officials on questions related to an ideology-pragmatism scale actually found that the CDU party officials were more ideology-oriented than the Socialist ones. While the older SPD officials of working-class origins were more ideological, the "younger leaders of higher socio-economic status and . . . educational level . . . and the officials who served in middle-class competitive districts were less ideological and more pragmatic." His finding that the "deemphasis on ideology in the SPD has been communicated to the lower party echelons" is the result of elaborate efforts by the party, including the use of programmed learning kits to rinse out the Marxist ideological heritage from its membership. In view of these efforts it is not surprising that the generational counter-reaction, and the present trend toward Marxian and other ideological programs, is particularly pronounced among the students and youth of West Berlin.[10]

The younger reformers who are coming to the fore in the SPD in the 1970's have given priority to turning pragmatist. As the former chairman of the party's youth group wrote, "If one thing is sure it is that today the study of the methods of a large American advertising agency is of more value in regard to an election outcome than the study of the program of another foreign Socialist party used to be decades ago." He urged his party to "weep no tears for the notorious oppositionists" who, because they placed prime value on being different, had wandered off to the NPD or other "outsiders' parties."[11] This sentiment characterizes the growth of positive Socialist attitudes toward power, which Herbert Wehner, in particular, has encouraged since the mid-1950's. But recently some other young leaders have been echoing the sentiments of older colleagues that the de-ideologization drive has gone too far. After a "decade of careful tactical steps" designed to "make it easier for party switchers to come over to it," the feeling is that a party with the SPD's structure could never beat one like the CDU at tactical adaptability. Since it still draws its major support from groups desiring further social change so as to gain their full rights, the party could not afford to "dispense with ideologically shaped long-term goals, lest it abandon to the conservative opponent the task of shaping the consciousness of its followers."[12]

Willy Brandt, the SPD's third chairman in the postwar period, became head of the party in 1958 after the death of Erich Ollenhauer, who had succeeded Kurt Schumacher in 1952. A whole generation of Social Democratic leaders sat on the Bundestag's opposition benches for almost two decades, and many never became ministers because time ran out on them. Most of the party's present leaders—such as Brandt, Herbert Wehner, Alex

---

[10] William E. Wright, "Ideological-Pragmatic Orientations of West Berlin Local Party Officials," *Midwest Journal of Political Science,* XI (August, 1967).

[11] "Gesellschaft der Zukunft," in Gunther Muller, ed., *Die Zukunft der SPD* (Hamburg, 1968), pp. 28–29.

[12] Joachim Steffen, "Nicht der Wähler, die SPD ist schuld," *Die Zeit,* May 28, 1968.

Moeller, and Karl Schiller—were born in the decade before 1914. Wehner, the organizational strong man, "remodeled" the party and now serves as chairman of the parliamentary party in the Bundestag. The Social Democrats switch more often between government and party positions than their CDU colleagues. For them important party positions can be more attractive than cabinet posts; these carry more power and prestige than they do in the CDU, which has consistently kept its organization under-developed. The SPD's present general secretary, Heinz-Jochen Wischnewski, resigned a cabinet position to assume his post, just as Wehner did.

THE FREE DEMOCRATIC PARTY (FDP)

The Free Democratic party is the only one of some ten smaller parties from the post-1949 period to survive the two-party trend, remaining continuously represented in the Bundestag and most Land legislatures. At times it has looked as if the FDP's persistence, and its success in fending off a majority electoral law, might institutionalize a three-party system. The Free Democrats owe their survival to a more enduring national constituency than the other small-party rivals, as well as to great tactical adaptability. The backbone of the FDP has been made up of portions of the religiously emancipated Protestant middle class who are dissatisfied with both major parties. Its following has been liberal, progressive, and "national liberal," with constant stress among these factions. Under conservative leaders, the FDP participated in several Adenauer and Erhard cabinets. But in 1969 it joined with the SPD to elect President Heinemann and to form an SPD/FDP cabinet.

What distinguishes the FDP from the two major parties are its frequent and rather sharp shifts in both policy and leadership. The Free Democrats have changed their national leadership frequently, with leaders and cabinet members always moving on and off the main stage. Originally the party was considered on the right wing of the Adenauer coalition, but now it falls to the left of the CDU on some issues and even left of the SPD on others, such as in its readiness to give greater recognition to East Germany. The Free Democrats previously thought of themselves as a liberal party, but since in the European context this has right-wing connotations, they now identify more with the progressive image. Most of the more conservative leaders who led into the earlier coalitions with the CDU have retired, and many of the FDP's original supporters have gone over to the CDU. FDP progressives made a determined bid for leadership after the formation of the Grand Coalition and succeeded in winning control of the party. The party is led by a triumvirate composed of party leader Walter Scheel and his deputies Herbert Mischnick and Hans Genscher. Since the FDP attracts many individualists who like to defy the majority consensus, the leaders always have a difficult time lining up the deputies behind party policy. In order to actually deliver the pro-Heinemann votes they had promised to the SPD, FDP leaders carried the delegates through a number of mock ballots to ensure a reasonably cohesive voting pattern.

The FDP's decision to accept Willy Brandt's invitation to join his cabinet was opposed by the "national-liberal" wing of the party, three of whose deputies, including Erich Mende, a former party leader, abstained in the vote on Brandt's Chancellorship bid. This made it evident that the coalition's slim lead of twelve Bundestag votes was not a reliable one. Subsequently many right-wing FDP Landtag deputies and local party leaders left the party. Reaction against Foreign Minister Scheel's leading role in negotiating the new Eastern policy provoked plans for a national-liberal splinter party, which might also appeal to disgruntled expellee voters. In October, 1970, Mende led two other right-wingers in leaving the party to join the opposition. This reduced the government majority from twelve to six votes, and raised the question of whether the FDP would fall short of the five-percent barrier in forthcoming Land elections. But a resurgence in FDP support diminished the possibility that even the FDP might fall victim to the five-percent barrier by the time of the next federal elections.

MINOR PARTIES

The decline of the minor parties proceeded inexorably. Whereas in 1950 there were almost a dozen political parties with a fairly wide following and representation in the Bundestag, in 1960 only three were left. The first casualties of political rationalization and the "5 per cent clause" were small regional parties. Some of these—like the Bavarian party (BP), the Center party in North-rhine-Westphalia, and the German party (DP) in Lower Saxony —were aided for a time by the CDU because they were useful in helping to establish majorities on the Land or national level. Nevertheless, they continually declined for lack of leadership and independent programs.[13] Others—such as the early Reconstruction Association (WAV), with a base of support in Bavaria, and the Expellees party (BHE), which had strength in areas where the expellees were concentrated—were special interest parties that declined as their constituencies were absorbed into the prosperous German citizenry. Until the early 1960's, some minor parties maintained a measure of influence on the Land level. However, the neo-Nazi Socialist Reich party (SRP)[14] and the Communist party (KPD) had lost most of their popular support by the time they were declared illegal in 1952 and 1956 respectively. Minor right-wing parties that were not made illegal by law, like the German Reich party (DRP), also steadily lost influence as the small nationalist revival, which reached its high point in 1951–52, ebbed in the face of official hostility and the unwillingness of Germans to commit themselves to hoary causes.

THE NATIONAL DEMOCRATIC PARTY (NPD)

The National Democrats for a while seemed to be an exception to the rule that radical splinter parties were becoming nonviable. A hypernationalist party with many former Nazis in its leadership, it was similar to right-wing predecessors like the DRP and SRP but was much more successful in appealing to the electorate; the NPD also avoided being outlawed as anti-democratic. Although it garnered only 2 per cent of the vote in the federal elections of 1965, it fared much better in Landtag elections during the 1966–68 period when opposition to the Grand Coalition was at its zenith. In these elections it polled nearly 10 per cent of the total vote, and in some localities went as high as 15 or 20 per cent. These victories permitted the NPD to jump the "5 per cent" barrier and enter most of the Land diets. For a while its success seemed to parallel the record of the National

[13] Otto Kirchheimer, "Notes on West Germany," *WP*, VI (1954), 306–21.
[14] Otto Buesch and Peter Furth, *Rechtsradikalismus im Nachkriegsdeutschland* (Berlin, 1958).

Socialists; they had climbed rapidly from 2.6 per cent of the total vote in 1928 to 18.3 per cent in 1930. Was history repeating itself?

The mere suggestion that it might caused the NPD to become the most intensely studied political party in Europe.[15] Observers found that the party tried to hold its hypernationalist appeals distinct from standard Nazi slogans. They were cynical, however, about the NPD's position as a conservative nationalist party committed to the constitution, since an avowed anti-democratic position would have invited suppression. The party managed to attract a much wider range of followers than its predecessors. Though they tended to dominate the national leadership, old fighters with a Nazi past were only one component. Other NPD members and deputies considered themselves more in the national-conservative tradition and may have been genuine in their disavowal of Nazism. But most unusual was the party's strong appeal to young people, many of whom had never experienced Nazism even as children. Some of the party's most aggressive candidates were men in their twenties, and its rallies also drew support from some sections of the rebellious youth who rallied to a symbol that was frowned upon by their elders. In its appeals, the NPD promised to put an end to the moral reproaches and discrimination the outside world ostensibly leveled against Germans because of what the Nazis had done in their name.

The factional struggles that have been the bane of most right-wing parties also plagued the NPD, leading to the expulsion of its first chairman. But the party managed to rally its forces and solidify its organization under Alfred von Thadden, who took over the leadership in 1967. Nine out of ten members in von Thadden's party presidium were former Nazis, but the "brown" coloration declined in the lower echelons of the party. Only a minority (35 per cent) of the 20,000 NPD members ever belonged to the NSDAP, and the several million NPD voters constituted almost a cross-section of the population. These voters were former supporters of minor parties, the SPD, and the CDU, in that order. Some believed that the relatively high proportion of ex-SPD

---

[15] For a comprehensive bibliography, see Lutz Niethammer, *Angepasster Faschismus* (Frankfurt, 1969), pp. 284–88.

voters resulted from the fact that "traditional nay-sayers" had become dissatisfied with the SPD as an oppositionist organ. Though the NPD adherents were somewhat better educated and some enjoyed above-average incomes, they were on the whole more dissatisfied with their lot. Their resentment was based on feelings of status deprivation, which they compensated for through the party's denigration of foreign workers, Jews, immigrants and other outsiders. Among the status-deprived groups attracted by the party were Bundeswehr soldiers and officers, whose high rate of sympathy for the NPD caused alarm. The party also did well in economically marginal areas; in general, its electoral appeal varied inversely with economic conditions. In 1969, a boom economy together with the persistent pounding of the party by all democratic forces caused the NPD's vote to plummet to 4.3 per cent, which shut it out of the Bundestag.

INTERESTS AND PARTIES

An analysis of West German interest group structure must take into account one factor which makes the situation very different from that in the United States: in Germany, many special interests are much older than the state, and some, like the Catholic church, even antedate the time when Germans became conscious of their national identity. In the United States, few groups or subcultures reject the main course of constitutional development. The vast majority of them, including even the major religious organizations, developed the bulk of their tradition only after the political institutions were already established. But in Germany, Bavarian farmers or Catholic Rhinelanders or Hanseatic merchants remain very much aware that their traditions have far deeper historical and institutional roots than those of the national political system.

A second category of German interest groups makes claims on the loyalty of members and seeks special treatment in public discussion because of factors related to the evolution of the German social system. Unlike the American, the German social system evolved from a feudal background, and in the process a tradition of loyalty to "estate" and social class developed which still affects the function of some interest groups. A typical example of an antiquated estate claiming privileges for historical reasons was the East Elbian Junkers, who during the Weimar period demanded special subsidies essentially because their forefathers had captured East Prussia from the Poles in the twelfth century. Other old socioeconomic groups—like the civil servants and, to a lesser degree, artisans and farmers—continue to this day to make claims for special treatment founded, at least in part, on rights accorded their estate during the feudal or preconstitutional periods. They compete with organizations based on social or class position, like the trade unions, which continue to appeal to the loyalty of their members and also bid for recognition in the political process, not only because of specific goals and the size of their membership, but also because they have played an historical role in opening up the full privileges of citizenship for members of their class.

Both of the aforementioned groups object to being compared to an association of used car dealers or a commercial fishermen's organization. Nevertheless, the newer kinds of narrowly economic interest groups set up to achieve pragmatic ends have become more numerous and more important as Germany has disestablished vested privileges and become an industrial society much like the United States. These newer associations with professional staffs, closely knit organizations, and experienced lobbyists are growing in influence rivaling the older groups. At the same time, many of these new interest groups have gained the right to participate in the political process by assuming a semipublic character as administrators of certain kinds of regulations. Thus German chambers of commerce, chambers of agriculture, and professional organizations have much greater power than most American equivalents and are in a position to make membership in related interest group organizations obligatory for all clients. All of these factors strengthen the position of the interest groups, and at times they emerge not only as powerful claimants on the political parties but even as rivals, who through their representatives in the legislature and their contacts in the administration will work independently when the parties do not seem sufficiently responsive.

The way German interests function politically can best be shown by a brief examination of two of the most important groups—the Catholic church and the Trade Union Federation.

Though both are officially neutral, they made their sympathies abundantly clear. In one 1957 survey, 83 per cent of
the German people associated Catholics with the CDU, only 1
per cent with the SPD; similarly 77 per cent associated the
trade unions with the SPD, only 1 per cent with the CDU.[16]
During election campaigns Catholic organs gave fairly open support to the CDU. Thus the Government Press Office reported in
1957 that "the main theme for the month of August in the Catholic Church press is the Bundestag election of September 15. Detailed reports highlight the great achievement of the present government in all domains." In addition Catholic bishops sent out pas-
toral letters which were read to a quarter of the German electorate
on pre-election Sunday, with messages like: "Do your electoral
duty! Vote only for men and women whose basic Christian principles are well known and whose public activity corresponds to
these principles." After the adoption of the Bad Godesberg program, the Social Democrats went to great pains to make themselves appear more acceptable to Catholic clergy and layman.
Toward this end they were even prepared to make concessions
on the principle of publicly supported denominational schools,
which they had long rejected. In 1965, the Socialist-led government of Lower Saxony became the first German Land government to sign a postwar concordat with the Vatican. Through
it the Land pledged itself to promote special Catholic educational
facilities from the grade school to the university level and not to
allow public communication media to be used for purposes hostile
to the Catholic church.

By making such concessions in a Land where the Catholics
made up only 20 per cent of the population, the party tried to
show that it could put aside its own inclinations where local traditions and demands seemed to warrant it. By doing so, the SPD
laid itself open to the charge of being "more papist than the
CDU." In due time SPD representatives appeared regularly at
Catholic congresses, and the percentage of Catholics voting SPD
increased measurably, though more in the cities than in the rural
areas. The "opening up" of the Catholic subcultures, which developed all over Europe in the wake of the Vatican Council, has

---

[16] Divo Institut, *Umfragen 1957* (Frankfurt, 1958), p. 50.

proceeded more slowly in Germany than in Holland. But the questioning of Catholic dogma and church authority also led the German Catholic Convocation of 1969 to pass resolutions openly critical of Pope Paul's birth control encyclical. One of the SPD federal cabinet ministers, George Leber, is a practicing Catholic. The fact that Leber also led one of the larger unions illustrates the extent to which the union-church polarization diminished during the decade.

The unions in the German Trade Union Federation have accepted the SPD's need to transcend its original working-class base. But they have been unhappy when the SPD's concern for other interest groups has caused it to give lower priority to such top union goals as the extension of co-determination within industry. Nevertheless, loyalty to the SPD led the unions, even the somewhat left-wing metal workers' union, to support the Grand Coalition's policies. An analysis of the metal union's newspaper showed a significant difference in the proportion of attacks on the government and the employers in periods before and after the SPD's entry into the Grand Coalition. In autumn, 1966, when the SPD was still in opposition, the paper launched thirty-six attacks against the government and ten against employers. During a similar period in autumn, 1967, the union organ criticized the Grand Coalition government fourteen times, while it took thirty-five swipes at employers.[17]

There are of course hundreds of other interest groups operating in Germany. Some of the more powerful ones are the Federation of German Industry, the farmers' organization, the various expellees' groups and *Landsmannschaften,* and the artisans' organizations.[18] At least three hundred of these organizations have offices in Bonn to keep in touch with political developments affecting their interest. Most of them, representing industrial and trade associations, operate much like their American counterparts. But their role in the political process is even more controversial than in the United States. The reason is that West

[17] Christa Hoffmann, "Der Kommunikationsfluss von einer Gewerkschaftsleitung zu ihren Funktionaren," *Hamburger Jahrbuch fuer Wirtschafts- und Sozialpolitik,* 1968 (Hamburg, 1968), p. 340.

[18] Rupert Breitling, *Die Verbaende in der Bundesrepublik: Ihre Arten und ihre politischen Wirkungsweise* (Meisenheim, 1955).

Germans have still not completely accepted the principles of a pluralistic democracy. Since many Germans developed their concepts of politics around hierarchical or monolithic models of the state, they are reluctant to concede that the public interest can be adequately defined through the freewheeling competition of "selfish" pressure groups. It is still felt that interest groups should present their requests to the state "from the outside," that is, that they should not directly influence decision-making in the legislature and the administration. However, the organized interest groups are clearly triumphing over their critics. Moreover, the procedures of the federal bureaucracy not only permit interest groups special access but even encourage them to amalgamate at the national level. The Rules of Procedure, binding on all the federal ministries, provide that their officials shall deal with representatives of central or peak associations, not with local interest groups. And the rules concerning which interest groups shall be consulted in the preparation of legislative drafts stipulate that only nationwide associations are to be involved.[19]

POLITICAL RECRUITMENT

Few factors can sap the crucial self-esteem of politicians more rapidly than the realization that the younger generation is unwilling to follow in their professional footsteps. The memoirs and autobiographies of the leaders of the middle-of-the-road parties of the Weimar period, like Stresemann, testify how the inability to recruit younger talent contributed to a lessening of faith in their own aims. Political recruitment, of course, did occur during this period, but dedicated young men were often drawn either directly to parties of the extreme left or right or to small "circles" and "brotherhoods" which served as intermediary recruiting grounds for the nationalist movements. As this development suggests, recruitment is a crucial political process not only quantitatively, in regard to the total participation elicited, but also in regard to the kinds of organizations that compete for the potential political activists.

In the Federal Republic, political recruitment has been the

[19] Thomas Ellwein, *Das Regierungssystem der Bundesrepublik Deutschland* (Cologne, 1963), p. 392.

function primarily of political parties and established interest groups. Established interest groups have at the lower levels worked primarily through the political parties, rather than overtly against them. Demonstrations by particularly volatile interest groups like the farmers, a frequent by-product of unrest in both Weimar Germany and the French Fourth Republic, have been relatively rare. Reunions of war veterans' groups have sometimes been used a forums for extreme statements by unreconstructed officers, but pressure from the Defense Ministry has kept them under control. The expellees' organizations whose members still lay claim to homelands incorporated into Poland and Czechoslovakia have been least controllable, with the Sudeten-German Landsmannschaften the most stubborn and outspoken.

Because most German parties were founded from the top down after 1945, they initially lacked enough qualified members to be put forth as candidates for lower-level elected offices. At first the CDU assigned even Bundestag candidacies to prominent interest group representatives who were not particularly active in the party. In fact, the CDU used to solicit suggestions from interest groups before making up its Land lists for the federal elections. Gradually, as the party developed larger party organizations on the local level, this has changed. Now candidates are expected to have held lower-level offices in the party. Thus there is more opportunity to screen their backgrounds and assess their ability. The SPD has always laid more emphasis on recruiting candidates from among dependable party members, but in the past this had led to unbalanced candidate lists composed mainly of union secretaries, journalists, and other white-collar employees. One of the party's aims, therefore, has been to attract a more diversified range of middle-class talents, and it has made some progress in this area. Thus the parties have gradually assumed a larger role in recruiting for higher-level offices, while the influence of the interest groups has diminished. This is a positive development in several respects. Many of the Bundestag and cabinet members with the most dubious backgrounds and credentials have been nominees of powerful interest organizations, especially those of the expellee Landsmannschaften.

Since most Germans display a marked resistance to attempts to enroll them as party members, the parties rely heavily on subsidiary organizations, whose members are about halfway to full party status. The CDU has such organization in the *Junge Union,* where sometimes balding "youth" in the 20–40 age bracket discuss policies and figure out how to promote each other to candidacies. More innovative in outlook are the student organizations maintained and subsidized by each of the major parties. They have provided a bridge between the parties and the emerging generation of intellectuals, but they have also frequently bitten the hand that fed them. Thus the Social Democrats in 1961 disowned their student organization, the *Sozialistischer Deutscher Studentenbund* (SDS), after it had ignored repeated demands from headquarters to tone down its radical pronouncements. The party pronounced SDS membership incompatible with party membership and chartered a new organization, the *Sozialistischer Hochschul Bund* (SHB). But by 1965, party headquarters was embroiled in a bitter dispute with this organization as well, and the Christian Democratic and Liberal student organizations, whose secretaries and publications are also heavily subsidized by the parties, have frequently flown in the face of party policies.

German parties have continued to be rather unsuccessful in convincing their followers to take out party memberships, even though they all attempt to be mass parties. The member/voter ratio is much lower for the German parties than for similar parties in Western Europe. The overall German member/voter ratio of 3 to 4 per cent has scarcely changed or improved over past decades, despite the mellowing influences of time and prosperity. The Social Democrats, who evolved the prototype of the mass party based upon faithful dues-payers, has had some success in maintaining a firmer membership commitment. About 7 per cent of SPD voters are also party members, and they now provide at least one-quarter of the party's finances. But in both the CDU/CSU and the FDP the ratio of members to voters is only about 2 to 3 per cent, and these members are so irregular in paying their dues that they account for less than 10 per cent of the parties' operating funds. That is why the SPD is referred to in Germany as a "membership party" and the CDU as a "voters' party." Significantly, the CDU has frequently won national elections without bothering to elicit much lower-level participation, but the relatively greater success of the SPD in Land

and local elections may be attributed to its more substantial membership organizations.

The SPD's advantage in municipal elections and its superior organization are overwhelming in all larger cities, and the urbanization trend is the most powerful long-term factor working in its favor. In 1969, the SPD controlled absolute majorities in the city councils of all except one of the twenty-six West German cities over 200,000 in population. In most of these cities the CDU elected scarcely half the number of city councillors that the SPD did, even though in national elections it often garnered a larger vote than the SPD. This is principally because national elections are fought mainly through the national mass media, whereas local elections still depend to a large extent on organizational strength. Besides, the Social Democrats can build on the fact that they have anywhere from five to fifteen enrolled members in the cities for every enrolled CDU member. In the total population, CDU membership in the big cities varies from 0.14 to about 0.50 per cent. Since about three-quarters of its members are Catholic, it fares better in predominantly Catholic cities like Cologne, but in Protestant cities like Hamburg or Bremen less than one inhabitant in five hundred belongs to the CDU.

TABLE 3–1:   CDU MEMBERSHIP AND CITY COUNCIL REPRESENTATION IN LARGE CITIES IN 1968

City	CDU PARTY MEMBERSHIP			CITY COUNCILLORS		
	Total	As Percentage of Population	Catholic Percentage	CDU	SPD	Other
Hamburg	2,558	0.14	27	38	74	8
Cologne	4,065	0.49	90	27	40	0
Frankfurt	1,639	0.24	72	26	46	9
Bremen	1,309	0.18	42	31	57	12
Hannover	1,287	0.31	69	18	33	4
Mannheim	1,487	0.46	86	15	22	11
Kassel	398	0.19	59	17	37	7

SOURCE: Guenter Rinsche, "Die CDU in den Grossstadten," in Dietrich Rollmann, *Die Zukunft der CDU* (Hamburg, 1968), pp. 192, 205.

POLITICAL COMMUNICATION

Political communication processes are shaped by complex patterns of interaction between political actors, professionals, and amateurs who define what news is and market it to the information-consuming publics. In Germany, some peculiar structural and attitudinal antitheses shape these processes. Thus a tendency among most German groups and organizations to insulate themselves from the world at large through bureaucratic defenses is countered by the very high value the society assigns to maintaining an unimpaired freedom to criticize public processes. In addition, a comparatively high level of consumer demand for political news is catered to by media which offer a limited variety of communication styles focused on a few centers of political developments. Finally, the highly centralized political system in Germany is balanced by a relatively decentralized communication system.

Communication styles among the German political elite are still marked by strong defensive reflexes. While political leaders are aware of the need to continually interpret developments for their followers, a widespread tendency persists of hoarding information as a commodity which is potentially classified if not secret. This is evident in the business sphere, where corporations provide stockholders with only a minimum of information in their annual reports. In the political sphere it is reinforced by remnants of ideological suspicion and by the tendency toward "government by experts." Information does not pass easily from the government party to the opposition or from the specialist members of a legislative committee to their lay colleagues. Institutions like legislative research bureaus, intended to help the average legislator become better informed, are underdeveloped. To keep tabs on the limited political doings in Bonn, an observer must subscribe to perhaps dozens of partisan and personalized newsletters put out by organizations and inside dopesters. The Federal Press and Information Office towers over the Bundestag to influence information flow toward uniformity. Informal rumor mills which are generated in reaction do not have their output leavened by stories emanating from commercial and cultural centers, which are located elsewhere.

THE PRESS

The Occupation period's licensing policy not only gave important positions in the mass media to reliable democrats; it also
decentralized the press, establishing all newspapers independently
on the local level. Consequently, Germany has fewer powerful
press chains than the United States and Britain, and the larger
newspapers tend to be more individual in character and editorial
viewpoint. The disadvantages of this system, however, are that
Germany lacks both a powerful prestige paper, such as *The New
York Times* or *Le Monde,* and a national newspaper distributed
throughout the country. But it does have good regional newspapers, including the *Sueddeutsche Zeitung* in Munich, which is
the most lively, the *Frankfurter Allgemeine Zeitung,* the most
sound and the closest to big business, and the *Welt,* published in
Hamburg and Essen, which is owned by the Springer chain. None
of these quality papers have circulations much over a quarter of a
million, and many other good papers do quite well with circulations
under 100,000. Still, they are far more important in shaping political opinion than the apolitical tabloid press, claiming a circulation
in the millions, that thrives on sensationalism on the model of
the British popular press. The total circulation of daily newspapers is about 17 million, a very good figure in comparison
to Great Britain (13 million) or even all of Weimar Germany
(14 million). Three-quarters of this circulation is distributed to
subscribers so that the pressure to produce sensational headlines
is minimized for all but the tabloid papers.

BROADCASTING

Radio and television have traditionally been public monopolies in
Germany, though by no means have they been simply organs of
government propaganda. Their relative independence results
from the fact that they are set up as independent public corporations on the Land and regional level and have been fairly
well insulated from pressure by the federal government. As in
most European countries, the mass communications directors do
not consider themselves bound by the taste of the majority, but
present cultural programs of a high level with the purpose of edu-
cating the public. The intellectuals in charge of these media are

also conscious of a responsibility to educate the public politically; hence they frequently present politically controversial programs.

About three out of every four West Germans have easy access to a television set, mostly in their homes, and between 1963 and 1968 the number of licensed receivers doubled to 14 million. An investigation of television-watching habits showed that regular television watchers spent some twelve hours a week in front of the set. In contrast to nonwatchers, television watchers spent thirty minutes less each day sleeping, forty-five minutes less on radio listening, and also spent less time on the proverbial evening stroll and in going to the movies. Even so in 1967, television had still not caught up with the other means of communication. Thus, on an average day in that year, 79 per cent of the total West German population over fourteen years of age read a daily newspaper, 70 per cent read an illustrated or other magazine, 68 per cent listened to the radio, and fifty-eight per cent watched television.[20]

The greatest press controversy of the past few years was caused by radical and liberal attacks against the right-wing papers of the giant Springer concern that dominate certain areas of the newspaper business. Thus the day after the 1965 election, the front page the tabloid daily *Bild-Zeitung* presented to its 8 million readers was heavily slanted in favor of Strauss and disparaging to the FDP and its leader, Erich Mende. The paper introduced "color" by quoting Strauss to the effect that he would try to ignore any resemblance between the FDP leader and the big steak he would devour that night.[21] Reporting styles like this helped provoke the student extremists, who subsequently carried their anti-Springer campaign to the point of burning some delivery vans and trying to invade the press mansions Springer maintained in Berlin and other cities.

At the opposite, or depoliticized, pole from the Springer papers are the hundreds of small local dailies and weeklies that concentrate on the local political and other stories that the big-city and super-regional papers pay little attention to. A German researcher, who did a careful study of the editorials in a week-

[20] Gerhard Schroeter, "Unsere Fernseh-Wirklichkeit," *Fernsehen in Deutschland* (Mainz, 1967), pp. 257–58.

[21] Hans Dieter Muller, *Der Springer-Konzern* (Munich, 1968), p. 341.

end edition in the small papers, found that editors were markedly unspecific, especially in their critical comments. Whereas two-thirds of the approving editorials mentioned names of persons or organizations, two-thirds of the critical editorials were circumspect enough *not* to identify the person or organization under attack. In the case of editorials criticizing public authorities and officeholders, a slight majority did mention names. But a full 90 per cent of the editorials criticizing nongovernmental local interests and persons failed to give the name of the person or group in question.

The general caliber of political reporting in the German quality newspapers is high, but a comparison with American newspapers suggests some interesting differences. By any international standard of newsworthiness, political coverage in both countries is only second best. In America it is sports coverage that is of prime importance, while in Germany it is high-brow culture that claims some of the best journalistic coverage. There the tantrums of a big-name theater director will usually edge out the complaints of a minister, if the director's theater is renowned

TABLE 3–2:   "NAMING NAMES" IN LOCAL POLITICAL EDITORIALS IN GERMAN NEWSPAPERS

	Critical References % (N = 97)	Approving References % (N = 73)
Editorials and comments which		
1. Named the persons or groups criticized or praised	36	66
a. Official authorities or officeholders	32	44
b. Nonofficial persons or organizations	4	22
2. Did not name persons or groups criticized or praised	64	34
a. Official authorities or officeholder	25	14
b. Nonofficial persons or editorials	39	20
	100	100

NOTE: Based on a sample of all German papers issued on Saturday, September 2, 1967.
SOURCE: Manfred Knoche, "Kommentar und Kritik im Lokalteil der Tagespresse in der Bundesrepublik," *Publizistik*, XIII (December, 1968), 356.

enough. Journalistic coverage of political happenings is biased in a similar way. Statements issued in and around a few recognized "stages"—the chancellery, the Bundestag, the party headquarters, and, abroad, the foreign ministries of the major powers —will always receive extensive news coverage and editorial comment. But developments in, say, local politics, or within interest groups or informal groupings, are given scant notice. German reporters are not apt to "dig" for news that is not covered in handouts or official statements—and that is one reason why the periodical with a contrary policy, the newsweekly *Der Spiegel,* has not only been a great success but has also assumed the nature of a political institution.

BIBLIOGRAPHY

OCCUPATION AND CONSTITUTION

Almond, Gabriel A., ed., *The Struggle for Democracy in Germany* (Chapel Hill, 1949).

Clay, Lucius D., *Decision in Germany* (Garden City, 1950).

Friedrich, Carl J., and H. J. Spiro, "The Constitution of the German Federal Republic," in E. H. Litchfield, ed., *Governing Postwar Germany* (Ithaca, 1953), pp. 117–51.

Gimbel, John, *A German Community under American Occupation* (Stanford, 1961).

Golay, John F., *The Founding of the Federal Republic of Germany* (Chicago, 1958).

Grosser, Alfred, *Die Bundesrepublik Deutschland: Bilanz einer Entwicklung* (Stuttgart, 1967).

Kauper, Paul G., "The Constitutions of West Germany and the U. S.: A Comparative Study," *Michigan Law Review,* LVIII (1960), 1091–1184.

Merkl, Peter H., *The Origin of the West German Republic* (New York, 1963).

Merritt, Anna J., and Richard L. Merritt, *Public Opinion in Occupied Germany* (Urbana, 1970).

Montgomery, John D., *Forced to Be Free: The Artificial Revolution in Germany and Japan* (Chicago, 1957).

Schwarz, Hans-Peter, *Vom Reich zur Bundesrepublik: Deutschland im Widerstreit der aussenpolitischen Konzeptionen in den Jahren der Besatzungherrschaft 1945–1949* (Berlin, 1966).

Schweitzer, C. C., "Emergency Powers in the Federal Republic of Germany," *WPQ*, XXII, 1 (1969), 112–21.

POLITICAL PARTIES

Bergstraesser, Ludwig, *Geschichte der politischen Parteien in Deutschland*, 9th ed. (Munich, 1955).

Bertsch, Herbert, *CDU/CSU Demaskiert* (East Berlin, 1961).

Braunthal, Gerard, "The Free Democratic Party in West German Politics," *WPQ*, XIII (June, 1960).

Buesch, Otto, and Peter Furth, *Rechtsradikalismus im Nachkriegsdeutschland* (Berlin, 1958).

Chalmers, Douglas A., *The Social Democratic Party of Germany: From Working Class Movement to Modern Political Party* (New Haven, 1964).

Edinger, Lewis J., *Kurt Schumacher* (Stanford, 1965).

Flechtheim, Ossip K., ed., *Dokumente zur parteipolitischen Entwicklung in Deutschland seit 1945*, 3 vols. (Berlin, 1962–63).

Frye, C. E., "Parties and Pressure Groups in Weimar and Bonn," *World Politics*, XVII, 4 (1965), 635–55.

Heidenheimer, Arnold J., *Adenauer and the CDU: The Rise of the Leader and the Integration of the Party* (The Hague, 1960).

Kaltefleiter, Werner, *Wirtschaft und Politik in Deutschland: Konjunktur als Bestimmungsfaktor des Parteiensystems* (Cologne, 1968).

Lowenberg, Gerhard, "The Remaking of the German Party System," *Polity*, I (1968), 87–113.

Maier, Hans, and Hermann Bott, *Die NPD: Struktur und Ideologie einer nationalen Rechtspartei* (Munich, 1968).

Merkl, Peter H., "Equilibrium, Structure of Interests and Leadership: Adenauer's Survival as Chancellor," *APSR*, LVI (1962), 634–50.

Muller, Gunther, ed., *Die Zukunft der SPD: Sozial-Demokratische Konzeption für die Zukunft* (Hamburg, 1968).

Pulzer, P.G.J., "Western Germany and the Three-Party System," *Political Quarterly*, XXXIII (1962), 414–26.

Rollmann, Dietrich, ed., *Die Zukunft der CDU: Christlich-Demokratische Konzeption für die Zukunft* (Hamburg, 1968).

Schellinger, Harold Kent, *The SPD in the Bonn Republic: A Socialist Party Modernizes* (The Hague, 1968).

Smoydzin, Werner, *NPD: Geschichte und Umwelt einer Partei* (Pfaffenhofen, 1967).

INTEREST GROUPS AND THE PRESS

Breitling, Rupert, *Die Verbaende in der Bundesrepublik: Ihre Arten und ihre politischen Wirkungsweise* (Meisenheim, 1955).

Deutsch, Karl W., and Lewis J. Edinger, *Germany Rejoins the Powers: Mass Opinion, Interest Groups and Elites in Contemporary German Foreign Policy* (Stanford, 1959).

Fernschen in Deutschland: Gesellschaftspolitische Aufgaben und Wirkungen eines Mediums (Mainz, 1967).

Hirsch-Weber, Wolfgang, *Gewerkschaften in der Politik* (Cologne, 1959).

Huddleston, John, "Trade Unions in the German Federal Republic," *Political Quarterly,* XXXVIII (1967), 165–77.

Muller, Hans Dieter, *Der Springer-Konzern: Eine kritische Studie* (Munich, 1968).

Safran, William, *Veto-Group Politics: The Case of Health Insurance Reform in West Germany* (San Francisco, 1967).

Spiro, Herbert, *The Politics of German Codetermination* (Cambridge, 1958).

4

Political Culture and Participation

The Founding Fathers of the Federal Republic had reason to fear that the institutions they were creating would be hated rather than loved. But these fears proved groundless. The institutions and symbols of the new system very quickly won acceptance by the population. After the early 1950's there was no longer any doubt that the political structures were coming to be regarded as legitimate by a rapidly increasing majority of the population. When confronted in survey interviews with alternative choices—single-party versus multi-party systems, dictatorial versus parliamentary institutions, and so on—more and more Germans spoke out in favor of those characteristics identified with "Bonn democracy."[1] However, when almost two decades after the founding of the Federal Republic, a sample of Germans were asked where they would go if they were given a free trip to Berlin or Munich or Bonn, only 7 per cent selected the capital city. Bonn was popular among civil servants, but less so among other groups. Interest varied directly with age: only 1 per cent of those in the 18-to-24 age group wanted to visit Bonn.[2]

SYMBOLS AND SYSTEM AFFECT

While the West Germans accept and largely respect their political institutions, they neither have particular pride in them nor enjoy

---

[1] Sidney Verba, "Germany: The Remaking of a Political Culture," in Lucian W. Pye and Sidney Verba, eds., *Political Culture and Political Development* (Princeton, 1965).
[2] *Hannoversche Allgemeine,* July 4, 1967.

identifying with them. Only 7 per cent of Germans reported feeling pride in their political institutions, compared with 46 per cent of the British and 85 per cent of the Americans.[3] Indeed, patriotic and national symbols are seldom employed conspicuously or spontaneously. It would appear utterly anachronistic if a German theater audience were to sing "Deutschland ueber Alles" after a performance the way British cinema audiences sing "God Save the Queen." The old anthem was readopted in revised form against the wishes of, among others, the first federal President, who felt its continued use would hamper the attempt to make a fresh start. Perhaps the best judges of German political attitudes are the flag manufacturers. In the Weimar period they did a brisk trade selling both flags with the republican colors and the monarchist black-white-and-red. In the Nazi period every German household had to have a good-sized swastika to display

TABLE 4–1:   THE ECONOMIC AND POLITICAL SYSTEMS: VALUATIONS AND AFFECT

A. *Is your standard of living better or worse than prewar?*

	1950 %	1954 %	1958 %	1961 %	1964 %
Better	7	18	31	44	56
Just the same	24	29	33	27	20
Worse	64	48	27	15	9
No clear position	6	5	9	14	14
	101*	100	100	100	99*

B. *Which is the most important freedom?*

	1949 %	1954 %	1958 %	1963 %	1970 %
Freedom of worship	12	16	16	14	10
Freedom of speech	26	32	44	56	58
Freedom from fear	17	17	10	10	11
Freedom from want	35	35	28	15	18
No comment	10	—	2	5	5
	100	100	100	100	102*

[3] Gabriel A. Almond and Sidney Verba, *The Civic Culture* (Princeton, 1963), p. 102.

TABLE 4–1 (cont.)

C. *Preference regarding political regime*

	1953 %	1956 %	1960 %	1965 %
For democracy	57	67	74	79
For monarchy	11	8	5	4
For authoritarian regime	8	4	2	2
Indifferent/Other	1	1	1	3
No opinion	23	20	18	12
	100	100	100	100

D. *What aspects of your country are you most proud of?* (1959–60)

	United States %	Britain %	Germany %	Italy %
Political institutions	85	46	7	3
Social legislation	13	18	6	1
Position in world affairs	5	11	5	2
Economic system	23	10	33	3
Character of people	7	18	36	11
Spiritual/religious values	3	1	3	6
Contributions to the arts	1	6	11	16
Contributions to science	3	7	12	3
Physical aspects of country	5	10	17	25
Nothing or don't know	4	10	15	27
Other	9	11	3	21
	158*	148*	148*	118*

* Totals exceed or are less than 100 because of multiple responses or rounding off.
SOURCES: *A, B, C*—EMNID Pressedienst; *D*—Gabriel A. Almond and Sidney Verba, *The Civic Culture* (Princeton, 1963), p. 102.

on proper occasions. However, manufacturers now report that private demand for the official black-gold-red flag is almost nil. Instead, they make pennants advertising "Bockwuerste" for sausage stands.

If the Germans largely eschew the conventional gestures of national identification, what symbols do elicit their loyalty and pride? It would appear that to a considerable extent they have redirected their loyalty to symbols and structures serving as sub-

TABLE 4–2:   ATTITUDES TOWARD ELECTIONS AND PARTY IDEN-
TIFICATION

A. *Feelings about voting and election campaigns*

	U.S.	Britain	Germany	Italy
Per cent of sample who report they:				
Feel satisfaction when going to polls	71	43	35	30
Sometimes find election campaigns enjoyable	66	52	28	18
Sometimes get angry during campaigns	57	41	46	20
Sometimes find campaigns silly or ridiculous	58	37	46	15
Never enjoy, get angry, or feel contempt during campaign	12	26	35	54

(Percentages exceed 100 because of multiple responses.)

B. *Willingness to discuss politics*

	U.S.	Britain	Germany	Italy
Per cent of sample who:				
Sometimes talk politics	76	70	60	32
Refused to report voting preference to interviewer	2	2	16	32
Don't feel free to discuss politics with *anyone*	18	12	32	34

SOURCES: *A*—Gabriel A. Almond and Sidney Verba, *The Civic Culture* (Princeton, 1963), p. 146; *B*—Pp. 116, 117, 120.

stitutes for the conventional national political ones; the economic system is one important object. The Almond and Verba study shows that many more Germans take pride in their economic system than do citizens of other countries. Whereas this pride can be justified in terms of postwar achievements, the Germans also placed a higher value on such elements as "character of the people" and "contribution to arts and sciences," where a displacement effect is more apparent.

The German search for substitute symbols has also gone in the direction of supranationalism. German elite groups in particular have been more and more inclined to identify with such European and Atlantic structures as NATO, the Council of Europe, and the European Community than they have with such national institutions as the federal presidency and the Bonn parliament. While it has not become the demand of a mass movement, pressure for direct election of members of a European parliament has probably been strongest in the Federal Republic, an indication of the fact that the nation-state has been surmounted as *the* unit of political organization in German politics. Unfortunately, substitute frameworks have not yet been fully developed. NATO was long regarded by many Germans as more of a substitute *Heimat* than a remote military bureaucracy. The alternative Heimat of a United Europe has also in its various organizational guises elicited considerable support. But since neither of these structures is mature enough to supply Germans with new passports and identities, the result has been to nurture underlying anxieties. Having traveled beyond the psychological confines of narrow nationalism, the Germans do not yet have the security of full membership in a supranational community.

The Atlantic alliance ideology to which they were long exposed has led most younger Germans to divide up the world mentally in a curious way. An investigator who studied the national stereotypes and prejudices of German youths found that they identified with a broad "in-group" composed of Americans, Germans, and the nationalities of northwestern Europe. A hostile "out-group" of nationalities included Russians, Poles, Jews, Mongols, and most of the Asian-African nations. An "in-between group" of nations—including the French, Italians, Japanese, and Hungarians—elicited ambiguous feelings.[4] Sophisticated members of the German intellectual elites cope with problems of national identification more creatively. Thus the avant-garde German composer Karlheinz Stockhausen has created a composition, "Hymnen," which is developed around mutations of parts of forty different national anthems. He chose to weave his piece around the anthems because these are "the most well-known, banal and obvious tunes that I can think of."[5]

[4] Heinz E. Wolf, "Deutsche Jugend urteilt über andere Laender," *Koelner Zeitschrift fuer Soziologie*, XVIII (September, 1966), 307.

[5] *Die Zeit*, December 8, 1967.

IMPRINTS OF DISCONTINUITY

Backers of the Grand Coalition government of 1966–69 hoped that the former Nazi party membership of its Chancellor, Kurt Georg Kiesinger, would be balanced by the anti-Nazi resistance record of the Vice-Chancellor, Willy Brandt. But critics have continued to use the personal records of its chief officials to attack the hypocrisy of a system that selected leaders whose own past failings disqualified them as personal examples for the youth. Thus, in 1968, the integrity of federal President Heinrich Luebke was attacked by students, who added the epithet "Concentration Camp Builder," to his signature in the "Golden Book" of Bonn University. The epithet referred to charges that Luebke had helped design concentration camps while working for an architectural firm during the Nazi regime. Luebke had in fact helped design buildings that were later used to house prisoner-workers, but it was a year before he directly spoke to the charges. In the meantime, the issue had been so blown up that civics teachers in schools "could scarcely discuss the institution of the presidency without mentioning it, if they wanted to retain their credibility."[6] Kiesinger, too, remained silent about his party membership and official work for the Nazi regime, until he was called as a witness in a war crimes case to support his allegation that even high officials of the Nazi government did not know about the extermination camps. Kiesinger testified that he had had no "official" information, that he knew only that something "ugly was happening" to Jews, who, he assumed at the time, were being shipped off to work in "munitions factories."[7]

After the Eichmann trial of 1961, the Documentation Center on Nazi Crimes worked overtime analyzing available wartime records and trying to secure supplementary ones, particularly from East Germany and the East European countries. The accused in these trials were not prominent Nazis but relatively un-

---

[6] Hans Joachim Winkler, "Ueber die Bedeutung von Skandalen fuer die politische Bildung," *Hamburger Jahrbuch fuer Wirtschafts- und Gesellschaftspolitik, 1968* (Hamburg, 1968), p. 239.

[7] Hans Speier, "Karl Jaspers on the Future of Germany," *Bulletin of the Atomic Scientists,* XX (December, 1968), 25–26.

known doctors, ex-SS functionaries, and concentration camp guards, who had been bypassed in earlier periods and had in the meantime reestablished quite normal lives as respectable burghers. German citizens all over the Federal Republic were shocked to find their respected family doctors or neighborhood grocers charged in newspaper reports with playing key roles in the death camps. In one trial a pathetic group of ordinary women in their sixties were put in the dock and charged as accessories to murder because they had followed doctor's orders as nurses in wartime euthanasia camps.

German editors, to their credit, reported the trial proceedings regularly and at length, even though they well knew that this was not the news fare most readers wanted.

When an effort was made to prolong the twenty-year statute of limitations so that those accused of acts committed before 1945 could still be prosecuted after 1965, surveys showed that over 60 per cent of the population were opposed, essentially because they wanted an end to "denazification," wartime reminders, and other symbols arousing guilt feelings. Also opposing the extension were some constitutional lawyers who argued that altering a criminal law with retroactive effect violated the spirit of the Basic Law, and that it was more important to preserve the principle of "government under law" than it was to prosecute a relatively few wartime criminals.

Federal Minister of Justice Ewald Bucher, who spoke against the extension in the Bundestag in March, 1965, had not only to meet a complex issue in the spirited Bundestag debate (of which excerpts are printed below) but also to defend the German judicial machinery. In preceding years, Communist attempts to bring the West German judiciary into disrepute had been very successful. Such high officials as the federal attorney general, many prominent judges, and even the chief of the Documentation Center on Nazi Crimes were discovered to have hidden either their membership in the Nazi party or formations, or, more serious, their participation in Nazi kangaroo courts during the war. The minister argued that the 6,000 convictions in West German courts of persons accused of crimes committed during the Nazi period—as against 5,000 convictions in courts convened during the Allied Occupation in the three western zones, and 12,000 convictions in East Germany—showed that judicial authorities had not been laggard; in fact, the extension was not really needed because proceedings had already been initiated against almost all persons on whom materials were available.

The majority of the Bundestag members, however, had come to feel that the Federal Republic could not afford to leave any doubt that it would carry prosecutions of wartime criminals as far as it constitutionally could. Deputies supporting the extension

---

DELIMITING RESPONSIBILITY FOR NAZI CRIMES

Excerpts from the Bundestag Debate on Extending Statute of Limitations for Murder (March 10, 1965)

BARZEL (Chairman, CDU/CSU Fraktion): . . . The German people did not beget a collective guilt. We have been saying that for twenty years and we will continue to do so. We have always identified with this people, with its whole history and with the honor of German soldiers. That too we will continue to do. We have always delineated cleanly between criminal acts and mistakes in political commitment . . . Only those guilty of crimes must go into court so that the court can determine the question of guilt objectively and finally . . . Mistaken political commitments are another matter. Freedom brings with it the possibility of wrong choices . . . There are no judicial institutions which could determine or measure responsibility for political errors . . .

BUCHER (Minister of Justice, FDP): . . . Then there is the ominous sentence: "We must live with the murderers" . . . I did not mean to say, as I have been accused, that living with a few murderers more or less makes little difference . . . The emphasis was on the word "must." We *must* do so . . . At Munich, when I was studying there, there was a Professor of Public Law—he held doctorates in both law and theology— who prattled to us students during every lecture about the "charisma" of the Fuehrer . . . Well, charisma can account for quite a lot. A man who is endowed with charisma naturally has the power to pronounce death sentences . . . And then came euthanasia, and the next link in the chain was a cleverly and artificially produced film called, "I Accuse." This film was obvious propaganda on behalf of the annihilation of unfunctional human life. Now we bring into court those who carried through these operations by giving injections or pills, and we say—assuming that they are found guilty—"these murderers we will not allow to live among us." But with the Professor, whom we can still meet today, we engage in interesting shop talk, and with the film producer, who is also still around, we talk pleasantly at a cocktail party. But with murderers we don't care to live! . . .

HIRSCH (SPD): This is truly not a matter of denazification, Colleague Unertl. The newspapers reported that you had said in Vilshofen that you were against a renewal of denazification. I can't imagine that you said that.

> (DEP. UNERTL: Yes, but also some other things that were not reported.)

That is really not at issue. We are all with you in opposition to a renewal of denazification.

> (DEP. UNERTL: Thank God.)

The sole issue is whether the statute of limitations shall be extended for murder . . . All Nazi crimes except murder are now beyond prosecution . . . The only question we must decide is extension of the statute of limitations for murder . . .

ARNDT (SPD): These deeds were not war crimes . . . War crimes are excesses that happen in the heat of battle or when generals or admirals carry things too far . . . The destruction of Dresden was a very great war crime, but it occurred as part of an eager drive for victory. But all that has nothing to do with this. For we weren't carrying out a war against Catholic Action . . . against the Confessional Church, against the feebleminded, against bedwetters, against the mentally ill in sanatoria, and we were not engaged in a war against Jewish women, children, babies, aged or men. This has no connection with war. This was a calculated, cold-blooded murder operation planned with the aid of the entire state machinery . . .

BENDA (CDU): Above all legalistic considerations those who support the motion are moved by the consideration that the moral feelings of a people would be corrupted in an intolerable manner if murders remained unatoned for even though atonement could be imposed . . . We all know that in connection with the events of the last war years Germans were not only criminals but also the objects of crimes. I have nothing against the understandable position of the Expellees . . . who want justice carried through there as well . . . I do have something against possible calculations that where there are such feelings there might possibly also be votes to win.

> (*Lively applause from the SPD and deputies of the CDU/CSU*)

. . . Then we naturally get the silly assertions of foreign pressure, then come the anonymous postcards from upstanding German patriots who in all their patriotism forget to sign their letters or postcards . . .

> (*Lively applause*)

Perhaps I will derive some enjoyment from collecting these and similar things received by other colleagues. From these one might be able to deduce considerable insights into the spiritual aberrations that occur within a people—and I repeat this, so that I shall not be misunderstood—which has surmounted the National Socialist experience. There is one thing that is gratifying about these anonymous notes. Our time is not one where people dare say these kinds of things openly. Those who want to say them must hide behind a cowardly anonymity.

> (*Applause*)

---

proposals stated that though the pressure of foreign opinion was great, it was not to this that they were yielding but to their concern for Germany's conscience. The Bundestag debate was followed by passage of a cabinet-endorsed bill under which murder charges could be filed for another four years by making the statute of limitations operative only from the creation of the Federal Republic in 1949, and not as of 1945.

CONSENSUS AND DISSENT

Generally speaking, the pattern of political behavior in the Federal Republic in the decade from the mid-1950's to the mid-1960's was much more similar to corresponding patterns in the United

States and Britain than to those of other large continental countries like France and Italy. In Germany, as in the Anglo-Saxon countries, the bulk of public political discussion and controversy took place within a relatively narrow sector of the political spectrum. Practically all political spokesmen or commentators, whether in the parties, the press, or even the interest groups, have their acceptance of political democracy, the constitutional framework, and the fundamental structure of a free society. Even before the Communist party was outlawed in 1956, its size and influence had diminished to the point where it resembled the tiny British Communist party more than the Communist mass movements in France and Italy. Even more striking was the absence of powerful Fascist or right-wing antidemocratic movements, like the neo-Fascist movement in Italy and the Poujadist party and semi-Fascist cliques in France, which played a significant role in preparing the downfall of the Fourth Republic.

The abundant production of the German economy made it possible to satisfy most of the people's material demands, and this has diminished their interest in ideological issues. The "end of ideology" was associated by Chancellor Erhard in the 1965 election campaign with the slogan-concept "The Fully Shaped Society."[8] He claimed that a society which had arrived at this stage "no longer consisted of classes and groups which sought to force acceptance of mutually exclusive goals, but had become cooperatively oriented and marked by the interaction of all groups and interests." In this view all German groups had become less conflict-oriented as the result of the series of experiences since 1918, but especially because they had achieved maximal development and recognition in the affluent period of the Federal Republic. A young conservative, writing in the journal *Civis,* emphasized that integration had come about through recognition of social interdependence and not through identification with reified symbols like "Volk" or "Nation." But the growth of consensus was felt by him to be based in good part in the overriding German concern for an efficient economy. "This consciousness of the interdependency of all upon all finds special expression in the focus

[8] Robert Spencer, "Erhard's Dubious Victory," *International Journal,* XXI (1966), 105.

of all sections of society upon the achievement potential of the entire economy. This consciousness is more strongly developed among us than in such other societies as the French, the Italian or the English ones."[9]

THE REVIVAL OF DISSENSUS

Ludwig Erhard's vision of an essentially conflict-free society, where prosperity and self-satisfaction would stifle ideological conflict, grew out of the postwar period when, even an economist argued, "economic efficiency and the standard of living . . . replaced self-determination as the principles of political legitimacy."[10] For a long time, the economy and its "miracle" overshadowed the polity, which had not brought unified nationhood, in German perceptions and feelings. Erhard's model of "The Fully Shaped Society" implied a diminishing need for political leadership, and he became the personal victim of that gross misinterpretation. His view of politics as a non-zero-sum game, where all participants could gain without expense to each other, made him personally impotent in power conflicts. The element of tragedy in his demise was heightened by the fact that it was the United States, the country Erhard most admired, which generated the additional pressures—its involvement in the Vietnam war and the high-pressure tactics of Lyndon Johnson—that upset the equilibrium on which Erhard's stewardship rested.

The failure of the "master economist," whose popularity was further damaged by the first serious economic recession in a decade, set off discontent and brought forth a revival of ideological articulation and politization that had been gathering momentum for some time. The conservative pragmatism with its emphasis on the private man and economic growth had become the *Zeitgeist* of the Federal Republic, but it failed to attract significant minorities who yearned for stronger commitments and ideals. About the time when material security came to be

[9] Werner Riek, "Erhard's Formierte Gesellschaft," *Civis* (June, 1965), p. 14.

[10] Hans Joachim Arndt, *West Germany: Politics of Non-Planning* (Syracuse, 1966), p. 123.

taken for granted and the political leadership's loss of control became evident, various subgroups that had been ridiculed for so long rallied for a comeback.

Even more markedly than in other countries, the years 1965–68 saw a rapid growth in strength of all manner of radical protest groups and movements. Though the student movement at the university level and the NPD successes at the polls were the most highly publicized components in this trend, neither serves as a satisfactory indicator of the total development. An examination of publishing contents and statistics would be more revealing. Thus heavy tomes dealing with complex problems in Marxian dialectics jumped in sales from the hundreds to the tens of thousands. Nationalist magazines that were having trouble surviving found a ready market again. Student newspapers, which had been rather devoid of serious political content, multiplied in all kinds of political and ideological persuasions and formats. The publishers of paperback editions of "heavy" critical authors increased some print orders into the hundred thousand range. Though intellectuals were most deeply involved as producers and consumers of this heady literature, readership groups appeared on the mass level as well. Mass-circulation magazines based on a combination of sexual license and radical politics, previously quite unknown in Germany, proved highly successful. A slick paper magazine aimed specifically at rebellious high-school students joined the ranks and did a thriving business.

Rather suddenly conflict, challenge, and dissent were in the air again—and in the streets as well, in the form of bloody clashes. The well-worn slogan "Bonn is not Weimar" seemed to lose some of its self-evidence as dissent spread. Some of the reasons for this development will be more closely examined in Chapter 10.

A GERMAN NEMESIS FIGURE

No figure has served as a more fulsome target of the intellectuals' attacks than the "negative symbol figure of German democracy" Franz Josef Strauss, the bull-necked Bavarian CSU leader who almost overnight earned the hatred of writers the world over by his crude attempt to suppress the critical voice of *Der Spiegel* in

1962.[11] It surprised no one that his name subsequently evoked spontaneous booing at conferences of the Congress on Intellectual Freedom, but more intriguing was the almost visceral reaction against him from the kind of German citizen who writes letters to the editor. Seldom in any democratic country has one personality managed to arouse such wide antipathies and anxieties among diverse publics. North Germans see in him the personification of the primitive Bavarian political style they have always scorned. Antimilitarists see in him, partly because of his actions as defense minister, an unrestrained advocate of military adventurism with no scruples about inviting atomic devastation. Those in whom past experiences have left a deep distaste for politicians who rely on emotional appeals have been appalled by the semiphysical compulsion Strauss resorts to in speaking to bully his audiences into submission. Those who fear excessive nationalism have been alarmed by statements, such as the one Strauss' wife made to an interviewer, to the effect that Strauss' real foes were "international groupings, in England, and in America, and generally everybody on both sides of the Iron Curtain who are enemies of Germany." Most appalling to many Germans is not so much Strauss' ruthlessness as his lack of self-discipline; the thought that he might someday come to power induces nightmares. As an editor of conservative journals has put it: "Although no one says so explicitly, the German public compares this man to Hitler. If he should succeed in returning to Bonn and one day become Chancellor then, according to the nebulous perceptions of the masses, the clock will once again have struck '1933.' "[12]

Some years ago Strauss was described as the only German politician who knew how to instill dissatisfaction in the prosperous Germans. When the NPD leaders showed that they also were adept at that game, Strauss interpreted their electoral succcess as "the answer to the years when everything German and all national sentiments were dragged through the mud." But in recent years

[11] Otto Kirchheimer and Constantine Menges, "A Free Press in a Democratic State?: The Spiegel Case," in W. M. Carter and A. F. Westin, eds., *Politics in Europe* (New York, 1965).

[12] Martin Bernstorf, "Wie maechtig ist Franz Josef Strauss?" *Civis* (May, 1965), 18.

Strauss' strategy has been to build up his reputation as a states-man and to eclipse the "Germany only" nationalists by rallying all Europeans with the cry that "our continent threatens—politi-cally and economically—to degenerate into an underdeveloped territory."[13] He would establish a "union of free European coun-tries" that would gradually develop its own nuclear weapons systems, and thus sidestep the goals of the nuclear nonproliferation program. An American, reviewing an earlier Strauss book, noted that it again sounded the "unmuted trumpet call of German nationalism," and that in the "Straussian grand design," Germany would eventually play a role in Europe that would "parallel that of Prussia in the German federation."[14] A German intellectual expressed a more basic objection: he felt that the Germans' mis-trust of national symbols would be increased if German politicians once again adopted the game of "playing the strong man." He accused Strauss of outright duplicity in speaking extravagantly in Paris of the need for a common German-French policy, while at the same time reviving irredentist hopes in articles written for the newspapers of German expellee groups that oppose recog-nition of the present frontiers in East Europe. As the critic pointed out, the two policies are completely irreconcilable since the French recognize those frontiers. He concluded sadly that "poisoning the national consciousness by raising false hopes and illusions seems to pay off in a political system where the telling of non-truths is highly rewarded."[15]

PARTICIPATION AND SUPPORTS

In comparing tables which relate various forms of political be-havior to cultural and economic indices, one would notice that the West German data conform to worldwide patterns in some areas but deviate in others. Thus, as one would expect from a high-income nation with a developed educational system, Germans exhibit a relatively good command of political information. But

[13] Franz Josef Strauss, *Challenge and Response* (New York, 1970), pp. 122 ff.
[14] Steven Muller, *Bulletin of the Atomic Scientists,* XXII (1966), 33.
[15] Georg Picht, "Grundlagen eines neuen deutschen Nationalbewusstseins," *Merkur,* XXI (1967), 9.

when it comes to their attitudes toward political symbols, parties, and institutions, the pattern of nonidentification that emerges is more like that found in some developing countries, where a large peasant sector lacks the communication and other links necessary for identification with the national political system. Data on German participation in civic activities, membership in political parties and clubs, or in informal neighborhood improvement associations show that most of them are very reluctant to play active roles in public life.[16] Thus, while some 10 to 20 per cent of voters in most West European countries are also party members, in Germany the ratio is only about 3 per cent.

Of course the Nazi experience has had considerable influence on political participation; many Germans (and their children) who were led to identify with that regime and its organizations later vowed never to risk being made fools of again. But other German traditions, or lack of them, have also shaped this pattern. Many structures which elicit civic participation in countries like the United States are either nonexistent in Germany or have quite different traditions. Take the churches, for example. In the United States, church membership is entirely voluntary, and all the funds needed for maintaining them are raised through voluntary donations. In Germany, by contrast, the churches are financed through state taxes levied on all members who were baptized in a particular denomination and did not officially renounce membership. Thus, because the churches are not dependent on cake sales and the like, they have not become the centers for the auxiliary groups which cluster around churches in the United States and which frequently also form the nucleus of local reform drives. And, in a broader area, there are almost no women's civic and political organizations, even though, curiously, the percentage of women officeholders is about the same as in the United States and Britain.

THE PARTIES' FINANCE PROBLEMS

The organizations most hurt by the curiously selective pattern of German political participation have been the non-Socialist parties. While the Socialists have been able to maintain a strong member-

---

[16] Wolfgang Hartenstein and Klaus Liepelt, "Party Members and Party Voters in West Germany," *Acta Sociologica,* VI, 1 (1962).

ship tradition and a respectable 6 per cent member-voter ratio, parties like the CDU and FDP have enrolled barely 2 to 3 per cent of their voters as members. This was usually enough to provide candidates for office, but when it came to maintaining local party activity and raising campaign funds, the non-Socialist parties had great problems. The CDU, for instance, would not have had any difficulty in an election year if it had the same donor-voter percentage prevailing in the United States—some 10 per cent—and if each donor gave perhaps DM 20, or half a day's income. But the dues and voluntary contributions amounted to hardly a tenth of the required sum. So, under Adenauer's leadership, the Christian Democrats and the Free Democrats took the seemingly easy way out: they relied on continuous subsidies from a political finance Conveyer organization, established by the German Federation of Industry, whose funds were derived from assessments levied on business firms through their trade associations.[17]

As long as they kept winning the solid electoral victories the CDU manager didn't worry about their small membership base at the grass roots. Then troubles began to pile up. In 1958 the Constitutional Court declared unconstitutional a provision for income tax deductibility passed by the coalition parties to make anonymous contributions from their business donors less problematic. Furthermore, the Conveyers often suspended funds when they were displeased by the parties' actions. Thus the FDP was cut off without notice when it quit Adenauer's cabinet in 1956. On another occasion, the Conveyers cut off subsidies to CDU headquarters after Adenauer had angered the industrialists by revaluating the currency. Thereafter, to the delight of the SPD, which had unsuccessfully sought to make electoral capital out of their financial dependency, the flow of funds to the CDU and the FDP diminished rapidly.[18] At this point the parties tried, without much success, to enlist more of their own members and donors. The voters had become accustomed to having Adenauer run an efficient government from the top down, and they could

---

[17] Arnold J. Heidenheimer, "German Party Finance: The CDU," *APSR*, LI, 2 (June, 1957), 369–85.

[18] Gerard Braunthal, *The Federation of German Industry in Politics* (Ithaca, 1965).

not understand why his party suddenly needed their help. Businessmen also insisted that they would contribute only if donations were tax deductible and if there were absolutely no chance that news of their financial support would become public. However, these stipulations clashed with the constitution and the court rulings.[19]

INPUTS VIA STATE SUBSIDIES

As a consequence of their difficulties, the parties began to consider the possibility of subsidies from the public treasury. In doing so they developed policies completely at odds with their ideological commitments. The FDP, normally committed to liberal, individualist values, became the strongest supporter of state finance. But the SPD, whose values were consonant with state finance, took a strongly negative position because it didn't need funds. The CDU wavered in between, although one of its deputies had taken the lead in introducing a small federal subsidy of DM 5 million which was shared among the parties after 1959 for "political education" work. Following the 1961 elections, the Free Democrats demanded increased subsidies as part of their price for entering Adenauer's fourth government and the not unwilling CDU gave way. In 1962, federal subsidies rose to DM 20 million, the sum being divided among the three parties represented in the Bundestag. In 1964 the coalition parties voted an increase once again, this time to DM 38 million. In the meantime, most of the Land parliaments and many communal organs followed suit, so that by 1965 well over DM 50 million of public funds was being divided among the political parties annually.

Many critics felt that the parties took too easy a way around the problem of getting their followers to share a tiny fragment of their prosperity with the party of their choice. Others, particularly the parties not represented in the Bundestag, attacked the distribution formula as unconstitutional insofar as it discriminated against new and small parties. In an interview the CDU treasurer gave to *Der Spiegel* in February, 1965, he sought to answer some of these criticisms.

[19] Ulrich Duebber, *Parteifinanzierung in Deutschland* (Cologne, 1962).

BURGBACHER: Well, may I ask you how you would organize the financing of a party, if that were your job?

SPIEGEL: On the basis of membership dues.

BURGBACHER: Marvelous! But what would you do if, even though the people vote for you, they refuse to become members?

SPIEGEL: Reduce expenditures. . . . What about contributions without any kind of tax deductibility?

BURGBACHER: Well, and you actually think the contributions would come in. Are you actually of this world, or where do you live? Do you actually think a man would give a contribution if it were publicly reported in the newspaper afterwards? . . .

SPIEGEL: You have explained the poor membership recruitment of the parties by saying that you can't force citizens to become party members. But won't your bill force the citizen to support parties which he actually may be opposed to?

BURGBACHER: If you asked the citizen if he would voluntarily like to pay for all the items contained in the Federal Budget you would hear all kinds of things. We only ask of the citizen that he help to finance the politics whose fruits he reaps. It is only thanks to the policies of these parties that the citizen is able to pay taxes in the first place, out of which they too are to be financed.[20]

In June, 1967, the Grand Coalition passed the German Parties Law, providing for a public subsidy of DM 2.50 for each vote received by parties that had polled at least 2.5 per cent of the total vote in the preceding election. The Parties Law, which replaced previous political finance legislation, also provided that the parties were required to disclose the names only of the private donors who gave more than DM 20,000 in any one year and the corporations that gave more than DM 200,000. "Under this fantastically generous formula, which all but made a mockery of the disclosure provision as a whole, just about none of the contributions of even the very largest corporate donors would need to be

[20] Der Spiegel, February 3, 1965.

publicized."[21] The SPD was thus virtually falling over backward to please its coalition partner. In a subsequent decision the Constitutional Court ruled that the coalition had gone too far on a number of counts. The court instructed the Bundestag to extend the subsidies even to parties polling as little as one-half per cent of the total vote; it also ruled that the high cut-off figure for private donor disclosures was not compatible with the provisions of Article 21 of the Basic Law.[22]

THE OPPOSITION-COALITION SYNDROME

The formation of the Grand Coalition by the CDU and the SPD in December, 1966, culminated a trend toward consensus among the major German parties; it also conformed to a European tendency to attach little importance to maintaining effective opposition parties within parliamentary systems.[23] Yet when the two

---

[21] Arnold J. Heidenheimer and F. C. Langdon, *Business Associations and the Financing of Political Parties: A Comparative Study of the Evolution of Practices in Germany, Norway and Japan* (The Hague, 1968), p. 87. On the German Parties Law, see also Arnold J. Heidenheimer, "Public Party Subsidization in West Germany and the U.S.," *Jahrbuch des oeffentlichen Rechts,* XVI (1967).

[22] The Parties Law requires political parties to file annual statements of the aggregate sources of their incomes. The following acknowledged income sources, including those of Land affiliates, cover the nonelection year 1968 (in millions of Deutschmarks).

Parties	Membership Dues	Office-holders' Payments	Contributions	Federal Public Subsidies	Other	Total
CDU	6.9	2.9	5.1	17.7	1.8	34.4
CSU	1.3	.9	2.1	5.3	.4	10.1
SPD	18.9	3.8	2.5	19.7	3.1	48.0
FDP	1.2	.7	2.1	4.6	1.4	10.0
NPD	.6	.2	.9	1.7	.4	3.8

SOURCE: *Bundesanzeiger,* October 21, 1969.

[23] Otto Kirchheimer, "The Waning of Opposition in Parliamentary Regimes," *Social Research,* XXIV (1957), 127–56.

dominant German parties formed a coalition government, following the postwar practice of parties in countries such as Austria, Holland, and Belgium, they set off an enormous wave of protest. Many journalists echoed leading political science textbooks on the need for an effective opposition to keep parliamentary government viable. Critics who had earlier been complaining that, as an opposition party, the SPD supported too many cabinet measures, now protested all the more loudly when the Socialists took the final step of joining the cabinet.

This sudden manifestation of a previously muffled regard for a parliamentary opposition is probably due to the strong and surprisingly persistent dialectical strain in German political conceptualization. When the SPD dropped its twenty-year opposition role, even rather apolitical Germans suddenly felt they had been deprived of an institutionalized antithesis, which they missed badly. This desire for an antithesis to counter the dominant thesis seems related to the sometimes single-minded German dedication to achieving dominant community goals. When they set out to build a national state after 1871, the Germans quickly created a more efficient state than anybody else. When they determined to rebuild their economy after 1945, they did so more effectively than any other European country. These mobilization efforts may have produced psychic needs for contingency safeguards. And that may be why the Germans, more than other peoples, like to have an antithesis available just in case the dominant thesis— represented in the postwar period by Adenauer, the CDU, and its policies—turns out to be abortive or hits a dead end. For example, cartels were quite popular in Germany as long as a "strong state" was around to control them. Now, when the SPD joined the government in a highly developed *Parteienstaat* setting, many citizens feared that an all-powerful government cartel would emerge, one which would not only lack effective institutionalized opposition but also do away with a potential impetus for counter-movements.

BIBLIOGRAPHY

Almond, Gabriel, and Sidney Verba, *The Civic Culture* (Princeton, 1963).

Bracher, Karl-Dietrich, "Staatsbegriff und Demokratie in Deutschland," *PVS,* IX (1968), 2–27.

Braunthal, Gerard, and Ulrich Duebber, "West Germany," in "Comparative Studies in Political Finance," *JP* (November, 1963), pp. 774–90.

Breitling, Rupert, "Offene Partei und Wahlfinanzierung," *PVS,* IX, 2 (June, 1968), 228–33.

Edinger, Lewis, *Politics in Germany* (Boston, 1968).

Hartenstein, W., et al., "Party Members and Party Voters in Western Germany," *Acta Sociologica,* VI (1962), 43–52.

———, and Günter Schubert, *Mitlaufen oder Mitbestimmen* (Frankfurt, 1961).

Heidenheimer, Arnold J., and F. C. Langdon, *Business Associations and the Financing of Political Parties* (The Hague, 1968).

Kirchheimer, Otto, "The Vanishing Opposition," in Robert Dahl, ed., *Political Opposition in Western Democracy* (New Haven, 1966).

Lehmbruch, Gerhard, "The Ambiguous Coalition in West Germany," *Government and Opposition,* III (1968), 181–222.

Liepelt, Klaus, and Alexander Mitscherlich, *Thesen zur Waehlerfluktuation* (Frankfurt, 1968).

McClelland, D. C., et al., "Obligations to Self and Society in the United States and Germany," *J. Abn. and Soc. Psychol.,* LVI (1958), 245–55.

Molt, Peter, "Wertvorstellungen in der Politik: Zur Frage der Entideologisierung der deutschen Parteien," *PVS,* IV (1963), 350–68.

Neumann, Elizabeth, ed., *Jahrbuch der öffentlichen Meinung, 1955–65*(Allensbach, 1965).

Pollock, James K., and John C. Lane, *Source Materials on the Government and Politics of Germany* (Ann Arbor, 1964).

Scheuch, Erwin, and Rudolf Wildenmann, eds., *Zur Soziologie der Wahl* (Cologne, 1965). This volume contains a number of significant articles, including one on German political attitudes by Scheuch, one on CDU finances by Uwe Schleth, and several 1961 constituency campaign studies.

Schmidtchen, Gerhard, *Die befragte Nation,* 2d ed. (Freiburg, 1965).
Schoenbaum, David, *The Spiegel Affair* (Garden City, N.Y., 1968).
Stackleberg, Karl G., *Attentat auf Deutschlands Talismann* (Stuttgart, 1967).
Verba, Sidney, "Germany: The Remaking of Political Culture," in Lucian W. Pye and Sidney Verba, eds., *Political Culture and Political Development* (Princeton, 1965).

5

Elections and
Voting Behavior

THE 1969 ELECTION CAMPAIGN

The 1969 election campaign was the most closely contested one in the twenty years of West German electoral history, yet right up to the end most voters doubted that there was any real alternative to a renewal of the Grand Coalition government. This was because no one knew whether the two smaller parties, the FDP and the NPD, could jump the 5 per cent barrier of the electoral law and what parliamentary strength each would have. It appeared reasonably clear that neither the CDU/CSU nor the SPD would win enough votes to form a one-party cabinet. But coalition possibilities depended *positively* on the relative success of the FDP, and *negatively* on the relative success of the NPD. If the NPD got into the Bundestag and the FDP did not, continuation of the Grand Coalition would be inevitable. If the FDP came off very well, it would have a stronger bargaining position for entering a government led by either the CDU/CSU or the SPD.

SIGNIFICANCE FROM THE VOTERS' PERSPECTIVE

The complexity of this situation prevented clear popular preferences from emerging. Voters who valued stability over other goals and were somewhat apolitical tended to favor a continuation of the Grand Coalition. This attitude was strongest among CDU/CSU voters, but was also very widespread among SPD followers. Those who wanted to end the Grand Coalition were, of course, divided on alternative solutions. Many FDP voters and the more reform- and issue-oriented supporters of the SPD favored the formation of an SPD-FDP coalition; they viewed the SPD/FDP alliance that led to the election of President Heinemann in March, 1969 (see below, p. 153), as the first step toward the forma-

127

tion of an SPD/FDP government. Other voters among both the CDU and FDP followers wanted to return to the "right-wing coalition" formula of the Adenauer period, with the CDU and the FDP serving together in cabinets. It is clear that one of the great hopes of the smaller parties—that the dissatisfaction with the Grand Coalition which had been so prevalent in 1967–68 would continue to spread—did not materialize. Whether support for the Grand Coalition actually increased during the campaign is uncertain; one survey reported that it did, another reported that it declined.

THE STRATEGIES OF THE PARTIES

The age-and-sex distribution of the 1969 German electorate favored the election goals of the CDU/CSU. Women and voters over sixty, who had always been more pro-CDU, constituted respectively 21 million and 11 million of the total electorate of 39 million. Women over sixty numbered 6 million, compared to the half-million young voters who had become eligible since 1965. This encouraged the CDU to emphasize the personality of its silver-maned Chancellor, whose supraparty appeal was strongest among these groups. And, in an attempt to pull back former voters who had strayed to the NPD in Land elections and to minimize further defections, the CDU stressed law-and-order issues in the campaign. Finally, the Christian Democrats emphasized issues that would attract former FDP voters who disagreed with the course of their party's new leadership. In essence, therefore, the CDU pursued what under German circumstances was something like an equivalent to the "Southern strategy" pursued by President Nixon in the United States election of 1968. The party was prepared to lose voters on the left, particularly among progressive Catholics and city-dwellers, in order to maintain and strengthen its position on the right.

Elements favoring the SPD in 1969 included the continuing trend toward urbanization, and the increasing readiness of Catholics, the more highly educated, and white-collar workers to disregard previous ideological taboos. The big question was whether the party's image would be more helped than hurt by its three years of participation in the government. The success of Social Democrats such as Economics Minister Karl Schiller and Foreign

Minister Willy Brandt impressed middle-class voters, as party strategist Wehner had intended it should. But the SPD had to realize that it might lose some of its left-wing and oppositionist adherents precisely because it had become too closely identified with the establishment. Thus the party had to stress the positions on which it differed from the CDU, especially its more progressive educational policy and its promise to seek new foreign policy alternatives.

The FDP initially combined an effective strategy, based on truly innovative appeals in areas such as foreign policy and the modernization of society, with the calculation that disaffection with the big-party coalition would rebound to its benefit. The Free Democrats foresaw that their emphasis on relatively radical goals would repel their more conservative followers, but they expected to attract progressive new voter groups from both the SPD and CDU. Their appeal was individualist; it held out the prospect that, because of the complex decision-making process after the election, an FDP vote might ultimately play a more crucial role than a big-party vote in forming a government.

The NPD's strategy was affected by the fact that the three other parties all concentrated on denigrating NPD leaders and policies, in an effort to keep the party below the 5 per cent margin. Having earlier proved it could attract voters as an offensive challenger, the NPD was increasingly forced to go on the defensive by denying that it was really neo-Nazi. It tried to appeal particularly to groups that felt left out in a modernizing postindustrial society—to farmers, to expellees who continued to resist accommodation with Poland and Czechoslovakia, and to groups like Bundeswehr soldiers who felt that society did not accord them adequate status. Many NPD candidates were Bundeswehr officers and noncoms.

The ADF (Action for Democratic Progress), the only other party of any significance in the election, was formed by a campaign alliance between the German Communist party (DKP) and two other left-neutralist parties that together had polled less than 2 per cent of the 1965 vote. The ADF sought primarily to attract radical workers and some components of the extra-parliamentary opposition. It was mainly a threat to the SPD's "left flank" and was given no chance of jumping the 5 per cent barrier. Most of the six other parties that entered lists in the election were idiosyncratic factions, none of which succeeded in attracting more than 50,000 votes.

CANDIDATES AND ISSUES

CHANCELLOR OR TEAM?

In their campaigns, both of the major parties sought to maximize their assets through known leaders and candidates. The CDU sought to repeat Adenauer's successful formula of capitalizing on the "Chancellor effect"—the tendency of many apolitical Germans to vote for the incumbent in high office almost regardless of party label. If they had been able to make 1969 another "Chancellor-election," the CDU would have benefited from a comparison of the two candidates, for Kiesinger had several important advantages over Brandt. His past as a former Nazi party member

TABLE 5–1:   ISSUE ORIENTATIONS OF PARTY ADHERENTS, 1968–69

		ADHERENTS OF THE			
		SPD	CDU/CSU	FDP	NDP
Issue Area	*Orientation*	%	%	%	%
Economic policy	Welfare-State	74	59	55	56
	Conservative	10	17	23	17
Role of religion	Laicist	64	35	65	68
	Clerical	20	47	19	20
Radicalism (Which most dangerous?)	Right Radicals	34	21	26	2
	Left Radicals	21	27	28	66
Foreign policy toward East	Mobile	38	25	43	28
	Immobile	48	55	45	60
Foreign policy toward West	Integrationist	53	59	48	31
	Nationalist	31	20	39	60

SOURCE: PAP Survey No. 9, Table 39.

TABLE 5–2:   SELECTION OF CHANCELLOR OR PARTY TEAM FO-
CUS OF VOTERS' DECISION-MAKING, SEPTEMBER, 1969

	"I WANT MY VOTE TO HELP DECIDE"		
	"who becomes Chancellor"	"which party team forms the government"	don't know
	%	%	%
CDU/CSU adherents	43	47	10
SPD adherents	15	79	6
FDP adherents	7	86	7
Men, 18–24	9	80	11
Men, 65 and older	35	56	11
Women, 18–24	22	68	10
Women, 65 and older	51	35	14
All West Germans	27	62	11

SOURCE: INFAS Report, October 10, 1969.

repelled fewer voters than Brandt's emigration during the Nazi
period.[1] Personally, the urbane and well-spoken Kiesinger succeeded in establishing direct contact with television viewers, especially women, in a way that Brandt did not. In 1965, Brandt had
tried a "Kennedy-style" campaign and failed. Finally, the CDU
candidate was running as the incumbent Chancellor, and Brandt
could not get as much mileage out of his service as foreign minister. Consequently, throughout the campaign, Kiesinger maintained a wide lead over Brandt as the favorite candidate. More
than one quarter of the SPD's followers preferred him to their
own candidate, whereas almost no CDU voters preferred Brandt
to Kiesinger.

[1] Brandt fled to Norway in 1933 and assumed Norwegian citizenship; he
resumed his German citizenship in 1947. When questioned in a 1954
survey as to whether anti-Hitler emigrants should be given high government office, 39 per cent of West Germans answered "No" while only
13 per cent gave an unconditional "Yes." By 1967, 23 per cent said
"No," 29 per cent "Yes," 31 per cent said "It depends on the individual,"
and 17 per cent had no opinion.

TABLE 5–3: POPULARITY OF CHANCELLOR CANDIDATES IN 1968–69 SURVEYS

Favorite Chancellor Candidate	SPD Adherents %	CDU/CSU Adherents %	FDP Adherents %	NPD Adherents %
Kiesinger	28	81	36	28
Brandt	42	2	11	6
Indifferent	30	17	53	66
TOTAL	100	100	100	100

SOURCE: PAP Survey No. 9, Table 17.

To restructure the situation in its favor, the SPD energetically emphasized that it was offering an experienced team, each member of which had proven himself in high Land and federal offices. Key ministers like Karl Schiller, who was more popular than Brandt and almost as popular as Kiesinger, were given prominence in the election propaganda, together with other important Socialists like Leber and Herbert Wehner. The implication of this juxtaposition was that SPD leaders were programmatically and personally committed to working together, whereas Kiesinger and Strauss had publicly engaged in frequent policy clashes. As Schiller said, "We did not enter the government in December, 1966, as stand-by Samaritans who would give a blood transfusion to a worn-down state party! Willy Brandt is the man who must lead us into the world of the 1970's."

More so than in earlier elections, the voter's perception of his role made it easier for the SPD team emphasis to be accepted. Surveys just before the election showed that by better than 2–1 voters believed they should decide primarily between *party slates of capable leaders* rather than between *Chancellor candidates.* Among CDU followers the two approaches to voting were almost evenly balanced; among older women, selecting the Chancellor was still the major consideration. But all other groups subscribed to the primacy of choice between party teams—young men by as much as 9–1 (see Table 5–2 above). A postelection analysis of the CDU criticized the party for failing to project the team image by emphasizing the role of other ministers besides

Kiesinger. It suggested that the professional socialization of some of the younger voters who had left the CDU predisposed them to a team image, whereas a "father figure like Kiesinger was not particularly appealing."[2]

ISSUES AND POLICIES

The carefully developed programs the parties presented had in most cases evolved from prolonged intraparty discussions among the party leaders; thus, no voter could complain that he was being forced to vote on trust and charisma alone. Although on many points the positions of the major parties were not too far apart, on numerous major and minor policy questions there were significant differences. But curiously, none of these differences were projected into fundamental campaign issues focusing national attention. The major reason for this was that for the preceding three years the SPD and the CDU had compromised on most of these policies in the Grand Coalition cabinet. Thus even areas in which major differences emerged after the formation of the Brandt cabinet—such as attitudes toward the GDR and the Oder-Neisse line—were not really discussed in the campaign. The big parties had carefully refrained from cutting into each other, for fear of becoming embroiled in mutual recriminations which would redound to the advantage of the FDP and the NPD. The NPD, of course, did attack the legitimacy of the other party positions, but its charges were not given wide coverage by the media and they failed to gain much attention.

Because surveys showed that most voters already regarded the SPD as the party best qualified to exercise leadership in domestic policy areas, the Social Democrats did not sensationalize popular issues. The party had succeeded in qualifying itself in terms of expertise and responsiveness long before the campaign began. Thus 57 per cent of respondents believed that the SPD would work strongly for "increased incomes together with stable prices," compared to 32 per cent who credited the CDU with the same dedication. Similarly the SPD held a 58–39 lead in regard to "educational improvements," a 56–41 lead in regard to "hospital

[2] CDU Rheinland, *Bundestagswahl 1969: Analyse, Konsequenzen*, p. 2.

modernization," but lagged 43–49 on the "maintenance of law and order."[3]

The CDU made some adjustments to improve its posture on issues where it was doing particularly badly; for instance, a month before the election, the party announced it was prepared to spend DM 20 billion to create a dozen new universities by 1980. But in the main, the CDU emphasized particular policy promises to specific interest groups like the farmers, the artisans, and the expellees. Both the CDU and the NPD competed for the votes of those expellees who turned away from the SPD when it edged toward recognition of the Oder-Neisse line. Indeed, the leader of the Expellees' Association, Reinhold Rehs, was offered a CDU candidacy immediately after he resigned from the SPD. In the past, such practices had helped tie beholden interest groups to the CDU, the model of a "catch-all party." This time, however, the local voters in what had been a safe CDU constituency refused to go along; Rehs went down to ignominious defeat, running 4,000 votes behind the CDU second-ballot total in his district.

It was ironic that tactical considerations led the party leaders to play down policy differences to such an extent, because this was the first campaign in the world which, under the rules of the new Parties Law, was predominantly and directly financed through specially designated public subsidies. Since the party pipers were now paying themselves, they could play what tunes they wanted. In the end money did "talk," because the one campaign issue that finally emerged was connected with finances. The issue grew out of a cabinet conflict over whether the mark should be revaluated upward in order to control domestic prices and maintain the balance of payments. Schiller had urged revaluation, but was defeated in the cabinet on a straight party-line vote. The dispute raised the question of how to distribute the credit and blame for the coalition's record between the two parties. The Socialists were encouraged to play up the revaluation issue, because for once most of the economists and bankers were on their side. Thus a highly complex issue was carried to the voters, who were aware that it related to every man's pocketbook but were

[3] PAP Survey No. 8, pp. 23–25.

in the main completely unequipped to understand the crucial technical arguments.[4] The dispute probably undermined Kiesinger's image as the omniscient Chancellor, since Schiller was able to sustain and bolster his side of the argument.

TO THE HEARTH OF THE VOTER

CAMPAIGN TECHNIQUES

Through interparty agreement the parties were pledged not to flood the country with election propaganda until the month before election day. Prior to the last month, the parties stated their positions in a reasonable manner in newspaper advertisements and on the free broadcasting time made available to them. The FDP earned top honors for its rational and well-argued appeals in this early period, according to a critic assessing the campaign in *Die Zeit*. "If on September 28 it were a matter of voting on the promotion style of the parties, then the FDP should be assured of an absolute majority. Just because of this one should not be surprised if it is the FDP which will suffer the greatest losses."[5] During this time the SPD sought to get its arguments across to housewives by creating a popular *Vacation Magazine*, whose political message became apparent only after the reader noticed that all the vacation anecdotes concerned relaxed and gracious SPD leaders. Another magazine, *For*, had a format designed to make the arguments of SPD-supporters like Günter Grass (who toured widely on behalf of the party) and Graf Bauddisin palatable to liberals. The party also circulated advertisements in which such quasi-aristocratic figures as the actor Kulenkampff and porcelain manufacturer Philip Rosenthal explained why they were supporting the Socialists.

During the concluding phase of the campaign the parties gave their advertising agencies virtual carte blanche to buy up any and all promotion opportunities. The CDU agency had reserved 80 per cent of the large, and 55 per cent of the medium-sized,

[4] INFAS Report, May 9, 1969.
[5] Willy Bongard, "Es Ist zum Heulen," *Die Zeit,* September 9, 1969.

outdoor billboards. Almost all of them were draped with Kie-singer's smiling face and the CDU's "drive-home" slogan, *"Auf den Kanzler Kommt es An!"* The Social Democrats spent the remaining portion of the DM 50 million they had budgeted for the campaign on a wide variety of propaganda techniques, including a thirty-two-page election booklet that was sent to the 20 million households in West Germany. By the end of the campaign almost all the voters had been "reached"; of those surveyed, 91 per cent acknowledged having seen party billboard ads, 75 per cent had read newspaper advertisements, 68 per cent had viewed television election broadcasts, some 60 per cent had seen Kiesinger and Brandt (4 per cent personally, the rest on television). Party magazines and leaflets reached some 30 to 40 per cent through the mails.

To establish their "brand images," each of the three incumbent parties selected official campaign slogans and colors:

CDU/CSU	Red	Sicher in die 70'er Jahre (Safely into the 1970's)
SPD	Orange	Die beste Zukunft die Sie waehlen koennen (The best future for which you could vote)
FDP	Black	Wir schaffen die alten Zoepfe ab (We're throwing out the old pigtails)

The CDU slogan gave a slightly forward-looking twist to the 1965 slogan of "No Experiments." It appealed to SPD and FDP adherents, as well as to CDU voters. The FDP slogan was the most dynamic and decisive sounding and became the most widely known. But it gained approval only among FDP followers and young voters.

The NPD emphasized circulation of its leaflets and tabloids to selected publics, such as farmers and expellees. It too received some public subsidies, though much less than the other parties. The NPD sought to marshal its followers in mass rallies and demonstrations, but these often had to be canceled because of counter-demonstrations organized by trade unions and youth. The Interior Ministry also expected massive attempts by the extra-parliamentary opposition (APO) to break up rallies of the established parties. These never really materialized, although there were some

APO protests of appearances by Strauss and Kiesinger. Nevertheless, Kiesinger made 440 personal appearances in the closing weeks of the campaign, while Brandt made only 160, though Brandt spoke more in the larger cities.

CHANGE IN VOTERS' INTENTIONS

Surveys indicated that at least one-quarter of the eligible voters changed their minds during the campaign. Whether and how these findings should be publicized was hotly disputed. Because of their unenviable performance in the 1965 campaign, the major survey institutes were susceptible to demands that they not publish their findings during the campaign, so as not to influence the voters through "band-wagon" effects based on possibly unreliable data. Although Wolfgang Hartenstein and others had marshaled arguments to prove that "band-wagon" effects were minimal in Germany,[6] the association of market research institutes voted under some official and party pressure that its member institutes should not publish aggregate survey findings during the last ten weeks of the campaign.

Nevertheless, the Second Television Network, which had lagged far behind its rival in its 1965 election coverage, scheduled a series of programs based on nonaggregated survey results. These findings disturbed many party leaders. The FDP had entered the semi-final campaign phase under the impression that it had attracted many sympathizers from the major parties in 1968 and early 1969. But in the summer, the television surveys showed that the party was losing adherents fast. An August survey indicated that it had already lost half of the voters who had been sympathetic earlier in the year. Other surveys were released sub rosa to create intended effects, and toward the end of the campaign outside newspapers not subject to the agreement, such as the London *Times,* published their own survey figures. Most of these surveys showed sustained trends from the CDU to the SPD, but this did not make the SPD happy; in 1965, most sur-

[6] Wolfgang Hartenstein, "Mit Prognosen Leben: Der Einfluss von Wahlvoraussagen auf das Waehlerverhalten," in *Interdependenzen von Politik und Wirtschaft: Festgabe fuer Gert von Eynern* (Berlin, 1968), pp. 285–306.

veys showed similar results but the Socialists lost the election nevertheless.

The FDP, which had entered the campaign with the most innovative goals and appeals, suffered the hardest buffeting of all. In its initially successful attempts to establish a new image— through its support of Heinemann, its German Policy, and its slogan—it engendered negative feedback where it hurt most, among its own members and secondary leaders. They had not expected the new leadership would aggressively follow through on its adopted program and numerous resignations ensued. Changing nuances in midstream, the party dropped the provocative "Pigtail" slogan for a blander one. Still later it reverted to a dynamic slogan that asserted, "You can change Germany—Bring the Grand Coalition to an End." Although the party was heading toward a coalition with the SPD, FDP leaders postponed announcing this until a few days before the elections for fear of slipping below the 5 per cent margin. By that time, the FDP's frequent changes during the campaign had revived widespread suspicion of the party as untrustworthy and opportunist.

THE VOTING RESULTS

Television viewers had to wait up very late on September 28, 1969, before they could be sure which party had the best chance of forming the new government. The final tally was as follows:

	Votes in Millions	Per Cent of Total	1965 Per Cent of Total
CDU/CSU	15.2	46.1	(47.6)
SPD	14.1	42.7	(39.3)
FDP	1.9	5.8	(9.5)
NPD	1.4	4.3	(2.0)
ADF	0.2	0.6	
Others	0.2	0.5	(1.6)
	33.0	100	100

For the first time, the two major German parties received a higher percentage of the total vote (88.8 per cent) than the Republicans and Democrats had polled in the preceding American election.

Although the CDU/CSU remained the leading party, President Nixon was somewhat premature in sending a congratulatory telegram to Chancellor Kiesinger. For the CDU/CSU fell short of a majority, and the government formation hinged on the small parties. The failure of the NPD to hurdle the 5 per cent barrier was widely applauded. But there were mixed feelings about the FDP, which had just managed to get by with 5.8 per cent of the total vote, a large drop from its 1965 tally of 9.5 per cent. The SPD was the only one of the three parties earning Bundestag representation to increase its percentage of the poll.

The Social Democrats made percentage gains over 1965 in all ten Laender, but they were especially successful in northern Germany. They gained some votes from the CDU and some from new voters. The CDU/CSU lost ground in all but two of the Laender. In these, Hessen and Baden-Wurttemberg, there were many dissatisfied FDP voters whose switch compensated the CDU for its losses to the SPD. The CDU incurred its heaviest losses in wealthy, highly developed Laender like Hamburg and Northrhine-Westphalia. The FDP lost heavily everywhere, in some Laender almost half of its 1965 vote. In Hessen it fell to 6.7 per cent of the total vote, compared to 28.1 per cent in 1949. It fared the worst in Bavaria where it received only 4.1 per cent and was beaten even by the National Democrats. The NPD suffered its decisive defeats in northern Germany and especially in Northrhine-Westphalia, where it was held to 3.1 per cent of the vote. In southern Germany, the party exceeded the 5 per cent mark in most Laender, even in Bavaria where Strauss' CSU had pitched its appeal far toward the nationalist pole in order to minimize losses.

Ironically the CDU suffered its worst setbacks in Cologne, the hometown of Adenauer and center of German Catholicism, and in other parts of the Rhineland. However, Rhineland CDU leaders attributed these losses to the CDU's strategy of trying to win potential NPD and right-wing FDP voters. "While the general success of this strategy cannot be questioned," they argued that it necessarily led to losses in areas where right-wing sentiment was small.[7] They also criticized the "completely useless verbal excesses" committed in line with the right-wing strategy, especially

[7] CDU Rheinland, *Bundestagswahl 1969*, p. 3.

by Strauss, who had labeled rebellious students as "animals" not worthy of legal protection. A postelection analysis showed that Strauss had lost both personal popularity and CDU votes in those non-Bavarian cities where he had campaigned on behalf of CDU candidates. Political scientist Rudolf Wildenmann judged that Strauss had lost 40 per cent of his popularity in the election, becoming "the negative counter-figure of the campaign."[8] FDP losses were particularly heavy in Laender where the local leadership had not accepted the party's leftward trend. The fact that the FDP was not involved in the Kiesinger-Schiller struggle over devaluation also hurt the party in the final stage of the campaign. But, most likely, the FDP failed to attract progressive new voters mainly because it left too many voters unsure too long about its commitment to an SPD-FDP coalition, if such a coalition proved feasible.

FACTORS DETERMINING VOTING BEHAVIOR

Nearly all of the variation found in West German voting behavior in recent elections can be explained in terms of class, religion, age, and sex. A comprehensive and subtle understanding of the influence of class and religious factors can be gleaned from the INFAS model, represented in Table 5–5. It divides the German population into six categories and eleven subcategories based upon class, religion, and organizational affiliation. In examining the sources of SPD support, one finds that non-Catholic union-affiliated workers vote SPD by more than three to one, while middle-class Catholics without union affiliation support the SPD in only one out of ten cases. The bulk of the German voters are to be found in the three largest categories of the *traditional left* component of the working class, the predominantly Protestant and a religious *traditional middle class,* and the middle- and working-class *traditional Catholic* sector. The traditional left sector leans heavily toward the SPD, the other two heavily toward the CDU. The model also identifies three smaller sectors whose political sympathies are more or less evenly split.

In the table which shows the changing popular vote positions

[8] *Der Spiegel,* October 13, 1969.

of the parties since 1949 (Table 5–4), one striking characteristic is the clockwork regularity of SPD gains since 1953, an increase of about 3 per cent each election. These gains have come through the SPD's successful wooing of voters in categories II, III, IV, and V in Table 5–5. Through its efforts to demonstrate in the Bad Godesberg program that it was no longer a class party and had overcome its traditional hostility to religion, the Social Democrats were able to appeal more successfully to Catholic workers and nominally religious members of the middle class. Constituency vote statistics between 1957 and 1969 confirm that the SPD was able to make the greatest gains in areas where Catholic industrial workers and middle-class employees in service trades were heavily overrepresented (Table 5–6A). By 1969, SPD gains in such areas were much higher than they were in areas pop-

TABLE 5–4:   POPULAR VOTE IN FEDERAL ELECTIONS, 1949–69 (AS PERCENTAGE OF VOTE CAST)

	1949	1953	1957	1961	1965	1969
CDU/CSU	31.0	45.2	50.2	45.3	47.6	46.1
SPD	29.2	28.8	31.8	36.2	39.3	42.7
FDP	11.9	9.5	7.7	12.8	9.5	5.8
NPD	—	—	—	—	2.0	4.3
Others	27.9	17.5	10.3	5.7	1.6	1.1
TOTAL	100	100	100	100	100	100
Turn-Out	78.5	86.0	87.8	87.7	86.9	86.8

ulated by the party's traditional followers, the working class. It gained 2.9 per cent in areas with a high percentage of workers, 3.4 per cent in those with a medium percentage of workers, and 4 per cent in those with a low percentage of workers. In other words, the SPD was making consistent inroads into two strongholds of the opposition—one composed of Catholic workers and urban middle-class groups, the other of secular status-conscious bourgeoisie.

By 1969, the only place the SPD had not made much headway was in the rural bastions of the traditional Catholic sector.

Constituencies with many Catholics and a lot of agriculture ranked lowest in regard to both the absolute SPD vote percentage and the SPD increase since 1957. The SPD vote in these areas was a little over half that in areas where Protestants and service trades were overrepresented. By the same token, the CDU vote

TABLE 5–5:   SIX SOCIO-RELIGIOUS GROUPS AND THEIR PARTY ATTACHMENTS

Category	Proportion of Electorate %		Strength of SPD Support %
I. Traditional left (working class, non-Catholic)	32		
a. Union members		18	77.4
b. Nonunion members		14	63.5
II. Left-oriented (middle class, non-Catholic, union members)	9		62.1
III. Middle-class oriented, non-Catholic nonunion members	10		
a. Socially mobile middle class		5	52.5
b. Workers with middle-class identification		5	49.3
IV. Catholic-oriented working-class union members	5		41.0
V. Traditional (non-Catholic) middle class	22		
a. Self-employed and others of middle-class parentage		12	18.6
b. Other middle-class nonunion members		10	32.0
VI. Traditional (practicing) Catholics	22		
a. Nonunion working-class members		7	28.7
b. Middle-class union members		3	21.5
c. Middle-class nonunion members		12	9.9

NOTE: Catholics who do not practice their religion are included in the "non-Catholic" classifications.
SOURCE: David R. Segal, "Classes, Strata, and Parties in West Germany and the United States," *Comparative Studies in Society and History*, X, 1 (October, 1967), 76.

was higher in proportion to the number of Catholics and the significance of agriculture. But while some Catholics are practicing Catholics, others have lost their sense of religious identification; the former are more numerous in the countryside, the latter in the cities. And it is the latter whom the SPD has been attracting in

TABLE 5–6: VOTE CHANGES IN DIFFERENT GROUPS OF CONSTITUENCIES

A. *SPD Gains, 1957–69*

Group of Constituencies Characterized by High Presence of —	1969 SPD Percentage of Total Vote	Gain over SPD Percentage in 1957 Election
Catholics, agriculture	27.3	8.8
Protestants, small business	46.9	9.6
Protestants, service trades	51.3	10.4
All Federal Republic	42.7	*10.9*
Protestants, agriculture	38.4	11.3
Protestants, industry	46.7	11.8
Catholics, service trades	44.1	13.5
Catholics, industry	40.0	13.6

B. *CDU Losses, 1965–69*

Group of Constituencies Characterized by —	1969 CDU Percentage of Vote	Change from 1965 CDU Percentage
Lack of agriculture, few Catholics	36.4	−1.5
Lack of agriculture, religiously mixed	38.8	−2.5
Lack of agriculture, many Catholics	45.2	−3.5
Some agriculture, few Catholics	41.8	−0.5
Some agriculture, religiously mixed	46.1	−1.2
Some agriculture, many Catholics	56.5	−3.0
Much agriculture, few Catholics	45.3	0
Much agriculture, religiously mixed	57.5	−0.5
Much agriculture, many Catholics	62.1	−2.0

SOURCES: *A*.—INFAS Report, "*Waehler 1969: Woher? Wohin?*", Table 9. *B*.—Max Kaase, "Determinants of Voting Behavior in the West German Elections of 1969," manuscript, 1969, p. 19.

increasing numbers, for in the rural areas and small towns the clergy still insulates most of its flock from effective recruitment. But if one controls for socio-economic structure, as is done in Table 5–6B, it is evident that CDU losses in 1969 increased with the Catholic percentage in the population, though most significantly in the urban areas. It is not coincidental that this growing shift of Catholic sympathies toward the SPD accelerated at a time when the churches recorded the largest number of membership withdrawals in three decades.

DE-IDEOLOGIZATION

Surveys exploring the significance of ideology among German voters did not bear out anticipated patterns. A 1969 survey, in which respondents were asked to declare their sympathies with an *ideological* position ("Politics is too materialistic. . . . What we need are ideals about which one can become enthusiastic.") and an *anti-ideological* position ("I have enough of political ideals and don't want to know anything more about *Weltanschauung*."), indicated surprisingly that ideologists were pretty equally distributed among the adherents of the three major parties.[9] Fifteen years earlier, SPD members would surely have been more committed to the ideological model, but in 1969, through generational change and an influx of new party members who were pragmatic and anti-ideological in orientation, the significance of ideology had waned.

The increasing similarity of the social and psychological background of the various parties' followers has probably also contributed to a weakening of party identification. This tendency may have been furthered by the partnership stance of the two major parties during the Grand Coalition period. Those who chose to follow what Dahrendorf has called the typically German pattern of avoiding conflict found that identifying more with the coalition than with a party was one way of avoiding conflict situations. Thus when SPD and CDU supporters were asked which of the two parties had accomplished more within the Grand Coalition, half of each group said that "both parties had made equal

[9] Institut für Demoskopie, *Waehlermeinung nicht geheim* (Allensbach, 1969), p. 130.

contributions."[10] Max Kaase has collected data showing that party identification actually declined during the campaign year. The proportion of those who said they adhered to a particular party dropped from 54 per cent in December, 1967, to 28.9 per cent in August, 1969, while only 18.7 per cent maintained a consistent party identification throughout the two-year period. Kaase concludes that "the stability of party identification as a psychological attachment to a given party as found in the United States was not found true for West Germany; rather, changes in party identification seem to coincide with changes in party choice."[11] Kaase and his colleague Rudolf Wildenmann are not content to identify this as a uniquely German phenomenon, due to factors suggested by those in Table 4–1 (p. 106). Rather, they question the general theoretical value of the party identification concept. They believe that a "party sympathy syndrome" is *directly* related to voters' perceptions of how parties stand on issues, especially economic ones.

"CONVERTING" THE VOTES

The simplest way of explaining the operation of the German electoral system and the government formation process is to describe what happened in 1969, allowing Willy Brandt to form an SPD/FDP government. The SPD (42.7) and FDP (5.8) shares of the vote fell short of a popular majority. How were they converted into enough parliamentary seats to permit majority backing for the new government?

West Germany has retained a modified system of proportional representation combining the single-member districts prevalent in the United States and Britain with Land party lists which introduce the proportional representation element. Half of the 496 Bundestag deputies (not counting twenty nonvoting deputies from West Berlin) are elected in single-member districts and half from the Land lists. Voters cast two ballots—one for the district deputy, another for a party list. The second ballot is more crucial

[10] *Ibid.*, p. 125.
[11] Max Kaase, "Determinants of Voting Behavior in the West German Elections of 1969," manuscript, 1969, p. 19.

in the final allocation and is the one used in most German electoral statistics references. The district deputies are elected on the plurality system. In recent years this has meant that they are all candidates of the CDU/CSU or the SPD. But smaller parties can get representations via the Land lists, if, *and only if,* they get at least 5 per cent of the national party vote. Thus, in 1969, the 5 per cent clause caused 1.4 million NPD votes to be "wasted" because not a single NPD candidate entered the Bundestag. At least twenty-five deputies would have been elected if the party had received an additional 250,000 votes.

How seat distribution is worked out can be illustrated by what happened in Schleswig-Holstein in 1969. This small Land in North Germany elects twenty-two deputies, eleven of them in districts and eleven through Land lists. In 1965 the CDU had won all but one of the directly elected seats. In 1969, however, the SPD wrested the district mandates from the CDU in three additional cities—Luebeck, Pinneburg, and Flensburg. In the Land as a whole, the 1,473,102 valid second ballots were distributed as follows: CDU, 46.1 per cent; SPD, 43.6 per cent; FDP, 5.2 per cent; scattered, 5.1 per cent. According to the proportional representation formula, the CDU was entitled to eleven of the twenty-two seats, so that it was assigned four Land list seats (the first four candidates) in addition to the seven deputies elected in districts. By the same formula the SPD was due ten seats, so it got six list seats in addition to the four directly elected deputies. The FDP was entitled to only one list seat. The corresponding picture for the entire country is shown below.

	Constituency Seats	List Seats	Total Seats
CDU/CSU	121	121	242
SPD	127	97	224
FDP	0	30	30

The SPD took thirty directly elected seats from the CDU/CSU, leading in the number of constituency seats for the first time.[12]

[12] Lewis J. Edinger, "Political Change in Germany," *Comparative Politics* II (July, 1970), 553.

That the CDU got an equal number of constituency and list seats was a statistical accident. All three parties got bonuses because the NPD and the lesser parties were closed out of the distribution by the 5 per cent clause.

After the election, the editor of the Springer paper *Die Welt* endorsed Kiesinger's pronouncement that a coalition without the CDU was politically impossible. *"Can there be a change of government in Bonn? Based on the election results a coalition against the CDU/CSU could be formed only with the greatest difficulty and against the dictates of reason. The CDU/CSU held its own very well after a campaign in which it was pushed into the defensive. And although the Social Democrats gained, they fell short of the expected goals."*[13] It was argued that the majority of twelve which an SPD/FDP coalition could muster was too slim, especially in light of the possibility that some right-wing FDP deputies might not cooperate. But the SPD and FDP leaderships agreed

TABLE 5–7:   AGE, SEX, AND VOTING BEHAVIOR, BADEN-WUERT-
TEMBERG, 1969

Sex and Age Group	Per Cent Voting for SPD	Change from 1965	Per Cent Voting for CDU	Change from 1965
Women				
21–29	40.2	+8.6	50.3	−4.2
30–44	36.6	+3.8	53.2	+2.0
45–59	31.8	+2.6	56.8	+2.8
60+	28.0	+2.7	63.0	+3.5
Men				
21–29	44.2	+6.3	42.8	−5.2
30–44	43.7	+2.9	42.1	+0.2
45–59	38.1	+0.9	43.2	+1.8
60+	34.6	+2.0	39.4	+2.2

NOTE: These data are based on representative precinct statistics where ballots were marked according to sex and age of the voter. In this Land, both the CDU vote and CDU gains were higher than in the rest of the Federal Republic.

SOURCE: *Statistisches Landesamt Baden-Wuerttemberg.*

[13] *Die Welt,* September 29, 1969.

they could not afford to pass up the opportunity. Ignoring a belated coalition offer from Kiesinger, the FDP began negotiations with Brandt and the SPD leadership after President Heinemann asked Brandt to take the initiative in forming the government. A few weeks later, on October 21, 1969, Brandt's name was presented to the Bundestag as Chancellor candidate. To achieve office he required an absolute majority, 249 of the Bundestag's 496 members. On the crucial vote he received 251 votes, only two more than the minimum. How he formed his cabinet is analyzed in the next chapter.

BIBLIOGRAPHY

Barnes, S. H., et al., "The German Party System and the 1961 Federal Elections," *APSR*, LVI (1962), 899–914.

Faul, Erwin, ed., *Wahlen und Waehler in Westdeutschland* (Villingen, 1960).

Fisher, Joel M., and Sven Groennings, "German Electoral Politics in 1969," *Government and Opposition*, V (Spring, 1970), 218–34.

Hirsch-Weber, Wolfgang, and Klaus Schuetz, *Waehler und Gewaehlte* (Berlin, 1956).

Janowitz, Morris, and D. R. Segal, "Social Cleavage and Party Affiliation: Germany, Great Britain and the United States," *American Journal of Sociology*, LXXII, 6 (1967), 601–18.

Kaase, Max, "Determinanten des Wahlverhaltens bei der Bundestagswahl, 1969," *PVS*, XI, 1 (March, 1970), 46–110.

Kitzinger, U., *German Electoral Politics* (London, 1960).

————, "The West German Electoral Law," *Parliamentary Affairs*, XI (1958), 220–38.

Klepsch, Egon, et al., *Die Bundestagswahl 1965* (Munich, 1965).

Merkl, P. H., "Comparative Study and Campaign Management: The Brandt Campaign in Western Germany," *WPQ*, XV, 4 (1962), 681–704.

Saenger, Fritz, and Klaus Liepelt, eds., *Wahlhandbuch 1965* (Frankfurt, 1965).

Vogel, Bernhard, et al., *Wahlkampf und Waehlertradition: Eine Studie zur Bundestagswahl* (Cologne, 1964).

"The West German Elections of 1969," *Comparative Politics*, II (July, 1970), entire issue. This special issue contains numerous excellent articles by both American and German authors on issues and voting behavior.

6

The Policy-Making Institutions

THE BONN SETTING

The physical and geographical disposition of capital cities tends to provide clues to the relationships of the political institutions that operate within them. In London, the proximity of the offices of the prime minister, most major ministries, and both houses of Parliament—all within a few hundred yards of each other in Whitehall and Westminster—reflects their intimate and subtle interrelationship. In Washington, although offices are more widely separated, there is a symmetry of sorts. Congress and the White House command different parts of the city, the older departments are strung out between them, and the newly powerful military and scientific establishments constitute a suburban outer ring. In the makeshift capital of Bonn, the attempt to read symbolic significance into the arrangement of government buildings almost defies imagination, because government came there last and had to build wherever space was available.

The Chancellery does constitute a pivot, with the parliament buildings a few hundred feet in one direction and the President's mansion about equidistant in the other. The Chancellery and the President's house were formerly mansions belonging to the rich; parliament is lodged in what was intended to be a teacher's college. But the location of the ministries is hardly indicative of the nature of executive-legislative relationships. They are spread out all over Bonn and the neighboring towns as well. The Press Office and the Foreign Ministry are closest to the Chancellery. The Justice Ministry surveys the scene from a castle on a distant hillside, while the Constitutional Court is over one hundred miles away in Karlsruhe. The Mercedes limousines that transport ministers about town carry special flags, and at the ministry entrances guards check the comings and goings of visitors. Identity cards are also checked at the entrances to the legislature, much more thoroughly in fact than they are when citizens enter or leave the country.

The Bundestag and the Bundesrat are lodged in adjoining series of buildings, originally built in 1930 and reconstructed in 1949. For twenty years most deputies had to share offices because of lack of room. The first unit of a new parliamentary building complex was finally opened in 1969, when a twenty-nine-story building with room for more individual offices and meeting rooms was completed on nearby parkland, which the city of Bonn had yielded grudgingly. In one sense it did establish parliamentary supremacy, since it is by far the tallest building in the Bonn conurbation, which at about the same time was administratively integrated within one municipal jurisdiction.

Some information about the Bundestag chamber will help cast additional light on the peculiar character of German executive-legislative relations. The chamber has been arranged like the large lecture hall that it might have been, with deputies' seats and desks covering most of the space, except for a raised platform at the front where the ministers and their top civil service aides sit facing the deputies. Even the most brilliant orators are hard put to gain the attention of the entire house. The arrangement discourages a free give-and-take and leads speakers to prepare formal lectures. Deputies have called it the worst parliamentary chamber in the world. Many complained that the elevated position of the government bench suggested that the executive had a privileged position.

Encouraged by Bundestag President Gerstenmaier, discussions were initiated in 1959 to renovate the chamber on the model of the British House of Commons, with the majority and opposition parties facing each other. But considerable difficulties were encountered. The members of the cabinet contended that (unlike British ministers) the Basic Law assigned them a special position quite distinct from their role as leaders of the majority party. This position was based on German practice going back to Bismarck, which was reinforced by a Constitutional Court decision in 1958. Finally, in 1969, a compromise was worked out. The government benches were lowered by about a foot, and the number of deputies' desks was reduced from 518 (one for each deputy) to 300.

THE PRESIDENCY

Political systems born by revolution in hierarchical societies have been hard put to devise an adequate republican substitute for the figure of the monarch. Though individual kings may have been loathed, the institution of the monarchy supplied a tremendously powerful symbol, which a large number of citizens needed in order to identify with the state. After 1918, many Germans, conditioned by generations of experience under an *Obrigkeitsstaat* (a state where authority derives from above), missed the security they had symbolically derived from the vestigial lord-vassal relationship. The Weimar Republic's difficulties with this problem were reflected in the fact that its first President, the Socialist Friedrich Ebert, had himself supported retention of the monarchy until just a year before he took office. Both he and his successor, Hindenberg, who remained a monarchist at heart even while in office, failed to institutionalize the Weimar presidency. In 1949, the Parliamentary Council tried once again, and the office it created has turned out to fit relatively smoothly into the constitutional structure, while at the same time supplying, in the persons of its initial incumbents, pleasant uncle figures whom most Germans grew to like and respect.

To secure this degree of acceptance, the presidency has been deprived of such important political powers as appointing the Chancellor in times of crisis, issuing emergency decrees, and serving as commander-in-chief of the armed forces. Most important, its incumbent is not expected to resolve conflicts between the cabinet and the legislature. Rather, his functions are mainly the routine of any head of state. He receives ambassadors, issues letters of appointment to officials, judges, and military officers, signs and proclaims treaties and laws, and possesses the power of pardon, but even these actions must be countersigned by a cabinet minister. In addition, he fulfills domestic political functions very much like those of the British monarch. He pro-

THE FEDERAL PRESIDENT

Article 54

(1) The Federal President shall be elected, without debate, by the Federal Convention. Every German who is eligible to vote in elections for the Bundestag and has reached the age of 40 years shall be eligible for election.

(2) The term of office of the Federal President shall be five years. Re-election for consecutive term shall be admissible only once.

(3) The Federal Convention shall consist of the members of the Bundestag and an equal number of members elected by the popular representative assemblies of the *Laender* according to the principles of proportional representation.

Article 58

Orders and decrees of the Federal President shall require for their validity the counter-signature of the Federal Chancellor or the appropriate Federal Minister. This shall not apply to the appointment and dismissal of the Federal Chancellor, the dissolution of the Bundestag under Article 63 and the request under Article 69, paragraph 3.

---

poses Chancellor candidates, appoints ministers on the Chancellor's recommendation, and can dissolve the Bundestag only under specifically outlined situations involving a deadlock between it and the executive. Quite obviously, this job is different from the presidency in the United States or the French Fifth Republic.

The method of electing the President was also designed to provide a widely accepted figure who would be insulated from popular influence. Because the drafters of the Basic Law wanted to avoid the Weimar situation where a popularly elected President could campaign for the office and vie with the legislature in his claim to represent the people, they provided for his indirect election through a special electoral college made up of all the members of the Bundestag and an equal number of representatives of the Land diets. This *Bundesversammlung* elects the President for a period of five years (compared to a seven-year tenure under Weimar), and an incumbent may be reelected only once. In 1949, the position went to a figure who very conveniently happened to be both the leader of the third largest party and a story book image of "the other Germany." Theodor Heuss, the first leader of the Free Democrats, was esteemed not only as a liberal politician of the old school but as a writer of essays and belles-lettres. During his ten years in office he established a reputation as an eloquent spokesman for humanitarian values. His reelection in 1954 was almost unanimous, and when he left office in 1959 most of the population of Bonn lined the streets to tender him a moving tribute.

Heinrich Luebke, who served as minister of agriculture under Adenauer, moved to the presidency in 1959 as a compromise choice. He has perpetuated attitudes of the Adenauer period. As a Catholic with rural roots, Luebke tended to moralize with a moderately conservative bias. Thus he defended traditional educational methods against critics and indirectly supported the continuation of a "hard line" policy toward the Communist bloc. Some felt that neither his personality nor his intellect qualified him for this high position, but attempts to prevent his reelection in 1964 came to nought. Luebke became increasingly involved in partisan politics as he became identified as an opponent of Chancellor Erhard and an advocate of the formation of a Grand Coalition in 1965–66. As a personal symbol of a rather rigid kind of moral orthodoxy, he became a target of ridicule to the country's rebellious youth and an embarrassment to liberals. He was no asset in the establishment's struggle to preserve and defend its legitimacy in the face of the rising tide of criticism during the late 1960's.

Gustav Heinemann—A New Model

Gustav Heinemann, who succeeded to the presidency on July 1, 1969, after the most closely contested election in recent history, differed from his predecessors in that he was in many respects a symbol of discontinuity and reversal of tradition. The first Social Democrat to be named to the presidency since Ebert was elected fifty years earlier, Heinemann was less of a one-party stalwart than any predecessor—he had changed party affiliation twice since 1949. Most important, he symbolized a decided turning

FROM PRESIDENT HEINEMANN'S INAUGURAL
ADDRESS, JULY 1, 1969

With the oath I have taken I assume the responsibilities of the office to which I was elected by the Federal Assembly on March 5, 1969. . . . As Federal President I have no statement of policy to make. I have ceased to be a member of the Federal Government and of the German Bundestag. I have given up all my functions in the Social Democratic party of Germany. In accordance with the intention of the Basic Law I shall from now on stand at the side of those whose task it is to take political decisions and to answer for them. Yet in this very hour the Federal President should be entitled to say a personal word. . . .

Our nation can show from its history much that may fill us with pleasure and self-confidence. We have made no mean contribution to the enrichment of mankind. But the name of our nation was also abused to unleash the disaster of the Second World War. Only if we ourselves persist in asking how this terrible chapter of National Socialism could come about will other nations no longer be able to hold that chapter of our history against us. . . .

The Federal Republic of Germany has deliberately been organized as a representative democracy. I consider that its system based on human dignity and human rights is the best foundation and framework for a state that we have ever had in our history. But it is not yet complete. All its guiding criteria such as free democracy, social justice and the rule of law require, in both state and society, constant endeavor and participation on the part of the emancipated citizen in the quest for daily improvement of these values. I know there are some who do not like to hear this. Some still feel attached to the authoritarian state. That state was long enough our misfortune and finally led us into the disaster of the Third Reich. . . .

Hence, it is no use deriding what is imperfect today or to preach the absolute as the program of the day. Instead, let us change conditions step by step, through criticism and cooperation. . . . I understand the impatience with all the inertia in human society and even the churches. I myself have been

an impatient person all my life. I still am. And to that extent
I understand even the radical groups among the restive young
generation. But it is just the latter whom, from my own impatience, I would call upon to reinforce the ranks of those who
have already set out before them on the long march of
reform and are determined to continue it.

---

away from the traditions, especially the foreign and military
policies, of the Adenauer era, and he did not hesitate to state
this plainly right after his election. Heinemann had been minister of the interior in Adenauer's first cabinet, but he resigned
from that office and from the CDU in 1951 because of his
principled opposition to Adenauer's policy of German rearmament. In the 1950's, he became the most outspoken critic of
Adenauer's "NATO first" policy, and for a while Heinemann
had his own splinter party. During the mid-1950's, he was re-
peatedly attacked as a crypto-Communist and went to court
twelve times to successfully reject libels that his party was
financed from Communist sources. In 1957, Heinemann dissolved
the party, joined the Social Democrats, and won a seat in the
Bundestag. There he drew on the support of his fellow Protestants
to challenge the CDU's position as the exclusive exponent of
Christian concerns.[1] In 1962 he represented *Der Spiegel* in its
legal battle against Franz Joseph Strauss, and in 1966 he re-
entered the cabinet to become the most successful minister of
justice in the Federal Republic's history.

The politicians who worked for Heinemann's nomination by
the Social Democrats, and for his election by a narrow SPD-FDP
majority in the Bundesversammlung, were very much aware that
his election might mean a stronger presidency with much more
political influence in the 1970's. In interviews Heinemann emphasized he would not be content merely to fulfill the figurehead
functions of the office, but would utilize its constitutional powers

---

[1] "Bundestagsrede vom 23. January 1958," in Gustav W. Heinemann, *Verfehlte Deutschlandpolitik: Irrefuehrung und Selbsttaeuschung* (Frankfurt, 1966). The publishers brought out a second edition of this toughly
titled collection on the eve of Heinemann's assumption of the presidency.

to the utmost, critically examining all nominations the Chancellor passed up for his signature. As a longtime member of the Confessional Church and an adherent of nonviolent values, Heinemann also announced that his actions would be measured by his conscience as well as by the traditions of the constitution. Asked whether there were any bills he would refuse to promulgate into law by his signature, he responded:

> That is a purely theoretical question, and I can answer it only with that kind of reservation. But one law which I would surely refuse to sign, because I could not reconcile it with my conscience, would be a constitutional amendment to reintroduce the death penalty. Another like it would be legislative authorization for providing the Bundeswehr with atomic weapons which would be under exclusive German jurisdiction. But I am quite confident that I shall not be put in a position where I shall be asked to sign such regulations.[2]

In emphasizing the moral dimensions of his official responsibilities, Heinemann was partly concerned about reestablishing contact with the rebellious German student population, whose political alienation disturbed him. He seemed to think they might be encouraged by the fact that a "loner" and "outsider" like himself had ascended to the highest constitutional position without sacrificing his principles.

THE CHANCELLORSHIP

Even convinced democrats have reluctantly come to accept that the German definition of democracy tends to mean "government for the people" more than it does "government by the people." The German penchant for order and their desire to be given at least a sure sense of direction cause them to place a premium on an individual who can keep firm control of the tiller. It is not only because he unified Germany that Bismarck remains by far the most admired historical German political figure. Despite reservations about his role in retarding progress toward parliamentarism and genuine political democracy, he is still widely

---

[2] *Die Welt,* July 1, 1969.

regarded as an ideal for German rulers, as was shown in commentaries on the occasion of the one hundred and fiftieth anniversary of his birth in March, 1965.

If, in 1948, an outside observer had accused the Parliamentary Council of drafting a Bismarckian constitution tailored to fit the personality of its presiding officer and second oldest member (who had himself grown up in the Bismarckian era), he would have been told that Konrad Adenauer had relatively little influence on the important drafting—as distinguished from the polishing—work of the council. The council concentrated on remedying the faults of the Weimar Constitution. If in the process they created an extremely strong Chancellor, they did so by indirection. For having decided that the President should not have any significant executive powers, power had to be concentrated within the cabinet. The drafters took for granted the continuation of a multiparty system, and they feared the system would break down, as it had under Weimar when ministers were frequently torn between loyalty to cabinet policies and pressures from their various parties. It was largely to prevent the breakdown of cabinet authority during crises that the Basic Law gave the Chancellor so much power to maintain executive stability against the legislature and to impose cabinet cohesion on its ministers.

His position is immensely strengthened by the fact that the Basic Law radically altered a traditional parliamentary practice: a Chancellor and his cabinet are no longer forced to resign if they lose a vote of confidence in the legislature. The Chancellor must resign after losing a vote of confidence *only if the legislature at the very same time elects by majority vote someone to take his place.* The adoption of this "positive" no-confidence provision was intended to prevent situations in which mutually hostile parties combine to bring down a ministry without being able to agree among themselves on a suitable replacement. In practice, this clause has made the position of a Chancellor who is also leader of a majority party virtually impregnable. As long as he retains control of his party, the legislature is unable to enter a no-confidence vote. On the other hand, the Chancellor may, on occasions of his choosing, ask the Bundestag for a vote of confidence, but even if he loses he need not resign.

Adenauer demonstrated how formidable a power instrument the chancellorship could be when the incumbent had iron will power, was the formal and effective leader of his party, and the dominant personality in his cabinet. His successor, Ludwig Erhard, showed that the Chancellor could also be a much less influential figure if he lacked the necessary attributes. It was partly because he felt that his portly economics minister did not have enough of a feel for power that Adenauer fought so bitterly to prevent Erhard's succession to the office. When Adenauer finally did yield in 1963, he insisted on retaining the chairmanship of the CDU, which he utilized for another three years to snipe at Erhard's conduct of the executive. The incomplete loyalty of Erhard's parliamentary following during this period was illustrated by the votes in the CDU/CSU parliamentary party in nominating him in 1963: 63 of 222 CDU/CSU deputies either abstained or voted "No."

To Erhard much of the spirit and tradition Adenauer had infused into the Chancellery and the federal government were alien. His earlier career as a business-school teacher and economic adviser had not provided him with the inside links to the bureaucratic elite that Adenauer had developed in the course of his long career in the Cologne administration. During his fourteen years as minister of economics under Adenauer, Erhard had focused his attention primarily on the economic policy field. There he held firm convictions, but not in many other policy areas. As an adherent of modified laissez-faire principles, he was inclined also to let decisions mature by themselves in a free marketplace of political ideas; his style was in sharp contrast to Adenauer's characteristic attempts to force through his own opinions. Thus Erhard was widely criticized for allowing President Lyndon Johnson to use tough bargaining methods to get him to make larger financial commitments than the Federal Republic could afford. Budget problems became increasingly acute when a recession in economic activity caused a decline in anticipated tax receipts. The cabinet, having made too many promises and commitments to external and domestic interest groups, was faced with a gaping deficit, which Erhard proposed to meet by reducing subsidies and expenditures. His cabinet began to disintegrate in October, 1966, when the FDP members resigned.

KURT KIESINGER AND THE GRAND COALITION

For some six weeks toward the end of 1966, the Federal Republic was thrown into a constitutional crisis that highlighted weaknesses in the provisions for selection of a new Chancellor. Turning a deaf ear to CDU suggestions that he resign, Erhard continued to preside over a CDU cabinet that lacked a Bundestag majority. The opposition parties, SPD and FDP, did have a four-vote majority, but they could not agree on an alternative candidate for Chancellor, as required by the "positive nonconfidence rule." Finally, Erhard agreed to resign if the CDU could select his successor. This was accomplished by having the CDU/CSU parliamentary party vote among several candidates proposed by the party executive—Minister-President Kurt Georg Kiesinger of Baden-Wuerttemberg, Foreign Minister Gerhard Schroeder, Fraktion Chairman Rainer Barzel, and Walter Hallstein. Voting on three ballots proceeded as follows:

	First Ballot	Second Ballot	Third Ballot
Kiesinger	97	119	137
Schroeder	76	80	81
Barzel	56	42	26
Hallstein	14	3	—
Vote Cast	243	244	244

It was no accident that the candidate who finally won on the third ballot, Kiesinger, had been away from the hothouse of Bonn politics for eight years, having returned to the Land political scene after having served in the federal parliament in the 1950's.

After lively intraparty discussion, a majority of CDU/CSU deputies agreed to support a "Grand Coalition" cabinet, although a strong group in the Social Democrats tried to argue for a "small coalition with the FDP. The cabinet assembled by Kiesinger consisted of eleven CDU/CSU and nine SPD ministers. Since Strauss had channeled Bavarian support to ensure Kiesinger's nomination, he had to be taken back into the cabinet as finance minister. All the other CDU ministers were holdovers from the Erhard cabinet, while the SPD ministers included the party's leadership group—party chairman Willy Brandt as Vice Chancellor and foreign minister, Herbert Wehner as minister for all-German affairs, and Karl Schiller as economics minister. It was the first time in thirty-six years that Social Democrats participated in a national cabinet.

In presiding over a cabinet composed of two nearly equal parties, Kiesinger obviously could not lay down guidelines on all policies, and in any case he was not attuned to the Adenauer style. But neither could he resort to Erhard's style of delegating most of his authority to other ministers and deciding conflicts by majority vote of the cabinet. Since the success of the coalition depended upon minimizing party polarization within it, Kiesinger had to help bring about cabinet consensus without resorting to a formal vote. Sometimes a cabinet vote could not be avoided, as in the dispute between Economics Minister Schiller and Finance Minister Strauss over revaluation in April, 1969. By extracting concessions from his own party, Kiesinger was able to maintain cabinet cohesion and accomplish most—although not all—of his party's original goals by the time the government was dissolved before the federal elections of September, 1969.

WILLY BRANDT AND THE SMALL COALITION

Like his predecessors, Willy Brandt became Chancellor after prolonged service in elected office on the local and Land levels, as well as in the federal cabinet. Like Adenauer he had been a big-city mayor; like Kiesinger the head of a Land government; like Erhard a federal minister. But although, at fifty-six, he was the youngest of West Germany's Chancellors, his life had spanned a much greater variety of social experiences. He looked in vain to the past for any successful Chancellors of either working-class origin or SPD coloration; therefore, he could gain little guidance from the records of past national leaders. The few left-of-center Chancellors of pre-Hitler Germany had served under circumstances which really offered no parallels to Brandt's situation. More relevant for him probably were the records of some Swedish and Norwegian Social Democratic prime ministers, whom he knew quite well. He also drew guidance from his own experiences as mayor and foreign minister, positions in which he had come

THE BRANDT GOVERNMENT AT WORK

When the new SPD/FDP coalition first entered office, Minister Horst Ehmke awakened the Chancellery from its long sleep with considerable ruthlessness, thereby spreading exaggerated hopes and fears. . . . Formerly an office which operated almost completely without publicity, the Chancellery suddenly became the subject of broad discussion. The opposition and the civil servants' associations bitterly complained that the dismissal and transfer of a number of politically significant officials constituted an abuse of power by the new masters. . . .

The Chancellery has now begun to develop an information system through which the anticipated initiatives of the various ministries are reported to the Chancellery, where they are computer-listed according to action dates, responsible ministry, and substantive contents and interrelationships. . . . The Chancellery absorbs these informations not purely for control purposes, but relays them to the ministries and the parliamentary parties.

Since then, the ministries are better informed about the proposed actions of other ministries, . . . whereas these lists enable the parliamentary parties to inject themselves at a relatively early juncture in the decision-making process.

The cabinet includes ministers with highly individualized personalities who have to be handled with care. There are important ministers with difficult personality structures, such as Schiller and Alex Moeller; there are ministers, such as Helmut Schmidt, Leber, Hans-Dietrich Genscher, and to an increasing extent also Walter Scheel, who have broad political interests which lead them to frequently enter the discussion of matters being handled by other ministries. In the cabinet, as elsewhere, some are more "equal" than others. There are old alliances, as between Schmidt and Moeller, political affinities as between Leber and Schmidt, whereas Genscher and Ehmke are united by their quick wit.

This cabinet is grouped around a Chancellor who invokes his uncontested authority with great restraint, indeed, according to some of his collaborators, at times with too much restraint. . . . Willy Brandt is well prepared for cabinet meetings. . . . He carefully absorbs the two-to-three-page memoranda which cover routine agenda items, and has developed a reputation, as Adenauer had earlier, for being an uncommonly conscientious student of dossiers.

Chancellery Minister Ehmke, who otherwise spares scarcely anyone from being the object of his sarcastic wit, treats Brandt with a degree of loyalty . . . which at times suggest a touch of veneration. And his collaborators react similarly. When, as occasionally happens, there is criticism of the slowness of some of the Chancellor's decisions, Ehmke springs to the defense: A cabinet which has to work under so many difficult conditions—small majority, an unclear economic situation, large and controversial foreign-policy decisions—could scarcely be led by anyone else. A Chancellor who was to attempt to determine the basic lines of policy by issuing orders would cause the government to blow up.

Rolf Zundel in *Die Zeit,*
September 8, 1970.

---

to rely heavily on a small staff of trusted personal advisers. In addition a well-organized SPD party organization made Brandt better prepared to cope with the office than Erhard or Kiesinger.

Where Adenauer had utilized the CDU as a "Chancellor party," Brandt was clearly a "party Chancellor." Indubitably, he owed his office to the electoral appeal of the SPD rather than to his own personality. The party had retained him as chairman despite his electoral shortcomings in the campaigns of 1961 and 1965. These common experiences had built a mutual acceptance and affection which none of the CDU Chancellors had developed with their colleagues. The team image that had been projected in the campaign reflected a fairly accurate picture of the interpersonal relationships at the top echelon of the SPD. But because Brandt and his advisers insisted that the cabinet ministers could not be selected according to the established SPD pecking order, several senior SPD parliamentarians were passed over in favor of younger candidates. Trusted advisers of Brandt, such as Horst Ehmke and Egon Bahr, were given key positions in the Chancellery even though they had been passed over in earlier elections to the party executive.

The tested decision-making techniques of the Social Democratic leadership served Brandt well in forming his cabinet. Though wishes of various party factions had to be reconciled with those of the Free Democratic coalition party, the composition of the cabinet was worked out in a much shorter time than ever before, even though only five of the fifteen ministers were held over from the preceding cabinet. The Free Democrats agreed to settle for three cabinet positions. Of the twelve SPD ministers, about half were drawn from the party's established parliamentary leadership, and the rest were selected because they represented important party interest groups such as the trade unions, urban interests, Protestants, and women.

THE CABINET

Parliamentary government developed with the acceptance of the convention that the executives in charge of government departments were to be chosen because they enjoyed the confidence of party majorities in Parliament, not because of their merit as the king's civil servants. In accordance with the rule that "the powers of the Crown must be exercised through ministers who are members of one or the other Houses of Parliament and who command the confidence of the House of Commons,"[3] a clear line was drawn in Britain between politicians and civil servants. One could either enjoy the tenure and pension rights of a permanent civil servant—in which case becoming a minister was out of the question—or one could go into Parliament with the hope of becoming a minister, but for only as long as one's party remained in power. It was not possible to switch back and forth between the two careers. In Imperial Germany, where parliamentary government never developed fully, this distinction was not drawn.

The situation changed very slowly from Bismarck's time, when practically all the "state secretaries" fulfilling ministerial roles were really civil servants responsible only to the Chancellor, who was himself the chief civil servant and only incidentally accountable to the Reichstag. In the Weimar period, though ministers were drawn predominantly from the ranks of parliamentarians, they were reluctant to relinquish the pension rights and other

[3] Albert Dicey, *Law of the Constitution,* 10th ed. (London, 1960), p. 431.

privileges they shared under public law with civil servants. In 1930 a special law had to be passed to make it evident that ministers were not covered by *all* the civil service regulations. But the distinction between parliamentary ministers and civil servants still remains difficult for the German legal mind to grasp, and a constitutional law text published in 1954 had to devote a paragraph to explaining that ministers do not *have* to be recruited from among civil servants. Nevertheless, their salaries, as well as that of the Chancellor, remain tied to civil service scales. The ministers receive one and one-third times, the Chancellor one and two-thirds times the salary of the top civil service bracket, plus expense allowances.

PARKINSON'S LAW (GERMAN VERSION)

Between 1949 and 1969, German cabinets consistently followed that variant of Parkinson's law which states that the number of ministries and the size of cabinets always grow larger rather than smaller. Adenauer had started with fourteen cabinet ministers in 1949, but the need to accommodate interest groups and coalition party representatives caused the number of ministries to mushroom. During the Kiesinger administration the cabinet was made up of the Chancellor, nineteen departmental ministers, and one minister without portfolio. When he formed his cabinet in November, 1969, Willy Brandt cut the number of cabinet departments down to fourteen again. He was able to carry through on this initiative because of the excellent recommendations that had been prepared by the Study Group on the Structural Reform of the Federal Government and Administration.[4]

Most of the functions of the five "abolished" ministries were consolidated, forming larger joint ministries. Thus the functions of the Family Ministry were largely absorbed by the Ministry of Health, the Treasury Ministry was merged with the Finance Ministry, the Ministry of Posts was combined with the Ministry of Transport. Because of the speed with which the reform was carried out, most of the affected interest groups did not have time

[4] Projektgruppe fuer Regierungs- und Verwaltungsreform, *Erster Bericht zur Reform der Struktur von Bundesregierung und -Verwaltung* (Bonn, 1969).

to mobilize their strength to save "their" ministries. The expellees' organizations tried to save the Ministry of Expellee Affairs, but since they had been outspokenly pro-CDU in the election, they had little influence in the new government and had to be content with massive criticism in the Bundestag. One interest group that had more adherents in high places in the SPD did manage to "salvage" a ministry scheduled for merger: the big-city mayors and communal officials, most of whom belonged to the SPD, succeeded in maintaining the autonomy of the Ministry of Housing.

In his cabinet appointments, Brandt named senior parliamentary figures to the ministries with the most power and prestige, while choosing heads of the secondary ministries with a keen eye to interest representation. The FDP leader Walter Scheel was granted his choice of the Foreign Ministry, while his party colleague Hans-Dietrich Genscher was named interior minister. Of the senior Social Democrats, Karl Schiller had undisputed title to continuing as economics minister, while two other respected leaders, Helmut Schmidt and Alex Moeller, took over the important Ministries of Defense and Finance previously run by Christian Democrats. The trade-union wing of the SPD was well represented by the appointment of two former union chairmen to the Ministries of Labor and Transportation. And a leading woman in the SPD, Kaete Ströbel, continued in her post as minister of health. The Housing Ministry became the province of urban interests, while the Agriculture Ministry was assigned to a conservative Free Democratic politician from Bavaria, Josef Ertl. Finally, different wings of the SPD were mollified by the appointments of Gerhard Jahn to the Ministry of Justice, Erhard Eppler, a Protestant intellectual, to the Ministry of Economic Cooperation, and Egon Franke, a powerful backbencher, to the Ministry of Inter-German Affairs. The difficult Ministry of Scientific Research was given to a nonparty expert, Professor Ernst Leussink.

PARLIAMENTARY STATE SECRETARIES

The Brandt government also widened the scope of an institution that had first been introduced in German government in 1967—the parliamentary state secretary. This innovation was based on the British practice of appointing one or more junior parliamentarians to help each minister run his department and maintain contact with Parliament and the public. Some of the appointees, such as Ralf Dahrendorf (FDP) to the Foreign Office and Klaus von Dohnanyi (SPD) to the Economics Ministry, were well-known figures; others were younger men to whom this offered scope for wider experience. Unlike the *permanent* state secretaries, who are civil servants, the parliamentary state secretaries must be members of parliament. Both can answer oral questions during the parliamentary question hour. But in the period 1967–69, both the Foreign Office and the Finance Ministry turned the job of representing the ministry during question hour almost completely over to the parliamentary state secretary. The Study Group on Structural Reform recommended elevating the parliamentary state secretaries to state ministers, so that these aides would fit directly into the hierarchies of their ministries and be able to assist ministers in the running of their entire departments, rather than just with specific tasks.

THE BUNDESTAG

ORGANIZATION

Like the United States Congress, but unlike the House of Commons, the Bundestag is presided over by an active party leader of the majority party. The office of Bundestag president is endowed with a good deal of formal dignity, and its incumbents have in the main been men respected by their colleagues for both their outstanding intellectual capacities and their strong will power. The chamber is run in a fairly decentralized manner on the basis of rules inherited from the Reichstag. Most important decisions regarding committee assignments, the scheduling of debates, etc., are made by broad agreement among the party leaders. The instrument through which they function is called, not very appropriately, the "Council of Elders," which includes the president, the three vice-presidents (representing the three major parties), and a number of delegates sent by each of the parties.

The average German deputy is considerably more difficult to

describe than his American equivalent. He may be a prominent businessman who was prevailed upon to go into politics when his local CDU was looking for candidates, or a man who had spent twenty years as a labor union secretary before being nominated by the SPD, or a teacher or journalist in either party,

THE BUNDESTAG

Article 38

(1) The deputies of the German Bundestag shall be elected by the people in universal, free, equal, direct and secret elections. They shall be representatives of the whole people, not bound to orders and instructions and subject only to their conscience.

Article 39

(1) The Bundestag shall be elected for a term of four years. Its legislative term shall end four years after its first meeting or on its dissolution. . . .

Article 43

(1) The Bundestag and its committees may demand the presence of any member of the Federal Government.

(2) The members of the Bundesrat and of the Federal Government as well as the persons commissioned by them shall have access to all meetings of the Bundestag and its committees. They must be heard at any time.

or a farmer sent into the CDU by the farmers' organization to look after agricultural interests, or the executive secretary of a trade association, or an official who had entered the civil administration through political channels, or frequently a lawyer, doctor, or intellectual. The greater variety of types is due to the fact that most interest groups in this traditionally class- and group-conscious country want to be represented by "some of their own," and the parties take care to include candidates with all kinds of backgrounds and expertise.

As Table 6–1 shows, the largest single group in the Bundestag as well as in both major parties is made up of officials on leave from government positions. This group is much more important

TABLE 6–1:   SOCIO-OCCUPATIONAL COMPOSITION OF BUNDES-
TAG (IN PERCENTAGES)

Occupations, Social Group	All Bundestag Deputies	CDU Deputies	SPD Deputies
Government officials and employees	22.3	22.7	23.1
Professions: lawyers, doctors, journalists, clerics, etc.	20.5	17.5	25.1
Employees of political parties and labor unions	16.1	9.6	28.1
Entrepreneurs, executives, business association officials	15.5	16.7	8.4
Farmers and farm organization representatives	11.5	18.3	1.5
Small businessmen, artisans	6.0	8.0	3.5
White- and blue-collar workers	5.6	4.8	7.4
Housewives	2.5	2.4	2.9
TOTAL	100.0	100.0	100.0

NOTE: Based on data for 1961–65 Bundestag.
SOURCE: Wolfgang Zapf, "Sozialstruktur deutscher Parlamente," in Fritz
Saenger and Klaus Liepelt, eds., Wahlhandbuch 1965 (Frankfurt, 1965).

than any similar one in Anglo-American parliaments, and it reflects the overlapping of administrative and parliamentary careers
that has always been possible in Germany. But the civil servants'
bloc is not quite as cohesive as the figures suggest; many are
basically party politicians who achieved *Beamten* status in the
postwar period. The second largest group, composed of members
of the professions, is even less homogeneous and cohesive. It is
of about equal significance in both major parties, though the SPD
has relatively more journalists and the CDU relatively more
lawyers.

The four next largest occupational groups in the table tend to
be directly representative of their organized interest groups, and
their differential distribution within the parties is significant.
Secretaries and officials of political parties and labor unions constitute the largest single category of SPD deputies, reflecting the
high degree to which that party has depended on union support

as well as the preference it has frequently given its own party organizers. In the CDU/CSU parliamentary party, a significant role is played by businessmen and farmers, often represented by officials of their trade associations, who play a key role in shaping economic policy in the specialized Bundestag committees. It is not surprising that the broader interest-group appeal of the CDU is reflected by its deputies since nominations—especially those on the Land lists—are drawn up with "representativeness" in mind. Many Germans would consider it odd to have a legislature composed predominantly of members of one profession, as the American Congress is dominated by lawyers. But that is because they identify lawyers primarily as members of the professional middle class, not as a group whose profession has socialized them into the roles of brokers and middlemen.

Only some German Bundestag deputies devote themselves as undividedly to their jobs as most American congressmen are obliged to. This vital group, however, includes the key party chairmen and secretaries, and the leading committee chairmen. These are the men whom Gerhard Lowenberg, in his detailed study of the Bundestag, identifies as the "professional politicians," constituting "at once the most disparaged and the most important part of the House."[5] In a broader sense the professionals constitute about 23 per cent of the members; in the narrower sense, those active solely in the Bundestag, they constitute a small group of about fifty members. The bulk of the backbench parliamentarians, however, are divided by Loewenberg into two nearly equal groups of interest representatives and MDB's with part-time private occupations. These deputies, encompassing about 60 per cent of Bundestag membership, include members who have important institutional or private outside interests that prevent them from investing all their time in furthering their parliamentary careers. Finally, a group of about 10 per cent of the membership is made up of civil servants and other public employees who sit in the Bundestag on a temporary basis while on leave from their permanent positions. Until recently, only the first group of members, the professional politicians, commanded staffs of personal

[5] Gerhard Loewenberg, *Parliament in the German Political System* (Ithaca, 1967), p. 118.

administrative or research assistants out of Bundestag funds. Such personnel resources are mainly centered in the parliamentary party or Fraktion offices and are drawn upon by members with the indulgence of party leaders.

The German Bundestag has been more bureaucratic than other parliamentary bodies, and has harbored more older members. In the 1950's, three-quarters of Bundestag members were over forty years of age when first elected and almost half were over fifty. This contrasted sharply with Britain where 70 to 80 per cent were under fifty and some 50 percent under forty at the time of first election.[6] In the 1960's, young party members were able to make stronger bids to hold up the automatic renominations of the veterans, and after 1965 the number of younger Bundestag entrants increased considerably. In that year, the average age of Bundestag members declined from 52.4 to 50.7 years, and the same trend continued in 1969, when many senior parliamentarians of all parties ran into determined opposition that brought party nominations to younger rivals. Only about 80 of the major-party constituency candidates (248 CDU/CSU, 248 SPD) faced nomination contests in 1965. By 1969, 120 contested nominations were carried to a vote at major party nominating conventions. This meant that one out of every four candidates emerged from a nomination struggle, and among SPD candidates this ratio was almost one out of three (74 out of 248).

After the 1969 election, the average age of Bundestag deputies dipped below fifty for the first time. The sixth Bundestag contains only thirty-two six-term veterans who have served continuously since 1949, and only about seventy-five deputies who were over sixty years at the beginning of the session. Almost a third of the house consists of first-termers, whereas in 1961 the proportion was less than a quarter. Together with the second-termers, they constitute about 57 per cent of the total membership. The success of the "under-45's" has produced a consistent rejuvenation in the membership. The number of these younger deputies has increased from 121 in 1961, to 159 in 1965, to 174 in 1969.

[6] *Ibid.*, p. 90.

THE FRAKTIONEN

The most important components of the Bundestag are undoubtedly the *Fraktionen,* the parliamentary parties with at least fifteen members. Party unity and discipline are strongly embedded in German tradition, and it is customary for the individual deputy to be very active within the party and its discussion groups. On most important matters party caucuses meet first to decide on the party position and then they appoint spokesmen to present their position in the plenary session. Work in the committees is less closely supervised by the party, but since committee members receive their positions through their Fraktion, they usually carry out party instructions. The parties also tend to vote uniformly on roll calls, though there is some difference between the behavior of the different party groups. The Socialist deputies have inherited a strong informal tradition of party discipline and seldom fail to follow the party position determined by the party majority. The Christian Democrats, representing a far wider variety of interests within a much looser party framework, have always declared that they do not impose party discipline. But even their rules provide that a deputy who believes he cannot follow the party position must announce this fact beforehand, and on matters of high priority, such as most foreign policy issues, the Christian Democrats have in fact voted almost as uniformly as the Socialists.

BACKBENCHERS AND THEIR MISGIVINGS

The increased number of younger, somewhat cocksure new entrants helped bring to the fore in the 1965–69 Bundestag many of the backbenchers' grievances and demands for reform. As one of them wrote shortly after assuming office:

> The younger ones were soon to experience that not all parliamentarians are equal. While they had to suffer catastrophic work conditions, which involve walking hundreds of meters in order to get their mail and engaging with their office-mate in the daily game of "who shall use the telephone now?," other colleagues were being picked up by luxury cars

bearing chauffeurs and secretaries. . . . The so-called plenary debates are a great disappointment for the young deputy. Rather than give the floor to a "newcomer," an old-timer is given the floor to make a fool of himself.[7]

Experiences such as these led to discussion of changes in the parliamentary rules (excerpts from this 1969 debate appear below). But some of the proposed reforms did not get past a parliamentary deadlock.

A "NEGRO REVOLT" IN THE BUNDESTAG

BLACHSTEIN (SPD): Way up there at the top there are the President and the Vice-Presidents, then come the Fraktion chairmen and their deputies, then come the committee chairmen and the chairmen of the party specialist groups. They have the more spacious offices; they also have trained specialized assistants and technical help. Then come the bosses of interest groups and trade unions with their own quite highly developed staffs. I would estimate that there are about fifty of these privileged deputies. And then come the 450 "Negroes," who have to perform their entire work load all by themselves,

(*Applause from all parties*)

from the getting of their mail, to the gathering of data needed to support their positions, to the preparation of their speeches, and everything that goes along with this . . .

MULLER (SPD): There is a great deal of talk about equality of opportunity in a democracy. But in that connection we forget that equality of opportunity is not provided in this house. . . . I can say here to German public opinion that it is basically a scandal the way I exploit my wife, without paying her any remuneration. During the past year my wife has written 3,700 personal letters for me without any payment. I cannot pay for that out of a DM 600 expense allowance.

(*Applause from deputies of the SPD and CDU/CSU*)

[7] Gunther Muller, "Erfahrungen eines jungen Abgeordneten," in Michael Hereth, ed., *Junge Republik* (Munich, 1966), pp. 57–58. And see Loewenberg, *Parliament in the German Political System*, p. 387, for relevant data.

PICARD (CDU/CSU): There are quite a few of us who are quietly amused that one or another of us procures the speech which he delivers here from within the very same ministry whose budget is under discussion.

(CALL FROM THE RIGHT: That's the way it is.)

MOMMER (SPD): Colleague Picard, you have just alleged that there are other colleagues who procure their speeches from ministries. Are you aware that this constitutes a grave accusation, and that you are not permitted to do that, unless you name names.

(*Applause from deputies of the SPD and from the Right*)

PICARD: Mr. Vice-President, let the parliament decide whether this is a grave accusation. I am not here in order to accuse anyone . . . I merely stand here to call things as they are. . . .

DICHGANS (CDU/CSU): Ladies and Gentlemen, it is our desire to give the "Negroes," as you have called them, somewhat more elbow-room. We would like to ensure that in addition to the official Fraktion spokesmen, who of course must inform the public about the position which the Fraktion as a whole takes, individual deputies should also get their word in, whether their considerations are correct or incorrect. . . . I have experienced cases here where five speeches each of a full hour's duration were held one after another. In that way you drive the deputies from the chamber.

(*Applause from the CDU/CSU*)

When the deputies know that in such debates they cannot get a chance to speak, when the deputies are here only as decoration, or as the French would say, *pour faire tapisserie,*

(*Amusement in the center*)

then you have an unworthy situation. You, ladies and gentlemen, will then have to accept the fact that our plenary sessions remain as poorly attended as they have so often been in recent times.

SPITZMUELLER (FDP): I too have experienced how scheduled debates were called off because the parliamentary whips agreed to discontinue debate on remaining topics because the preceding points had taken up too much time. Then one day I blew my top and at 10 o'clock at night I said, "You can decide whatever you like, but I am going to speak." And then we had a debate at 10 o'clock in the night.

Since one of the costs of the Grand Coalition was a restraint on interparty criticism, the backbenchers of the two major parties came to focus more of their gripes and dissatisfaction on the parliamentary leaders. Eugen Gerstenmaier, the somewhat authoritarian veteran Bundestag president, offered a fulsome target, especially since the carefully rigged pyramid of privileges was attributed largely to him. He was the one who had insisted that the Bundestag ushers be dressed in formal clothes and that the other deputies rise when the president entered the chamber. Gerstenmaier had grown accustomed to manipulating the trappings of power; he had thrown his considerable influence around rather freely both in and outside of the Bundestag. In 1968, it emerged that he had used influence to make sure the amendment of a restitution bill authorizing payments to victims of National Socialism would cover his own case. In the American Congress such interference would be taken for granted as a perquisite of leadership. But in Germany this was a touchy case, and the publicity elicited enough criticism to alarm the politicians, who were aware that the NPD could exploit the issue as part of its attack on parliamentarianism. When he looked to support from his fellow parliamentarians, Gerstenmaier encountered an evasive silence largely because of the hostility he had aroused over the years through his self-righteously moralistic style and high-handed manner. Under tremendous pressure from the CDU leaders, he resigned from his cherished office with only the sheerest of face-saving resolutions.

The new Bundestag president, Kai-Uwe von Hassel, a Christian Democrat who had previously served as defense minister, shrewdly identified himself with the backbenchers' reform demands. In March, 1969, in the course of another debate on Bundestag reform, he earned great applause from the rebels by saying that deputies had not been sent to Bonn to waste their time on the many small errands they had to handle for lack of assistance. Several packages of important reforms were passed in the succeeding months aimed at both increasing the work capacity of the backbenchers and equalizing opportunity among deputies. Thus each individual deputy was empowered to hire a secretary or other assistant to help him in his duties, and an additional 100 professional assistants were to be engaged by the Bundestag.

Both the debate and question-hour time were kept open by the adoption of rules limiting plenary speeches to fifteen minutes (with some exceptions if the Fraktionen specifically requested them), and confining each deputy to no more than two written questions per week. In addition, the Bundestag executive and Council of Elders were combined and given the responsibility of planning the parliamentary schedule for several months in advance.

THE COMMITTEES

Most of the Bundestag's real legislative work is done in committees. Here, as in most other aspects of legislative procedure, the German practice lies halfway between the American and the British. In Britain, the traditionally dominant cabinet's suspicion that standing legislative committees would develop into dangerous competitors, both to party leaders on questions of policy and to individual ministers as originators of legislation, checked the trend toward the development of specialized standing committees. According to British practice, the parliamentarian is supposed to be a jack-of-all-trades and not an expert trying to compete with the civil servants, whom, as minister, he may one day have to direct on questions of broad policy. In the United States, under the separation of powers, no such inhibitions have prevented congressmen from attempting to become sufficiently expert to trip up the bureaucrats. And the committees have emerged as powerful centers, in which interest groups frequently reject or rewrite bills submitted by the executive agencies. Germany combines the British deference toward executive initiative with something of the American tendency toward expertise. Thus the parties try to fill their committee places with experts, many of them ex-officials and interest group representatives who can compete with the civil servants in their own technical and legal language.

Comparative statistical evidence bears out the importance of committee and party meetings in the German legislative process. Thus in 1954 the British House of Commons, where committee and party meetings do not play a very large role, did the bulk of its work in 170 plenary sessions totaling 1,408 hours. The same year the French National Assembly, which spent more

TABLE 6–2:   QUANTITATIVE MEASURES OF BUNDESTAG WORK, 1949–69

	BUNDESTAG SESSIONS OF				
Activity	*1949–53*	*1953–57*	*1957–61*	*1961–65*	*1965–69*
Plenary sessions	282	227	168	198	247
Party meetings	1,774	1,777	675	727	788
Committee meetings	5,474	4,389	2,493	2,986	2,400
Investigating committees	174	34	0	37	19
Bills					
Introduced	805	877	613	635	654
Passed	545	507	424	427	463
Oral questions	392	1,069	1,375	4,786	10,480
Pages of printed parliamentary record (in thousands)	14.3	13.6	9.8	10.1	13.9

time in committee meetings, met in plenary sessions 132 times for a total of 796 hours. The United States House of Representatives also did the bulk of its work in committee, with 123 plenary sessions that year totaling 533 hours. The Bundestag, however, went furthest in concentrating work in committee and party meetings. Its plenary meetings, usually held on only two days a week when the Bundestag was in session, numbered only about fifty-five. However for every plenary session that year, the Bundestag had no less than twenty committee and nine party meetings.[8]

LEGISLATIVE AND CONTROL FUNCTIONS

The Basic Law allows the executive to compete with both houses of the legislature in introducing bills, and in fact most legislation originates with the ministries. The German legislator who drops a bill into the hopper has a better chance of getting it passed than his British equivalent, who has to draw lots for such an oppor-

[8] "Wie die Parlamente tagen," *Das Parlament,* December 12, 1960, p. 11. See also Loewenberg, *Parliament in the German Political System,* p. 404.

tunity. But even so, the German deputy must compete with the civil service bill drafters, who have all the authority and resources of the ministries at their disposal. Thus, of the 463 laws passed in the four years of the Fifth Bundestag (1965 to 1969), 14 originated in the Bundesrat, 80 were introduced by Bundestag members, while 74, or more than 80 per cent, were submitted by the cabinet. In fact, executive dominance of the legislative func-

LEGISLATIVE PROCESS

Article 76

(1) Bills shall be introduced in the Bundestag by the Federal Government, by members of the Bundestag or by the Bundesrat.

(2) Federal Government bills shall first be submitted to the Bundesrat. The Bundesrat is entitled to state its position on these bills within three weeks. . . .

Article 77

(1) Federal laws shall be passed by the Bundestag. After their adoption, they shall, without delay, be transmitted to the Bundesrat. . . .

(4) [In regard to bills where the Bundesrat has only a suspensory veto] Vetoes adopted by the majority of the votes of the Bundesrat . . . may be rejected by a decision of the majority of the Bundestag. Should the Bundesrat have adopted the veto by a majority of at least two-thirds . . . the rejection of the Bundestag shall require a majority of two-thirds. . . .

Article 81

(1) . . . the Federal President may, on the request of the Federal Government with the consent of the Bundesrat, de-clare a state of legislative emergency with respect to a bill, if the Bundestag rejects the bill although the Federal Govern-ment has declared it to be urgent. . . .

(2) If the Bundestag, after the state of legislative emer-gency has been declared, again rejects the bill or passes it in a version declared by the Federal Government to be unaccept-able, the bill shall be deemed to have been passed insofar as the Bundesrat consents to it. . . .

tions is so taken for granted that German newspapers often report that the cabinet has sent a bill to the legislature with a headline like "Cabinet Decides to Pass Traffic Law," thus causing the unsophisticated reader to take passage by Parliament almost as a matter of course.

This in fact would be true in only a few areas. In most, especially where important interest groups have managed to rouse their followers both in and outside the majority party, cabinet bills often undergo rough treatment before passage. At the beginning of 1960, for example, Finance Minister Etzel announced that the budget could stand no more than a 4 per cent pay increase for government employees. The civil service organizations denounced this as altogether insufficient, and the opposition parties immediately announced they would press for a 9 per cent increase. In the Interior Committee, made up mostly of members with a civil service background, a majority, including the CDU chairman, adjusted the cabinet bill to the 9 per cent figure. But some weeks later in the plenary session, the same CDU committee chairman, having in the meantime consulted his party leaders, introduced a motion on behalf of the CDU calling for a 7 percent increase, and this was finally passed. During the same period the labor minister was having a difficult time with his bill to reform the medical insurance system; it elicited violent opposition from both the trade unions and the medical associations and split the CDU so badly that even the Chancellor's personal intervention failed to bring about an acceptable compromise.

The Bundestag has been hard put to develop proper techniques and styles for controlling the cabinet's policies. The concept of the proper role of the opposition as a critic of the government has proved especially difficult to establish. "There is unfortunately little need to substantiate the fact that in the Federal Republic there exists no special demand for being shown various sides of a question," writes the author of a leading German government text. "There is more preference for exclusive emphasis on one side which appears to indicate pursuit of a firm and clear policy." This prejudice against the political critic was probably aggravated when Schumacher, one of the first "generation" of leaders, consistently opposed almost every major policy backed by Adenauer. Also responsible, as the discussion of the Bundestag chamber illustrated, is an absence of that tradition which in Britain is symbolized by the fact that the Leader of Her Majesty's Loyal Opposition possesses an official title and a salary. The Social Democrats gradually grew tired of being regarded as unfruitful naysayers and, in line with their reorientation after 1959, changed their parliamentary tactics as well as their overall strategy. In an effort to emphasize their "positive" contribution, they often limited criticism to questions of implementation rather than policy, and they came to vote against government measures almost as infrequently as they had once voted for them.

AN EVALUATION OF THE BUNDESTAG

. . . A group of Members has sat in Parliament through three, four, and even five terms, gaining influence with seniority. With every passing year, the chances have improved that their style will become the habit of their successors. . . .

But the very ease with which the institution has responded to the political environment has also produced incongruities between public perceptions of Parliament and parliamentary performance. . . . There is little respect for the type of professional politician who conspicuously leads Parliament. The sense of public participation in politics through Parliament is not well developed, and parliamentary decisions do not carry any special legitimacy by virtue of being the decisions of a representative body. An administrative view of politics prevails which values expertise and efficiency, and disparages the influence of special interests and partisanship.

The Members of Parliament are themselves influenced by these culturally conditioned attitudes. They feel a far stronger incentive to develop their legislative specialties, for example, than to engage in political discourse with the general public. Parliamentary leaders and whips have concentrated on developing an informal body of procedural norms which facilitate their negotiations among themselves, but they have felt no obligation to formalize any aspect of the new arrangements to make them publicly visible. . . . They have permitted the decision-making process which takes place in the convenient privacy of the committee room or the party caucus to displace the public deliberations of the House. In short, the

Members regard their party leaders, or their interest-group patrons, as their chief constituents, and they treat the general public with the reserve and discretion more typical of the bureaucrat than the politician.

> GERHARD LOEWENBERG,
> *Parliament in the German*
> *Political System*
> (Ithaca, 1967).

The parties do present, of course, alternative views in debate, which Bundestag rules allow to occur during discussions of the budgets of relevant ministries and on the basis of interpellations introduced by thirty members. But since plenary sessions occur relatively seldom, there is not enough time for many large-scale debates in the course of a year. When they do take place, the speeches have usually been weighed extensively in party committees beforehand, which hardly makes for spontaneity. Enough parliamentarians have taken the trouble to develop forceful speaking styles so that the general level of debating has improved somewhat, and the galleries are better occupied than they used to be. With few exceptions, however, using debates to influence the government through aroused public opinion is not very effective. "The prestige of parliament is not great enough for its debates to have a great influence on the shaping of popular opinion, and consequently the government parties don't take them terribly seriously."[9]

The 1969 reform of the Parliamentary Rules sought to encourage more lively debates by reenforcing the requirement that speeches be delivered extemporaneously and not simply read from manuscript. Fraktion spokesmen could still speak as long as forty-five minutes, but the standard limit for a speech during debate was to be fifteen minutes. Another important rule, adopted against the wishes of the CDU/CSU, provided that committee hearings could be held in public if committee majorities so decided. This promised to enliven Bundestag proceedings consider-

[9] Thomas Ellwein, *Das Regierungssystem der Bundesrepublik Deutschland* (Cologne, 1963), p. 138.

ably, especially in view of the increasing trend toward television coverage. After 1964, plenary sessions were televised more often, with forty-six hours of live transmission in 1968. The special hearings on the Emergency Laws received even more extensive coverage—almost 100 hours of live transmission. Should this trend toward more public plenary debates and open hearings continue, it could engender effective antidotes to various "anti-parliamentary" proclivities in the population. It might even elicit more orders for the printed parliamentary records, of which only about 1,000 copies have been requested by nongovernmental parties. However, excerpts from parliamentary debates have been circulated to a much larger audience through the periodical *Das Parlament,* which is often used in civics classes.

The special investigating committee is a control instrument seen frequently in the United States but very rarely in the Federal Republic. Its potential for staging pseudo-trials in which personal reputations are bombarded by sensational charges revives even more unpleasant memories for Germans than for Americans. A number of these committees were set up to investigate several postwar scandals, but their sensational work reminded many observers of ill-fated precedents during the Weimar Republic. Disliked everywhere, the demagogue is still the nemesis of German politics.

The Germans are more enthusiastic about a peculiarly British parliamentary institution, the question hour. It was introduced experimentally in the 1950's, occurring only once a month. A 1960 rule change provided for question hours at the beginning of each plenary meeting, allowed written questions to be submitted as late as the day before, and permitted supplementary questions. Since this development occurred at a time when the Bundestag was trying to reassert some prerogatives that had wilted under Adenauer, the question hour quickly took on dramatic as well as informative functions. Ministers and state secretaries, the top-level civil servants who unlike their counterparts in Britain may answer queries for the ministers, were frequently upbraided if their responses were deemed evasive or condescending. As it has developed in the Bundestag, however, the question hour has lost its British character of a series of "happenings" characterized by brevity. Although questions are initiated by individual deputies, the whole party tends to get involved on issues that are highly political. Thus some question hours have dealt with only one topic, with dozens of deputies volunteering supplementaries on a series of closely related subjects. In one question hour in May, 1965, for instance, State Secretary von Hase of the Press Office was interrogated about spending DM 200,000 of government funds to place unsigned pro-Erhard advertisements in 500 daily newspapers four months before elections. In the course of a half-hour exchange on the matter, von Hase received no less than thirty-eight questions from twelve deputies of all three parties.

THE BUNDESRAT

The second chamber in the German parliament is unique: it is, in effect, a continuous congress of state (Land) ministers who vote in accordance with the instructions of their governments. This throwback to an organizational form similar to that of the princes' chambers of Imperial Germany grew out of efforts to build up the Laender to check the German tendency toward

---

THE BUNDESRAT

Article 50

   The Laender shall participate through the Bundesrat in the legislation and the administration of the Federation.

Article 51

   (1) The Bundesrat shall consist of members of the Governments of the Laender which shall appoint and recall them. Other members of such Governments may act as substitutes.

   (2) Each Land shall have at least three votes; Laender with more than two million inhabitants shall have four, Laender with more than six million inhabitants shall have five votes.

   (3) Each Land may delegate as many members as it has votes. The votes of each Land may be cast only as a block vote and only by members present or their substitutes.

---

centralization of power in the national government. As presently constituted, the Bundesrat consists of forty-one members of Land cabinets—five each from the four Laender with populations of more than 6 million (Northrhine-Westphalia, Bavaria, Lower Saxony, Baden-Wuerttemberg), four each from the three Laender with between 2 and 6 million inhabitants (Rhineland-Palatinate, Schleswig-Holstein, Hessen), and three each from the three small Laender with less than 2 million (the Saar, Hamburg, Bremen). In line with the legalist, single-will doctrine that it is unreasonable for a state to have two contradictory wills, the Land votes must be cast as a unit. When the Land government is based on a coalition, as most are, the policy of the strongest Land party usually prevails.

The Basic Law assigns the Bundesrat much greater legislative power than its Weimar predecessor. Its approval is required for all constitutional amendments and for all federal legislation affecting the administrative, taxation, and territorial interests of the Laender—rather a broad category. On all other kinds of legislation it can enter a suspensive veto, which, however, can be overridden by an equivalent majority of the Bundestag. In addition to this impressive (by continental European standards) legislative authority, the Bundesrat approves federal government ordinances, shares in the election of judges to the Constitutional Court, and possesses considerable reserve powers to deal with any serious conflict either between the executive and the Bundestag or between the federal and Land governments.

The very nature of its makeup insures that the overwhelming share of Bundesrat work is done in committees. Almost all Bundesrat members are Land ministers for whom the Bundesrat role is a secondary one, which they attend to during brief visits to Bonn once or twice a month. By the time the delegates arrive, proposals have already been worked out in committees, and in 99 per cent of the cases where only one committee report is presented, the proposal is adopted by the plenary session.[10] Obviously, the question of *who* writes the committee reports is crucial here. The fact is that although Bundesrat members oc-

---

[10] Karlheinz Neunreither, "Politics and Bureaucracy in the West German Bundesrat," *APSR*, LIII (September, 1959), 716.

casionally participate in committee sessions, the bulk of committee work is done by their alternates, who are permanent Land civil servants, not politicians. Since the upper chamber has at most three weeks to consider legislation submitted by the government (and frequently much less), the Land ministers have very little opportunity to form judgments other than those based on the recommendations of their civil service advisers. Indeed, a German law professor has written that "In the committees . . . there is in process of growth a tight world of its own . . . in which the permanent civil service and changing delegates from the Land ministries are in their own metier, the world of a bureaucracy with its own law."[11]

However, seen within the traditional German context, the Bundesrat provides an ideal meeting place where federal and Land officials can work out differences on federal legislation—as well as federal ordinances based on legislation—affecting their respective spheres of responsibility. Though it seems complex, their arrangement provides for a rational division of labor, while also introducing checks to unlimited power; the Bundesrat may be viewed as "providing a stage for the antagonism between the Land and the Federal bureaucracies, while at the same time forcing them to some kind of advantageous cooperation."[12]

In effect, the Bundesrat has sought to reinforce it delicate position by utilizing only half of its constitutional powers and exercising its legislative prerogatives largely under camouflage. It has sought to avoid being caught between the powerful party machines by, for instance, placing the election of its presiding officer "above politics," rotating this honor according to a fixed scheme. On the whole, it adopted the coloration of the nonpartisan bureaucrats who are officially only its assistants. "A kind of exaltation of the administrative functions of the Bundesrat has taken place, while its political functions are more or less disparaged."[13] In line with bureaucratic aversion to public controversy, it has shunned frank conflict with the Bundestag—only one or two, usually minor, laws fail each year because of its

---

[11] Werner Weber, *Spannungen und Kraefte im westdeutschen Verfassungssystem* (Stuttgart, 1951), p. 91.

[12] Neunreither, "Politics and Bureaucracy," p. 726.

[13] *Ibid.*, p. 728.

negative vote—and instead attempted to get its way in the secret councils of the interchamber Conference Committee. The Bundesrat tends to call the Conference Committee into effect whenever it does not want to approve a law, but even there the Land ministers argue less on the merits of the issue than on "grounds of administrative infeasibility."[14] Thus the Bundesrat "obscures its political intentions by cloaking them in recommendations of a technical character so that they will be more readily endorsed by the relatively inexpert lower house. Staff members of Bundesrat Committees claim that this procedure is highly successful."[15] The Land representatives do try to protect the interests of the Land government from the increasing enroachment of the federal government; they do not want to be relegated exclusively to the position of carrying out federal laws. At times the Laender even engage in some adroit horse trading which angers the national party leaders. But this kind of Bundesrat action makes the headlines only occasionally. On the whole, its policy of "obscuring political issues in administrative forms"[16] has, in effect, turned it into a sort of federal-Land administrative council which is remote from the public (polls have shown that only one out of nine Germans knows what the Bundesrat is) and insulated from the major political currents of the day.

PROVISIONS FOR DEADLOCKS

Adenauer's domination of his party and his cabinet, together with the CDU's strong numerical position, have shielded the Federal Republic from the kinds of crises the Weimar Republic suffered as a result of deadlocks among differing branches of the government and other breakdowns in the decision-making machinery. The Constitutional Court, whose role is discussed in Chapter 8, has played an important part in arbitrating conflicts over constitutional powers between governmental organs. However, with a change in the distribution of political forces, it is quite possible that situations will develop which cannot be resolved by the normal techniques. The Basic Law includes special provisions for a number of such situations.

One of these (ART. 63) covers the situation that arises when

---

[14] *Ibid.*, p. 722.   [15] *Ibid.*, p. 724.   [16] *Ibid.*, p. 728.

the President's nominee for the chancellorship does not succeed in getting the requisite support of an absolute Bundestag majority. If another candidate can get the support of an absolute majority, he is elected. If, however, the Bundestag remains deadlocked for two weeks, another ballot is called for, and the President may either appoint the candidate with the largest number of votes (even if short of a majority) or dissolve the Bundestag. The dissolution power may also be used in one other related situation (ART. 68). If a Chancellor loses his political support in the Bundestag and is defeated on his own motion of confidence, he may within twenty-one days ask the President to dissolve the Bundestag and call new elections. It is conceivable that Chancellor Brandt may need to invoke this provision if his parliamentary majority becomes too precarious.

The Basic Law also provides a variety of techniques for overriding decisions of particular organs or checking the abuse of power. Thus the President may be impeached by one-fourth of the members of either the Bundestag or Bundesrat "for willful violation of the Basic Law or any other Federal Law" (ART. 61). He may then be tried and, if found guilty, removed by the Constitutional Court. A Constitutional Court decision can of course also be overridden by amending the constitution, which, however, requires an absolute two-thirds majority in both houses of the legislature (ART. 79). In conflicts between the federal government and the Laender over the way the Laender administer federal legislation or allegedly violate federal law, it is the Bundesrat which has the decisive voice (ARTS. 37, 84). With its consent the federal government may send out commissioners to give direct instructions to the Laender bureaucracy.

DISSOLVING THE BUNDESTAG
Article 68

If a motion of the Federal Chancellor for a vote of confidence is not assented to by the majority of the members of the Bundestag, the Federal President may, upon the proposal of the Federal Chancellor, dissolve the Bundestag within twenty-one days. The right to dissolve lapses as soon as the Bundestag by the majority of its members elects another Federal Chancellor.

BIBLIOGRAPHY

LEGISLATURE

Eschenburg, Theodor, *Der Sold des Politikers* (Stuttgart, 1959).

Glum, Friedrich, *Das parlamentarische Regierungssystem in Deutschland, England, und Frankreich* (Munich, 1950).

Grieves, Forest, "Inter-Party Competition in the Federal Representatives of Government 1945–65: A Methodological Inquiry," *Western Political Quarterly*, XX, 4 (December, 1967), 910–18.

Johnson, W., "Questions in the Bundestag," *Parliamentary Affairs*, XVI (1962), 22–34.

Keim, Walther, ed., *Der deutsche Bundestag: Eine Bestandaufnahme, 1949–69* (Bonn, 1969).

Kirchheimer, Otto, "The Composition of the German Bundestag," *WPQ*, III (1950), 590–601.

————, "The Waning of Opposition in Parliamentary Regimes," *Social Research*, XXIV (1957), 127–56.

Kralewski, Wolfgang, et al., *Oppositionelles Verhalten im ersten deutschen Bundestag, 1949–1953* (Cologne, 1963).

Laufer, Heinz, *Der parlamentarische Staatssekretaer* (Munich, 1969).

Loewenberg, Gerhard, *Parliament in the German Political System* (Ithaca, 1967).

Neunreither, Karlheinz, "Politics and Bureaucracy in the West German Bundesrat," *APSR*, LIII (September, 1959), 713–31.

————, *Der Bundesrat* (Heidelberg, 1959).

Pikart, E., "Probleme der deutschen Parlaments Praxis," *Zeitschrift fuer Politik*, IX (1962), 201–11.

Prittie, Terence, "The German Federal Parliament," *Parliamentary Affairs*, X (Spring, 1955), 235–39.

Pinney, Edward L., *Federalism, Bureaucracy and Party Politics in Western Germany: The Role of the Bundesrat* (Chapel Hill, 1963).

Ritter, Gerhard A., *Deutscher und britischer Parlamentarismus* (Tuebingen, 1962).

Stammer, Otto, et al., *Verbaende und Gesetzgebung: Die Einflussnahme der Verbaende auf die Gestaltung des Personalvertretungsgesetzes* (Cologne, 1965).

Steffani, W., "Funktion und Kompetenz parlamentarischer Untersuchungsausschuesse," PVS, I (1960), 153–76.

EXECUTIVE

Eschenburg, Theodor, *Staat und Gesellschaft in Deutschland* (Stuttgart, 1956).

Heidenheimer, Arnold J., *Adenauer and the CDU: The Rise of the Leader and the Integration of the Party* (The Hague, 1960).

Knight, Maxwell E., *The German Executive, 1890–1933* (Stanford, 1952).

Loewenstein, Karl, *Political Power and the Governmental Process* (Chicago, 1956).

Meyn, Hermann, "Zur Transparenz der politischen Ordnung der Bundesrepublik," *Aus Politik und Zeitgeschichte* (October 4, 1968).

Ridley, E. F., "Chancellor Government as a Political System and the German Constitution," *Parliamentary Affairs*, XIX, 4 (Autumn, 1966), 446–61.

Schmidt, Hannelore, "Die deutsche Exekutive 1949–1960," *European Journal of Sociology*, III–IV (1962–63), 166–76.

Speier, Hans, and W. P. Davison, eds., *West German Leadership and Foreign Policy* (Evanston, 1957).

7

Federalism and Finances

FEDERALISM, GERMAN STYLE

Many characteristics of the relationship between the West German Laender and federal government will seem unusual to a reader who thinks of federalism in terms of the American model. That the Laender pass much of their legislation in accordance with federal "framework laws," that the Land bureaucracy carries out both Land and federal administration, and that the Land ministers participate directly in the shaping of federal decisions through the Bundesrat—all these are indices of the very significant differences between the American and German federal structures. In fact, it has frequently been asked whether the German arrangement can be really classified as "federal" at all. A leading British student of federalism, Professor K. C. Wheare, is among those who have answered the question in the negative. Following American practice, Wheare argues that the true principle of federalism is based on a division of power in which "the general and regional governments are, each within a sphere, coordinate and independent."[1] The peculiar aspects of German federal-Land relationships discussed earlier (see pp. 72–74, 182–85) lead him to conclude that the German system is not really federal, but a special example of a decentralized unitary state.

Critics have contended that Wheare's federal model contains too much of an ethnocentric bias in favor of the United States and other Anglo-Saxon countries. One critic argues: "The rigid requirement of the mutual independence of the executive and legislative institutions of both levels is at best a product of historical

[1] K. C. Wheare, *Federal Government,* 3d ed. (London, 1953), p. 11.

circumstances, and not an indispensable part of a general definition of federalism." The German arrangement, according to this
point of view, is characterized by coexistence and voluntary cooperation leading to a functional separation under which the federal government is assigned the bulk of legislative power while
the states exercise most administrative powers. Hence the West
German arrangement emerges as an example of "executive-
legislative federalism."[2] Whatever the terms employed, the discussion of the merits of the American and German types of federalism continues unabated. Von Merkatz, a German politician
who served as federal minister for Bundesrat affairs—an office
which from the American point of view has little justification—
reaffirmed his faith in the native model. "I know on the basis of
my own observations in the United States, that the system there
is constantly criticized for its lack of any kind of systematic base.

LAND AND LOCAL GOVERNMENT

Article 28

(1) The constitutional order in the Laender must conform
to the principles of the republican, democratic and social
government based on the rule of law within the meaning of
the Basic Law. In the Laender, counties and communities, the
people must have a representative assembly resulting from
universal, free, equal and secret elections. . . .

Article 30

The exercise of the powers of the state and the performance
of state functions shall be the concern of the Laender, insofar
as this Basic Law does not otherwise prescribe or permit.

Article 31

Federal law shall supersede Land law.

Article 70

(1) The Laender shall have the power to legislate insofar
as this Basic Law does not confer legislative powers on the
Federation.

[2] Peter H. Merkl, "Executive-Legislative Federalism in West Germany,"
APSR, LIII (1959), 732–41.

Our principle of the close interdependence of the federal government and the Laender has developed historically and has throughout proved its worth."[3]

The German arrangement originated in the compromise through which the German Empire emerged under Prussian leadership. "It was painful enough for the non-Prussian states to see the symbols of political power move to Berlin; but they were considerably more apprehensive at the thought of Prussian administrators setting up offices of the national administration in their cities and towns. So they attempted to preserve their integrity by restricting the new national government as much as possible to the new political center, Berlin, and insisting that policy emanating from this center should be administered wherever possible by local officials."[4] Whether the individual states could prevent themselves from becoming overshadowed under this arrangement depended mainly on their ability to guard their tax revenues and to maintain a strong political position.

Under the Empire the states retained control over most direct taxes, but during the Weimar period the Reich took important state taxes over for its own use, and the Laender were dependent on Reich funds in times of crisis to keep their administrations going. Politically, the problem of equilibrium was crucially affected by Prussian predominance in power and population. Although the Prussian kings who inherited the Imperial mantle tended to dominate the national scene, at least they respected the formal rights of the lesser kings and princes. After 1918 the kings and princes were removed, but Prussia still had more population than all the rest of Germany put together. This fact, together with the strong centralist bias of the Weimar Constitution, tended to weaken the functioning of federal institutions during the interwar period. When Hitler abolished the Laender in 1934, their political significance had already all but disappeared.

The determination to break up Prussia was one of the few important points the Allies could agree upon in 1945. But in the

[3] Ossip K. Flechtheim, ed., *Bund und Laender* (Berlin, 1959), p. 51.
[4] Karlheinz Neunreither, "Federalism and the West German Bureaucracy," *Political Studies,* VII (1959), 235.

formation of new Laender, each of the occupying powers followed its own inclinations. In the south the Americans re-created Bavaria and combined smaller territories to form the Laender of Hessen and Baden-Wuerttemberg, both of which had some historical traditions. On the left bank of the Rhine, the French combined the former Bavarian province of Palatinate with parts of Hessen and Rhenish Prussia to form Rhineland-Palatinate. The British combined other formerly Prussian areas to create the large and heavily industrialized state of Northrhine-Westphalia, while farther to the north they used other ex-Prussian areas to create the Laender of Lower Saxony and Schleswig-Holstein. Together with the two city-states of Hamburg and Bremen and (since 1956) the Saar, these constitute the Laender of the Federal Republic. The attachment of the people to their Laender varies considerably, diminishing as one moves from south to north. Polls have shown that only one out of four West Germans would be upset if the Laender were abolished. In 1954–55, the people of Lower Saxony favored dissolution by four to one, those of Northrhine-Westphalia two to one, and those in Bavaria split evenly. If there are any genuine states' rights advocates in Germany, they tend to be the Bavarians.

FEDERAL AND LAND FUNCTIONS

After the creation of the Federal Republic, the German administrative system tended to reshape itself in conformance with earlier patterns. The strong Laender bureaucracies created by the Allies did not deter this trend; even under the Empire effective, centralized control had been achieved without greatly expanding the size of the national administrative apparatus. Until the Nazi period, most administrative functions had remained with the Laender, and indeed a good part of the Land administration's tasks consisted of executing Reich laws. Both the national government and the Laender preferred a system under which the Reich exercised the bulk of legislative power, while the Laender retained control over administration. This allowed maximum uniformity in basic policy with a considerable amount of latitude in local application. Part of the national administration consisted of ministries for the few areas in which the Reich had exclusive jurisdiction, but mainly it was made up of authorities who acted as top level planning and supervisory agencies in fields where actual administration was carried out by the Laender. Of course, to achieve a high degree of uniformity the national government set up norms for the Land administrations, concerning both internal structure and organization.

Administration in the Federal Republic works in much the same way. The staffs of most federal ministries are relatively small; only the Foreign Ministry, part of the Finance Ministry, the post office, and the federal railroads possess their own administrative substructure. For the rest, administration of federal programs is carried out by the Laender either as a matter of traditional prerogative, or as a service rendered at the special request of the federal government. There are thus four different methods of administration: (1) execution of federal laws by federal administration, for example, the railroads and the post office; (2) execution of Land laws by Land administrations, for example, the police and education authorities; (3) execution of federal laws by Land administrations as a matter of right, for example, labor and social welfare offices; (4) execution of federal laws by Land administrations at the request of the federal government, for example, the agencies maintaining the Autobahnen and waterways. The overall effect of this arrangement is that although an overwhelming share of public expenditure is spent on programs based directly or indirectly on federal legislation, the majority of civil servants work for the Land administrations. Thus, if one excludes the railroads and the post office, only about 10 per cent of public officials work for the federal government, about a third are in the employ of local government, and well over one-half belong to the Land administrations.

How do the Germans avoid problems like those encountered by the United States in such areas as Southern state enforcement of federal voting guarantees or civil rights laws? The fact is that the German federal administration has extensive control over Land administration of federal laws. Where the Laender carry out federal laws, the federal government may issue binding administrative regulations, may demand the rectification of inadequacies, and may send agents to investigate cases. As a last resort, it may, with the approval of the Bundesrat, force the

Laender to comply; the Basic Law provides that the federal government or its commissioner shall have the right to give orders to all Laender and their authorities.

This arrangement produces a much more homogeneous administrative system than someone acquainted with the American type of federalism might expect. The tendency toward uniformity leads the Laender officials to accept federal administrative regulations as a framework even when there is no obligation, that is, in relation to the administration of their own Land laws. Such regulations must have the approval of the Bundesrat, which, however, seldom opposes them. On the contrary, all the Land governments believe it in their own interests to accept such federal regulations, so as to achieve administrative homogeneity and avoid haphazard differences between the Laender. After considering this development, some Germans have come to the conclusion that administrative rationalization has "led the Laender to derive their powers from the Federal Government and its laws, just as much as the counties and the cities derive theirs from the Land governments and their laws. They are as much subject to federal supervision as the cities and the counties are to Land supervision."[5]

TAX SYSTEMS AND PUBLIC FINANCE

Anyone surprised to find that the Basic Law includes a discussion of the beer tax should consider that in Germany the national government's share of taxes increased steadily at the expense of the Laender and communities—from 40.3 per cent in 1913, to 67.6 per cent in 1928, to 78.5 per cent in 1937—reaching a climax in the Nazi wartime period, when no less than 95 per cent of taxes was collected by the national government. The authors of the Basic Law (and the Allies) were determined to halt this trend; they took great pains to specifically allocate tax sources, and also sought to prevent overlapping revenue claims and to spell out responsibility for tax administration. The result is a

[5] Heinz Kreutzer, "Bund und Laender in der Bundesrepublik Deutschland," in O. K. Flechtheim, ed., *Bund und Laender* (Berlin, 1959), p. 20.

"finance constitution," which is so well integrated that a German expert referred to this section of the Basic Law "as the specifically Prussian contribution to a constitutional liberal-democratic state, which otherwise bears more the hallmarks of Rhenish-Bavarian influences. It is surely no accident that the intellectual father of the finance constitution is a former Prussian finance minister."[6]

FEDERATION AND LAENDER

Article 35

All Federal and Land authorities shall render each other mutual legal and official assistance.

Article 83

The Laender shall execute the Federal laws as matters of their own concern insofar as this Basic Law does not otherwise provide or permit.

Article 84

(1) If the Laender execute the Federal laws as their own concern they shall regulate the establishment of the authorities and the administrative procedure insofar as Federal laws consented to by the Bundesrat do not otherwise determine.

(2) The Federal Government may, with the approval of the Bundesrat, issue general administrative rules.

(3) The Federal Government shall exercise supervision to ensure that the Laender execute the Federal Laws in accordance with applicable law. For this purpose the Federal Government may send commissioners to the highest Land authorities and, with their consent or, if this consent is refused, with the consent of the Bundesrat, also to the subordinate authorities.

Article 87

(1) The foreign service, the Federal finance administration, the Federal railways, the Federal postal services, the administration of Federal waterways and shipping . . . the

---

[6] Karl M. Hettlage, "Die Finanzverfassung im Rahmen der Staatsverfassung," *Veroeffentlichungen der Vereinigung der deutschen Staatsrechtlehrer*, XIV (1956), 13.

administration of the Federal defense forces shall be conducted by a direct Federal administration with its own administrative substructure.

Article 106

(3) Receipts from income tax and corporation tax shall accrue . . . to the Federation and the Laender in a ratio of 35 per cent to 65 per cent.

(4) . . . The requirements of the Federation and the Laender in respect of budget coverage shall be coordinated in such a way that a fair equalization is achieved, any overburdening of taxpayers precluded, and uniformity of living standards in the Federal territory ensured.

Most Germans were appalled at the suggestion that they should follow the American practice of allowing the various governmental levels to administer concurrent tax powers independently. Hence, as hitherto, the federal and Land finance administrations are closely integrated for collecting income and corporation taxes. The chief Land finance officials who administer collection of these taxes are chosen jointly by the federal and Land Finance ministries, while their salaries and the costs of maintaining the collection machinery are also shared. As the state secretary of the Finance Ministry has put it:

> Today we have one income tax, with two partial claimants, with a split administration active as a Land administration of the Land part, and as a Federal agent for the federal part of the tax. This is curious enough. But if we had adopted the other method, we would have had two distinct income taxes collected by two claimants, as in the United States where 35 of the 48 states collect their own income taxes parallel to the federal one. As to the retarded and economically dubious nature of such a double and unequal taxation of income I need not comment here. . . .[7]

Although separate tax collection was avoided, the states' autonomy in financial and administrative matters, which the Basic Law encouraged, did create noticeable interstate differentials.

[7] *Ibid.*, p. 24.

The differences in per capita state tax receipts did not reach American ratios of three to one or four to one, but they were significant. As Table 7–1 indicates, wealth and income levels differ considerably, and a poor Land like the Saar could expect only about three-fifths the revenue from the same tax rate applied in a rich Land like Baden-Wuerttemberg. According to the "American" model of federalism, one might have expected the poorer Laender to pay lower teachers' salaries and to maintain schools of a lower quality than those of the richer. In 1969, American state expenditures on education did indeed vary between $400 and $1,000 per student, with noticeable differences in the quality of school and university education. The Germans consider differentials of this range intolerable. As the finance minister said in the course of a 1968 debate:

> No student cares whether he attends a university in North-rhine-Westphalia, or in Lower Saxony, or in Bavaria. Decisive for him and for all of us is that there are enough universities, that they are as nearly equal in quality and capacity as possible, and that they are distributed in a proper way throughout the Federal Republic.[8]

And indeed, in contrast to the difference in the prestige attached to doctorates from, say, the University of Idaho and the University of Michigan, in Germany a degree from the University of Kiel (which happens to be in a poor Land) is fully as good and respected as one from the University of Heidelberg (located in a rich Land).

The near-equality of per capita expenditures of Laender is maintained through various "equalization" techniques, which operate in a much more fundamental and sustained manner in Germany than in the American federal system. Through the *vertical equalization* program, a portion of the jointly collected revenues are earmarked specifically to help bring the tax income of the poorer states up toward the average. The Finance Reform of 1969 provides that up to 25 per cent of the Land portion of the turnover tax be routed directly from the federal treasury to

[8] Finance Minister Strauss in Bundestag session of July 17, 1968.

these poorer Laender. In 1970, this amounted to some DM 2 billion. A sizable proportion of this money went to sustain West Berlin with its above-average expenditures and below-average receipts.

TABLE 7–1:   WEALTH AND TAX INCOME OF THE LAENDER

Land	SHARE OF FEDERAL REPUBLIC'S		Per Capita Income Tax Receipts (1970 Estimate, in DM)	Tax Income as Per Cent of Laender Average After Horizontal Redistribution (1970 Estimate)
	(a) Total Population (1967)	(b) Taxable Personal Wealth (1967)		
Saar	1.1	0.7	388	95.3
Rhineland-Palatinate	5.0	3.9	433	92.0
Lower Saxony	9.8	7.5	459	92.1
Schleswig-Holstein	3.5	2.7	469	93.0
Bavaria	18.5	18.2	558	92.5
Northrhine-Westphalia	24.5	30.2	633	101.3
Hessen	9.0	8.9	649	103.1
Baden-Wuerttemberg	16.7	16.2	668	102.9
Bremen	1.5	1.5	813	126.8
Hamburg	4.6	6.5	1141	144.1

Upon the insistence of the financially weaker Laender, the Finance Reform of 1969 also continued the *horizontal equalization* program, through which in previous years the richer Laender had paid billions of marks directly to the poorer ones. This program is designed to bring the poor states up to a level where their per capita tax receipts are *at least 92 per cent of the all-Laender average*. As a spokesman for affluent Hamburg said in the Bundestag debate:

The sacrifice brought by the financially stronger Laender will amount to between DM 580 and DM 750 million. May I spell out what this means for my own Land? For Hamburg that will mean paying DM 218 million annually, or 5 per cent of our total budget. . . . I believe that these figures clearly refute the continuing talk . . . that what is dominant around here is the status quo thinking of the rich. . . .[9]

The Finance Reform of 1969 (which State Secretary Hettlage, quoted above, helped prepare) also reflected criticism that certain crucial functions could not be left as the exclusive domain of the Laender. In particular, three problems—the expansion of higher education facilities, regional economic development, and the improvement of the agricultural infrastructure—were deemed areas in which the Laender should yield their claim of exclusive jurisdiction. Instead they recognized *Joint Tasks* (*Gemeinschaftsaufgaben*), in which the federal government would help plan as well as finance. As the finance minister put it:

The universities are responsibilities of the Laender. But the creation of new universities cannot be allowed to remain dependent solely upon the capabilities and circumstances of the various Laender. Rather, planning has to take place with respect to the needs of the entire Federal Republic . . . Implementation of the Joint Tasks shall be based upon plans which are jointly developed by the *Bund* and the Laender. . . . Fifty per cent of the finances will be supplied by the Bund and fifty per cent by the Laender.[10]

The Finance Reform of 1969 further pared away the financial power of the Laender by strengthening the position of the cities. As in the United States, the cities had become dependent on extracting state funds to maintain many of their services. The Finance Reform paved the way for legislation allowing communities to claim as a matter of right specified portions of certain business and income taxes collected by the Laender. Thus, a

[9] Senator Heinsen in Bundestag session of March 17, 1969.
[10] Finance Minister Strauss in Bundestag session of July 17, 1968.

uniformly administered income tax would be shared by federal, Land, and community governments. German citizens would continue to fill out only a single form, in contrast to the predicament of many Americans who have to pay three or more different kinds of income taxes and fill out as many different forms each spring.

Since 1969, several levels of government have shared the two taxes which together bring about two-thirds of the total tax income. The most important of these, the corporate and individual income tax, is divided between the local (14 per cent), the state (43 per cent), and the federal (43 per cent) governments. The other, the turnover tax, is divided 70–30 between the federal government and the Laender. Thus, in 1970 the anticipated tax sources of the three levels of government were as follows:

TAX YIELD (IN BILLIONS OF DM)

Type of Tax	Federal Government Share	Laender Share	Local Government Share
Income tax share	26.6	26.6	6.8
Turnover tax share	24.6	10.5	—
Other taxes	28.7	11.9	11.8
TOTAL	79.9	49.0	18.6

LAND POLITICS

For the most part the structure of the Land governments closely resembles that of the federal government. They are based on the parliamentary system and (except for Bavaria) have unicameral legislatures (*Landtage*). Elections to the Landtage vary according to the laws in a particular Land, but all are based on the principle of proportional representation. The executive is composed of a minister-president and a cabinet, but the powers of the former are considerably more limited than those of the Chancellor in Bonn. Land cabinets usually are fairly small, and the ministers are appointed by the minister-president on the advice of parties participating in the government. Because the prime function of Land governments is administration rather than policy-making, the parties represented in the government tend to nominate leaders with administrative experience for the cabinet positions. The Land ministers' salaries are pegged at a specific fraction, 70 per cent, of the salaries of federal ministers. Since these in turn are determined by prevailing civil service scales, the salaries of civil servants and political decision makers on both federal and Land levels are closely linked.

Many Land ministers wield considerable power, especially those concerned with areas where the federal government plays a small role. For example, Land ministers of the interior set down police policies, and Land ministers of education and culture handle such perennially "hot" issues as the religious integration of public schools. Since the Catholic church presses for the maintenance of separate public schools for Catholics and Protestants, school controversies frequently break out, and Land ministers of education can quickly become very well known. However, most of the work of other ministers tends to revolve around the more prosaic problems of administering policies that are basically determined in Bonn.

In many Laender, changing coalition arrangements have caused frequent government changes. During his period of dominance Adenauer sought to force all CDU Land parties to leave coalitions with the SPD, and in the mid-1950's most Land cabinets were either composed on the "Bonn pattern" or SPD-dominated.[11] In the 1960's something of a reverse trend set in, and all kinds of party coalitions now occur on the Land level. The FDP, for instance, was allied in 1965 in three Laender with the Social Democrats and in four with Christian Democrats. There were also several Land cabinets made up of SPD and CDU ministers. The recruitment pattern for Land ministers might surprise Americans—they are often brought in from another Land because of their expertise. Their lack of grass-roots political support is not a serious handicap since the party provides all the support they need, while intimate knowledge of the structure of a

[11] Arnold J. Heidenheimer, "Federalism and the Party System: The Case of West Germany," *APSR,* LII (1958), 809–28.

particular Land is less important than in the United States because so many aspects of administration are uniform throughout the country.

Although Land parliaments have the same four-year term as the Bundestag, Land election dates do not coincide with federal elections but occur one or two at a time on different dates. This contributes to lower voting turnouts and different voting patterns than in the federal elections. Thus, until the mid-1960's, the Social Democrats consistently did better in Landtag campaigns, mainly because their voters were more disciplined than the marginal CDU voters who were brought out by Adenauer's appeal but often did not bother to vote in Land elections. But gradually, the Landtag elections have mirrored the same trend toward a two-party system that has emerged on the federal level. In the early 1950's, the combined CDU and SPD share of the Northrhine-Westphalia Landtag vote amounted to 69.2 per cent; it had risen to 89.7 per cent in the mid-1960's. In Bremen and Schleswig-Holstein, predominantly Protestant Laender where the CDU was originally weak, the change in the corresponding figures is even more significant—from 48.1 per cent to 83.5 per cent, and from 47.3 per cent to 84.2 per cent respectively. Although they held out longer on the Land than on the federal level, small and especially regionally based parties have gradually disappeared even from the Landtag. Except for several North German Laender, the FDP has also lost much of the strength it showed in the early Landtag elections.

Bavaria constitutes the only significant regional phenomenon in German politics, and even that isn't as distinctive as it used to be. Quite a few of the numerous smaller parties which twenty years ago ran candidates only in Bavaria have disappeared. However, the Christian Social Union, the Bavarian affiliate of the CDU, remains a token of Bavarian individuality. The CSU is the only Land branch of any of the three major parties bearing a different name from the federal party. It also boasts that its party organization is independent of the federal CDU and maintains a Bundestag Fraktion which is not integrally a part of the CDU. For many years this Bavarian independence was relatively nominal, but after Franz Josef Strauss became leader of the CSU he emphasized its distinctiveness in order to establish a personal power base. Thus CDU Chancellors have been forced to bargain for CSU support for cabinets just as they have with other coalition partners. The internal politics of the CSU is notable particularly for its bitter factionalism, which provides plenty of color that is reported widely in the newspapers of other areas with less dramatic politics.

LOCAL GOVERNMENT

Though many German cities can look back to periods of medieval splendor when they ranked among the leading political powers in Germany, today—except for the city-states of Hamburg, Bremen, and West Berlin—their status depends on the Laender. Because of the diversity of regional development, many different kinds of governmental forms have been adopted on the municipal level. The Rhineland cities, for instance, under Napoleonic influence developed a very centralized system which might best be called the *dominant mayor* pattern. The mayors elected by the city councils for terms of twelve years were unchallenged heads of the city administration, as well as presiding officers of the city councils. Chancellor Adenauer held this type of position as Buergermeister of Cologne from 1917 to 1933. In the Prussian areas of North Germany, by contrast, the municipal government was based on the *Magistrat* type, with executive power in the hands of a plural board of magistrates elected by the council which also served as the upper house of a bicameral municipal legislature. In South Germany yet another system (the *council* type) prevailed under which the city council, made up of the elected members and the chief city administrators, was a unified organ responsible for both legislation and administration. All three of these systems included the figure of the Buergermeister, but he had much less power under the latter two systems. In their own way, the Nazis wrought uniformity through the German Municipal Government Act of 1935 which abolished all elections on the local level. Mayors and city councillors were appointed after consultation between local and national Nazi leaders and the Reich Ministry of the Interior, and became agents of the Nazi party and the national government.

The postwar period was characterized by a tendency to return to the pre-Nazi system, modified however by an attempt on the part of the occupying powers to break up undue concentrations of communal power. The British, especially, sought to reduce or abolish the power of the mayor and magistrates by splitting the political and administrative functions of the chief local officials and vesting all executive and legislative power exclusively in the council (on the British model). They abolished the magistrate boards, reduced the mayor to the position of chairman of the city council, and centered administrative powers in a nonpolitical city manager (*Gemeindedirektor*) who was made responsible to the elected city council. This *council-manager* system has prevailed in Northrhine-Westphalia and Lower Saxony. Schleswig-Holstein, on the other hand, returned to a Magistrat system, but a weakened one in which the collegial executive is no longer also a second legislative chamber, while its members are subject to recall by the city council. Most cities in Hessen operate with the same system. The French also tried to get the Germans in their zone to abandon the dominant mayor form (even though it had been inspired by Napoleon), but they were less successful, and Rhineland-Palatinate reinstalled the dominant mayor system in 1948. Fewer problems were encountered in South Germany where the Americans found the old council system an acceptable way to distribute powers. Thus in Bavaria and Baden-Wuerttemberg, elected city councils combine legislative with executive powers, while a mayor, elected either by the council or the citizens, is the chief administrative officer responsible to the council. This *council-mayor* system is distinguished from the system prevalent in Northrhine-Westphalia and Lower Saxony by the fact that the mayor and not the city manager is the main bearer of administrative responsibility. There is still another type of city government in Hamburg, Bremen, and West Berlin. In this system, which combines the functions of municipal and Land governments, the council elects a collegial executive, the *Senate,* that is headed by a governing mayor.

West German county government in rural and small town areas also varies according to regional patterns. The leading organs here are the county council (*Kreistag*) and the county director (*Landrat*). In some areas the Landrat is more politician than administrator, and in others he combines the two functions. The

German tradition of interdependence, which often squeezes county directors into the state official hierarchy and integrates local administration into the Land system, tends to limit the degree of self-determination that local government can achieve. Although the county directors have become more autonomous as the result of postwar reforms providing for their appointment or election on the county level, the Laender have substituted indirect supervision for the direct hierarchical controls they once possessed. The Laender's principal control mechanisms include (1) reserving policy decisions to Land agencies, (2) establishing standards for staffing county agencies, (3) staffing offices of the county director's office with Land civil servants, (4) increasing the county's dependence on Land grants-in-aid, and (5) assigning functions to specialized field units that remain under direct ministerial control.[12] In any case, the cities are financially dependent on the Land treasuries. The kind of equalization which operates horizontally among the Laender operates vertically among communities, with the Land holding the pursestrings. The average German city is dependent on Land subsidies of varying sorts to cover about one-fifth of its budget. In the early 1950's, the cities were angry that the Laender were not equitably sharing increases in tax revenues. As a result of their pressure, the federal parliament in 1956 amended the Basic Law (ART. 106) to strengthen the communities' claims to certain kinds of taxes, and to provide for some sort of fixed key for the division of Land tax receipts between Land and municipal treasuries.

Local government advocates have not been able to win for the cities and counties greater constitutional recognition of their role as the "third power" in administration, which would place them on an equal footing with the federal and Land governments. Indeed, local government authorities have not yet succeeded getting many of the Laender to abolish what they regard as the obsolescent middle-echelon district administrations. These subsidiary Land government offices exist in all the Laender except the city-states and Schleswig-Holstein; among other duties, they supervise communal police, education, and public health activities

[12] Herbert Jacob, *German Administration since Bismarck* (New Haven, 1963), p. 185.

which are carried out with the support of Land funds. The communal politicians argue that these organs are undemocratic, since they are not directly responsible to any parliamentary organ, and are largely unnecessary in that their functions could be transferred to the Land ministries and communal governments. However the orthodox German view continues to differentiate between the higher claims of the state (the Land) and the communities. "The state has not become merely a 'holding corporation' for the communities and the communities have not taken over the role of the state. There has been a democratization of administration on all levels, insofar as free elections for the local and state legislatures are guaranteed . . . and in that these exercise a control over the administration. But the state is superior to the communities integrated within it, as its legislation, administration and legal system prove."[13]

BIBLIOGRAPHY

Bellstedt, Christoph, *Die Steuer als Instrument der Politik: Eine vergleichende Untersuchung der Steuerpolitik in den USA und Deutschland* (Berlin, 1966).

Brecht, Arnold, *Federalism and Regionalism in Germany* (New York, 1945).

Culver, Lowell W., "Land Elections in West German Politics," *WPQ*, XIX, 2 (June, 1966), 304–36.

Flechtheim, Ossip K., ed., *Bund und Laender* (Berlin, 1959).

Heidenheimer, Arnold J., "Federalism and the Party System: The Case of West Germany," *APSR*, LII (1958), 809–28.

Merkl, Peter H., "Executive-Legislative Federalism in West Germany," *APSR*, LIII (1959), 732–41.

Neunreither, Karlheinz, "Federalism and the West German Bureaucracy," *Political Studies*, VII (1959), 232–45.

Noldner, K., "Foederalismus und Unitarismus im Bundesstaat, dargestellt am Beispiel der Finanzverfassung," in Heinz Dietrich Ortlieb and Friedrich-Wilhelm Dorge, eds., *Wirtschafts- und Sozialpolitik* (Opladen, 1967).

[13] Erich Becker in Hans Peters, ed., *Handbuch der kommunalen Wissenschaft und Praxis* (Berlin, 1956), I, 118.

Peters, Hans, ed., *Handbuch der kommunalen Wissenschaft und Praxis,* 3 vols. (Berlin, 1956–59).

Preece, Jan, *Land Elections in the German Federal Republic* (London, 1968).

Reich, Donald, "Court, Comity and Federalism in West Germany," *Midwest Journal of Political Science,* VII, 3 (August, 1963), 197–228.

Varain, Heinz, *Parteien und Verbaende: Eine Studie ueber ihren Aufbau, ihre Verflechtung und ihr Wirken in Schleswig-Holstein 1945–1958* (Cologne, 1964).

Wells, Roger H., *The States in West German Federalism* (New Haven, 1961).

8

Bureaucracy and Planning

BUREAUCRACY AND SOCIETY

The shaping influence of a branch of government on political traditions will depend not only on its power position vis-à-vis the other branches of government but also on the degree to which it can influence patterns of behavior in everyday life. The average American is of course aware of the existence of bureaucrats in Washington and the state capitols, but, except during times of war and depression, his contacts with officialdom are apt to be limited. Many of the government employees he does encounter, such as the school principal, the county clerk, or the agricultural field agent, may themselves be only vaguely aware of their place in an official hierarchy outside of their local office. Whether for good or bad, this is a reflection of the fact that competitive, individualist values and great decentralization have kept American public servants from creating an *esprit de corps* of their own. In Germany this situation has traditionally been very different. There, the administrative branch is the oldest of existing political institutions, and for a long time Prussian civil servants even considered their experience and impartiality a sufficient substitute for a formal constitution.

It has been well remarked that "in dealing with the 'civil service' in Germany one is dealing with a concept which is vastly wider than that used by most other countries."[1] Under German law the employees of all public law institutions, communities, counties, and public facilities are all part of an integrated body of public officials—a body that includes not only administrators and government clerks, but also teachers, railroad conductors,

[1] Brian Chapman, *The Profession of Government* (London, 1959), p. 67.

and the men who read the gas meters. All vie for the status and security of the *Beamte,* the professional civil servant with tenure. Also, the inhabitants of most German provincial towns will more frequently be in contact with officials of the central government bureaus, which, in contrast to American practice, tend to be dispersed all over the country. Moreover, civil service ranks and titles have for generations dominated German middle-class society to such an extent that German businessmen used to compete with each other in philanthropy and public spiritedness in the hope of being granted the honorary title of "Commercial Counsellor," which would put them on a social par with the higher officials. And to this day, civil service salaries remain an almost universal measuring rod, with everyone from the Chancellor down receiving compensation pegged to the pay of a specified Beamte rank.

The status of its officials, its interpenetration with society, and its reputation of incorruptibility long allowed the German administration to claim the position of a preferred instrument for making political decisions. Many Germans, no matter how opposed they might be on principle to its hierarchical traditions, still cannot help feeling a greater confidence in the ability of the administration to make correct, impartial decisions than of remote, party-influenced parliamentarians. In the United States, bureaucrats tend to seem more remote than local politicians; in Germany, the reverse is true. German citizens are in close contact with the administrative apparatus, not only because of the large number of services that are traditionally state run (railroads, utilities, health services, etc.), but also because most aspects of economic and social life tend to be supervised by officials. This was particularly true of the immediate postwar period, which was not ideal for the Allied attempt to convert the administration into a bulwark of local democracy. Localized decision-making, which the Americans in particular tried to develop, was resisted by officials who believed that only a system based on hierarchical coordination could rationally and equitably allocate the resources.

THE CIVIL SERVICE

The Beamte is a permanent professional civil servant who has achieved his position only after passing through rigorous training periods and examinations. Not all public servants are Beamten. Those who are simply public employees (*Angestellten*) or manual workers (*Arbeiter*) may be ineligible for Beamten status because of the lowly function of their jobs, the temporary nature of their employment, or because they lack some of the specific qualifications which allow Beamten to claim lifetime tenure and pensions. Such pensions range from a minimum of 35 per cent of regular pay after ten years' service to 75 per cent of regular pay after thirty-five years' service. Within the public service as a whole there are four broad grades—the regular, middle, superior, and higher services. For the middle and superior grades, which include everybody from secretaries, through inspectors, to supervisory officials, requirements include a training period of from one to three years with subsequent examination. For the higher service, requirements include the completion of university studies (usually in law), passing the *Staatsexamen,* and a three-year training period climaxed by passing a second broad state examination.

In return for security and high social status, the Beamte has traditionally been bound by a code of behavior whose premise is that, unlike other salary earners, he is the representative of the state and must at all times exhibit exemplary behavior and self-sacrifice. Thus it was long accepted that those entering the Beamte status voluntarily limited their civil rights. The Beamte must be ready to take on nonpaid side work, change his place of residence, or work up to twelve hours above the regular weekly norm. He is bound not only to exercise correct and conscientious behavior on the job but also to behave in private life so as to command the respect and confidence his profession requires. The Beamten Law also enjoins him to look after the "reputation of members of his family," which is held to include assuring "modest behavior by his spouse." The provision that he is allowed to accept gifts only with the permission of his superiors was ignored, during the 1950's, by a fair number of federal officials who seemed to be under the impression that methods which prevailed in business life should also apply in the public service. A sizable number of prosecutions, particularly against members of the Finance, Defense, and Traffic ministries, but including also a case in the federal Chancellery, served to stem this minor wave

TABLE 8–1:   DISTRIBUTION OF PUBLIC SERVICE CATEGORIES BY LEVEL OF GOVERNMENT, 1963

| | EMPLOYED BY | | | |
Category	Federal Government	Land Governments	Local and County Governments	Total
Beamten and judges	67,757	552,606	119,289	738,652
Angestellte	84,662	295,374	260,218	640,254
Arbeiter	90,722	101,769	186,415	378,906
TOTAL	243,141	949,749	565,922	1,757,812

SOURCE: *Statistisches Jahrbuch fuer die Bundesrepublik Deutschland 1964* (Stuttgart, 1964), p. 442.

of corruption. The German public did not react with as much indignation as it once might have, a reflection of the fact that the Beamte is no longer considered infallible.[2]

The denazification and other reforms carried through by the Allies in the postwar period aroused a considerable amount of righteous indignation among dismissed officials who held that their basic right to lifelong tenure had been arbitrarily violated. They claimed that the Allied action was illegal under German law and sought not only reinstatement but back pay. Of the 53,000 civil servants removed in the Western zones, only about 1,000 remained permanently excluded through German official action. Most of the rest were gradually taken back into various official agencies, and the others enlisted the civil servants' associations to put great pressure on the Bundestag to enact leg-

[2] Theodor Eschenburg, "The Decline of the Bureaucratic Ethos in the Federal Republic," in Arnold J. Heidenheimer, ed., *Political Corruption* (New York, 1970), pp. 259–65.

islation in their favor. They were known as the "131'ers," after the article of the Basic Law which provides that the status of civil servants who lost their jobs after 1945 was to be settled by law. There were basically two categories in the post-1945 group: (1) those dismissed because of Nazi activity and (2) those officials who had previously served in the Eastern sections of Germany now outside the Federal Republic's boundaries. The law the Bundestag passed in 1951 neatly evaded the political problem by lumping the two groups together and giving their members priority in reinstatement to public positions as well as generous retirement options. A Constitutional Court decision of 1954, however, indirectly rapped the civil service over the knuckles. The court found that the thorough nazification of the civil service had in effect turned the service into a tool of the Nazi regime. While recognizing that Article 131 bound the Federal Republic to provide some sort of care, it held that dismissed officials had no automatic right to reclaim positions in what was essentially a new postwar employment situation. But in practice few were denied a fresh start. In the Foreign Office, for instance, those officials who had been dismissed for anti-Nazi activities fared quite well after 1949. But on the other hand, of the majority who had retained their positions in the Hitler era, "only a few were actually rejected because of concessions they made to National Socialism."[3]

In addition to attempting to remove Nazis, the Allies had also sought to democratize the German civil service by breaking down its caste structure to allow the admission of "outsiders" with qualifications other than the traditional legal training or long service on lower levels of administration. The Americans regarded the caste structure of the civil service as a fossilized remnant from the period of absolutism with a strong *esprit de corps* that perpetuated undemocratic and reactionary political values. They felt that the special status held by the Beamte led not only to dangerous claims of privilege against outside criticism, but also to internal administrative stratification which tended to perpetuate irrational methods of administration.

---

[3] Samuel Wahrhaftig, "The Development of German Foreign Policy Institutions," in Hans Speier and W. P. Davison, eds., *West German Leadership and Foreign Policy* (Evanston, 1957), p. 32.

German reaction to this criticism was predominantly hostile. Beamten spokesmen argued that it was no accident that the Americans saw eye-to-eye on this problem with German Socialists. "American liberalism, with its trend toward a minimization of the state, has found common ground with Marxists who want to 'socialize' the *Beamtentum*. Both want to do away with the remnants of class rule and to achieve a 'classless society.' " The Americans were said to be badly misguided in seeking to destroy in Germany what they were trying to foster at home: a feeling of dedicated service among public employees. They were considered ignorant for failing to realize that the legal prerequisite for German Beamten was made necessary by the continental type of legal system. "American officials do not seem to recognize that case law was abandoned in Germany in the seventeenth century. This may be deplorable, but adoption of the Roman law system requires for its application the legally trained civil servant."[4]

Only a minority of Germans, mainly "outsiders," agreed with a liberal Stuttgart lawyer who countered that the German Beamte was still excessively concerned with continuing his former rulers' role as "carriers of the state's honor." He called for the abolition of the "marriage-like vow of fidelity through which the Beamte dedicates his entire service to the state," as well as for the abolition of distinctions between Beamten and other civil and private employees, and also a de-emphasis of pension privileges. "The high premium placed on the generous pension forces the Beamte to make do with unsatisfactory or dishonorable working conditions, for no matter how much he disagrees with the legislator or his superiors he dare not leave his job, thereby forfeiting pension rights for which he has worked for years."[5] Such arguments, however, failed to prevail in the Bundestag. Instead, strong Beamten organization influence caused the adoption of a new Beamten Law without any fundamental reforms. The traditional internal stratification, the difficulty of entering as a noncareer applicant, and the emphasis on perpetuating the distinct character

---

[4] Ernst Kern, "Berufsbeamtentum und Politik," *Archiv des oeffentlichen Rechts,* LXXVII, 108.

[5] Otto Kuester, "Zur Frage des Berufsbeamtentums," *Archiv des oeffentlichen Rechts,* LXXVII, 364.

of the Beamtentum through pension and other privileges have been modified in only minor ways.

A REPUTATION GAP

To some it seems that postwar reforms have left the German civil service fundamentally unchanged as an institution. Thus an English student of comparative administration wrote in 1959 that "the German public official's status is unique in western Europe" because the German respect for the expert causes the official to be placed on a pedestal and idealized to a far greater extent than in other countries. Even in somewhat monarchic and Germanic countries like Sweden, Denmark, Austria, and Holland, the public official may be "trusted, respected, and in some ways reluctantly admired," but unlike his German colleague he is "not assumed to have a monopoly on political wisdom nor to typify all that is best in the national character."[6]

The traditional elite character of the German civil service is seen as one of the factors that might make it a model applicable to certain developing countries, for in India, Ghana, and Nigeria, a well-trained civil service helped perform some of the tasks of nation-building, just as their equivalents had done in Germany. The federal division of powers in Germany may also be an attractive model for such countries since "it allows the central regime to keep control over policy-making while the constituent states administer the central mandates. In the face of powerful centrifugal forces, new nations may find that administrative federalism offers an attractive solution to some of their thorniest political problems."[7]

In Germany itself, however, much of the old pride and interest in administrative achievements has declined. Upon returning to Germany in the mid-1960's, Fritz Morstein Marx, the outstanding scholar of administration, observed that public interest in administrative achievements was hardly greater than in most developing countries. He found that the standard of German bureaucracy fell

[6] Chapman, *The Profession of Government*, p. 310.
[7] Herbert Jacob, *German Administration since Bismarck: Central Authority versus Local Autonomy* (New Haven, 1963), p. 214.

short of its image abroad, where experts admired the efficiency it had displayed in earlier eras.[8]

When Chancellor Kiesinger was in office, he entertained the idea for a while of establishing a central civil service college similar to the French *Ecole Nationale d'Administration,* so as to familiarize high-ranking German civil servants with modern administrative procedures. It was his contention that because the civil service remained rooted in the administrative notions of the nineteenth century, West Germans were hard put to nominate officials to international organizations who would be on a par with their colleagues from other countries. But his criticism of "the mildew which has settled on the higher ranks of the civil servants in this country"[9] did not have any immediate results. Although a lawyer by training himself, Kiesinger was critical of the jurists' monopoly of the better positions. Interior Minister Ernst Benda also told a civil service conference that the 30 per cent of higher civil servants who were trained lawyers could not continue to look down at experts with other training as "outsiders." He demanded that rules prejudicial to their advancement and promotion exclusively by seniority be altered.[10]

In the course of time some German Beamten have begun to emerge from behind their anonymity and to criticize directly their superiors. On one occasion Chancellor Erhard was berated in person when he went to speak to a civil servants' convention. In 1968 the Tax Officials Association, which was losing 700 of its members each year to private industry, complained bitterly about the tortuous, irrational, and socially unjust tax system they had to attempt to administer. At about this time the public was up in arms about the greatest tax swindle in German history, pulled off by rank amateurs who took advantage of German officials' reverence for anything with an official-looking stamp on it. The swindlers easily got DM 11 million of tax rebates and were exposed only when they used a slightly irregular abbreviation in a fake official letter. This case promised to do to the

[8] Fritz Morstein Marx, "Verwaltung in auslaendischer Sicht," *Verwaltungsarchiv,* LVI (April, 1965), 106.
[9] *Christ und Welt,* August 25, 1967.
[10] Ernst Benda, "Beamtentum in unserer Zeit," *Das Parlament,* December 12, 1968.

image of German officialdom what the *Hauptmann von Koepenick* had done for the German military—make them look ridiculous.

The month after this swindle was uncovered the tax officials launched a public campaign demanding reforms in the tax regulations, which they claimed had become so complex that injustices were unavoidable. They put out a leaflet telling the public that "You are paying too much tax because you can no longer find your way about in the tax jungle." They declared their readiness to strike because of poor pay and being made the scapegoats for poor legislation. Finance Minister Strauss responded scornfully to their demands. But the *Frankfurter Allgemeine* wrote that the activities of the leaders of the association, "who wanted to cooperate, could have been channeled in a different direction long ago if preparations had been made for the necessary amendments to tax legislation."[11] Some months later Interior Minister Benda agreed that "the contemporary administration style is condemned to be heavy-handed because of the excessive number of regulations . . . I have the impression that we show too little trust in our public officials, by prescribing for them the minutest detail and treating them as immature persons." He called for a greater delegation of responsibilities and decision-making powers "down" the administrative ladder in the expectation that this might awaken much latent talent.[12]

HOW BRIGITTE BROUGHT HOME THE BACON

For years Brigitte Glinga had worked as an ordinary hairdresser, taken the tram to work and paid taxes. Then she decided to soft soap the tax office and live from taxes.

In May, 1966, she founded the firm Hansa Export and informed the Duesseldorf tax office that her firm had purchased DM 5,420,955 worth of coal from the Cologne "Glueckauf" firm and exported it to the Amsterdam firm van der Berge. She asked if the tax officials would kindly transfer to her account DM 216,838 as turnover tax rebate for exporters. They were so kind!

[11] *Frankfurter Allgemeine Zeitung*, August 19, 1968.
[12] Benda, "Beamtentum in unserer Zeit."

Certainly a tax official examined the "undertaking" but all was in the best of order. The firm Glueckauf existed only in Brigitte's letter. Hansa Export had not moved a single ton of coal over the border and no turnover tax had been paid, qualifying for a rebate. All this just never dawned on the investigator.

What the captain's uniform achieved in the Hauptmann von Koepenick swindle at the beginning of this century, an authentic office stamp achieved in the Duesseldorf tax office. A customs office located at Dammer Bruch 12 affirmed in a communication, adorned with the customs' eagle, that the coal had been exported. An official later complained that with an official stamp on the document one has to assume that a document is in order. The customs office, Dammer Bruch 12, had closed its doors in 1954.

Because the millions rolled in so beautifully, further sham firms were founded, seven in all. On two more occasions examinations were carried out, but everything seemed to be in order. The attractive Brigitte could already afford a Jaguar and Mercedes 230 SL.

When in November, 1967, the tax office complained that the customs certificates were indeed stamped but not signed, Brigitte Glinga wrote to herself. Under the letterhead *Zollamt Dammer Bruch* she informed herself that "according to the regulations to be applied to the customs law and General Customs Regulations (Zollad) a signature is not necessarily required. Certified: Hamhofer, ZollAss."

Now the light dawned in Duesseldorf! A customs assistant is abbreviated to merely "ZAss"!

A REBIRTH OF PLANNING

While Ludwig Erhard remained the principal articulator of West German economic policy from 1948 to 1966, planning was a dirty synonym for ill-conceived attempts to interfere with market mechanisms. During this time the German government took great pains to disguise its economic activities, whereas the French government played them up. As Andrew Shonfield noted:

> When the German government intervened to accelerate the growth of certain sectors of the economy, it went to

great length to present the matter . . . as if it derived from or supplemented, some primary private initiative, whereas in France the natural tendency was and is to insist on the public character of such initiative.[13]

In the mid-1960's, a German advocate of planning was very pessimistic about the chances of rehabilitating economic and political planning processes in the Federal Republic.

> Who can ordain planning procedures in an economy that has just experienced a miraculous boom by a modern version of laissez faire? Politically any overt extension of programming or planning is less feasible now than it has ever been . . . It is uncertain whether pure politics will, under present circumstances, be capable of reintroducing the issue of economic planning as an issue of democratic progress into West German discussion.[14]

However, a rapid though step-by-step relegitimation of planning mechanisms occurred after Kurt Schiller replaced Erhard as the Federal Republic's economic miracle man and when the Social Democrats took over the government leadership in 1969. The first important step was taken by the CDU/SPD government in June, 1967, when it passed the Law to Promote Economic Stability and Growth. On the basis of this law, the government soon passed a medium-term Federal Financial Plan that projected budget expenditures for the four-year period 1967–71. The most immediate goal of this measure was to restore order to federal finances, which had become badly unbalanced during the latter part of the Erhard period. But the plan's long-range goals were to adjust financial policy decisions to economic resources and needs and to ensure increased public investment with a view to the tasks of the future. This financial planning mechanism soon won high praise from German and foreign specialists. By 1969 a German study group concluded that it had become, along with

---

[13] Andrew Shonfield, *Modern Capitalism* (New York, 1965), p. 275.
[14] Hans Joachim Arndt, *West Germany: Politics of Non-Planning* (Syracuse, 1966), pp. 122–23.

the American Planning Programming Budget System (PPBS), one of the leading models in the Western world.[15]

Since the medium-term Federal Financial Plan was operated through a cabinet subcommittee directed by the Ministries of Economics and Finance, there was some apprehension in the rest of the administration that these two ministries would develop into "super-ministries." But if the other ministries, as the "wholesale consumers of public funds," were to participate directly in the financial planning, the plan would lose its central thrust. The Project Group for Administrative Reform also identified some other shortcomings in its 1969 report. It pointed out that the Financial Plan did not contain information about nonmonetary national capacities, such as those relating to research capacity or important political areas not involving large direct expenditures. The group considered the possibility of transferring the Financial Plan bureau from the Finance Ministry to the Chancellery, in a position analogous to that of the U.S. Bureau of the Budget under the Office of the President. However, it concluded that this proposal would create additional difficulties without promising to solve enough of the identified problems.[16]

The Group recommended that the Financial Plan remain in operation, but that it be augmented by a bureau of Political Planning in the Chancellor's office. It made a strong plea for improved planning mechanisms as a prerequisite for more meaningful "conceptual politics." Basing their recommendations predominantly on information theory, the authors pointed out that there were great shortcomings in information flow in the German governmental process. And they emphasized how important it was to link information evaluation with decision-making and follow-through evaluation. To this end, the group developed three possible models for a Political Planning Office. It suggested that the director of planning capacities be a close and high-level collaborator of the Chancellor's, who could deal with other ministers on an equal level and involve the Chancellor himself in planning processes as much as possible. Chancellor Brandt's selection of Horst Ehmke as minister without portfolio to serve

[15] Projektgruppe fuer Regierungs- und Verwaltungsreform, *Erster Bericht zur Reform*, p. 192.
[16] *Ibid.*, pp. 198–203.

as coordinator in the Chancellery was an important step toward implementation of these recommendations.

However, one respected official—who in other contexts has often advocated keeping a sharp line between civil servants' expertise and political decision-making criteria—publicly criticized the proposal. He argued against placing the Political Planning Office in the Chancellery because it would further intensify the great concentration of power there. Instead, he suggested that the Planning Office be attached to the parliament or established as a highly insulated autonomous institution with a legal basis similar to that of the Public Accounting Office.[17]

URBAN AND REGIONAL PLANNING

To understand the different conditions under which public officials in Germany and the United States attempt to deal with problems of sprawling urbanism, let us compare parallel efforts in Munich and Boston. In his excellent article, Rolf Grauhan noted that in 1960 both cities elected new mayors, Hans-Jochen Vogel in Munich and John E. Collins in Boston, and he examined what happened when they sought to develop comprehensive planning and redevelopment for their metropolitan areas.[18]

Both urban areas had grown swiftly in the preceding and subsequent periods. Munich almost tripled in population between 1950 and 1965, and the number of automobiles in the city quintupled. But its public officials had one advantage: the situation was easier to handle because most of this growth had taken place within the borders of a single political jurisdiction, the city of Munich, containing fully three-quarters of the population of the metropolitan area. In Boston, however, Mayor Collins was in charge of a municipal administration that could legislate for barely one-third of the Boston region's population. And because

---

[17] Josef Keolble, "Wider die Expertokratie," *Die Welt,* November 8, 1969.
[18] Rolf Grauhan, "Stadtplanung und Politik," *Politische Vierteljahresschrift,* VII (November, 1966), 392–406. See also Hubert Abress, "Stadtentwicklung und Stadtplanung," *Zeitschrift fuer Politik,* XIII (1966), 183–200; and Wolfgang Hartenstein, "Die Anziehungskraft der grossen Stadt," *Raum und Siedlung,* 1967/11, 259–61, who emphasizes some differences between Munich and other large German cities.

city boundaries had remained static since 1911, the actual area of the City of Boston encompassed only 5 per cent of the whole metropolitan area. Local governments in seventy-six other autonomous communities presented competing decision-making centers. By contrast, in Munich the surrounding communities were only involved in "far-out" problems, like the selection of land for a new regional airport.

TABLE 8–2:   BASE LINES FOR URBAN PLANNING

	Munich	Boston
AREA (IN SQUARE MILES)		
Within city limits	118	42
Outside city limits	403	923
TOTAL METROPOLITAN AREA	521	965
POPULATION (IN MILLIONS)		
Central city	1.2	0.7
Outside city	.4	1.2
TOTAL	1.6	1.9
Date of last incorporation to central city	1942	1911

To get the institutional vehicle he needed for his planning program, Mayor Collins had to undertake a much more ambitious campaign, but he created a less impressive body than the one Mayor Vogel had been able to establish rather easily. To replace the old autonomous Boston City Planning Board with a new Boston Redevelopment Authority, Mayor Collins needed an act of the Massachusetts legislature. Mayor Vogel merely needed the approval of his city council for a reorganization plan that placed the Munich city planning office directly under his jurisdiction.

After that, things moved along well in Munich. The city planners created a city development plan for the next thirty years, and in 1962 the completed draft was submitted to sixty Munich institutions and civic associations for comment. The plan was presented to the city council as the composite proposal of the entire municipal administration, and after its near-unanimous passage it became binding as the Plan of the Land Capital Munich.

In the state capital of Boston, Mayor Collins was moving faster than most American mayors, but much more slowly than Vogel. Thus the Boston Redevelopment Authority was legally quite independent of the city government, and the public proposals it submitted were not backed by the full authority of the city administration. Then came the problem of coordinating with the numerous other communities in the metropolitan area. By 1963, they were just getting coordinated enough to set up a Metropolitan Planning Council that held purely informative meetings for local government officials. Boston did better than most American cities, but its accomplishments couldn't compare with those of Munich, which a few years later was able to install a brand new subway system and put in a successful bid for the 1972 Olympics, showing itself to be a city that could cope with a vast influx of outside visitors.

The resistance against successive attempts to persuade local governments to surrender their powers or even identify to larger metropolitan governments has, in the United States, caused almost all such efforts to fail. In Germany some mergers and incorporations were carried out by fiat under the Nazis. But such rationalization measures can also occur under democratic rules if a party organization is strong enough to overcome local loyalties and traditions. Thus, in Rhineland-Palatinate a Christian Democratic Land government angered many of its rural constituents by pushing through a bill consolidating hundreds of the smaller and unviable hamlets and pygmy villages. And in the densely populated Ruhr area, the Social Democrats, who control almost all the city councils, have agreed to support a plan to abolish several large and many smaller cities, with a view toward creating a "supercity" of 5 million people that would extend from Dortmund to Duisburg.

BIBLIOGRAPHY

Arndt, Hans-Joachim, *West Germany: Politics of Non-Planning* (Syracuse, N.Y., 1966).

Brecht, Arnold, "Personnel Management," and Rodney L. Mott, "Public Finance," in E. H. Litchfield, ed., *Governing Postwar Germany* (Ithaca, 1953), pp. 263–93, 326–60.

Chapman, Brian, *The Profession of Government* (London, 1959).

Cole, Taylor, "The Democratization of the German Civil Service," *JP*, XIV (February, 1952), 3–18.

Eschenburg, Theodor, *Staat und Gesellschaft in Deutschland* (Stuttgart, 1956), pp. 760 ff.

Federal Ministry of Finance, "Remarks on the First Pluri-Annual Federal Financial Plan for the Period 1967–1971," *German Economic Review*, VI, 3 (1968), 258–69.

Grauhan, Rolf, "Stadtplanung und Politik: Vergleichende Beobachtungen zum Stellenwert der Planung in der Verwaltung einer amerikanischen und einer deutschen Grossstadt," *PVS*, VIII, 3 (November, 1966), 392–416.

Grauhan, Rolf, "Der Oberbürgermeister als Verwaltungschef," *PVS*, VI, 3 (September, 1965), 302–29.

Herz, John, "Political Views of the West German Civil Service," in Hans Speier and W. P. Davison, eds., *West German Leadership and Foreign Policy* (Evanston, 1957), pp. 96–135.

Hollander, G. E., "The Public Interest Pressure Group: The Case of the 'Deutsche Staedtetag,'" *Public Administration*, XLV, 3 (Autumn, 1967), 245–59.

Jacob, Herbert, *German Administration since Bismarck: Central Authority versus Local Autonomy* (New Haven, 1963).

Naschold, Frieder, *Demokratie und Organisation* (Stuttgart, 1969).

Rugg, D. S., "Selected Areal Effects of Planning Processes upon Urban Development in the Federal Republic of Germany," *Economic Geography*, XLII (October, 1966), 526–35.

Saintonge, R. A. Chaput de, *Public Administration in Germany* (London, 1961).

Steinbuch, Karl, *Falsch programmiert* (Stuttgart, 1968).

Zapf, Wolfgang, "Zum Sozialprofil der hoeheren Beamtenschaft," in Zapf, ed., *Beitraege zur Analyse der deutschen Oberschicht* (Munich, 1965).

9

The Powers of
the Judiciary

Even more than other continental peoples accustomed to a codified law structure, the Germans tend to regard the body of law as a unified system which covers all possible contingencies arising out of the frailty of man in human interaction. While the citizens of more pragmatic political cultures, such as the Anglo-Saxon countries, tend to utilize the machinery of law only after having exhausted less formal means of settling disputes, like compromise and arbitration, the continental European, convinced of the rightness of his case, will go to court as a matter of course. He sees the judge not as a fallible fellow human who must decide between conflicting claims and precedents, but as an expert trained to apply detailed code provisions and an aloof representative of an abstract justice.[1] Writers, social philosophers, and a surprisingly large number of average Germans have tended to agree with Hegel when he wrote: "How infinitely important, how divine it is, that the duties of the state and the rights of the citizen, just as the rights of the state and the duties of the citizens, are legally determined."

The modern German civil law code was adopted at the end of the nineteenth century, a century later than in France. It was the fruit of stupendous labor by many legal scholars who paid intensive attention to problems of classification and arrangement. Consequently, the code, though more useful than the French in that it provides more exhaustive information, has a very elaborate and complicated structure.[2] Those who use it have to be

---

[1] Herbert Spiro, *Government by Constitution* (New York, 1958).
[2] Max Rheinstein, "Approach to German Law," *Indiana Law Journal*, XXXVI (1959), 546 ff.

thoroughly trained. In the course of their training, generations of German law students have been immersed in the ideological assumptions on which the code is built. Implicit is the premise that the written law is self-sufficient, that the codes, together with the statutes which implement and amend them, constitute a key capable of deciding all problems that come before the court. Judges are expected not to seek answers outside the provisions of the written law. This orientation nurtured and accentuated a positivist tradition which had led German legal scholars to emphasize that the law is what the sovereign says it is. Since German jurisprudence has tended to emphasize that sovereignty rests with the state (in contrast to the French, who emphasized the role of the nation), justice and the interests of the state became difficult to dissociate.

For want of constitutional traditions or other expressions of community consensus, the Germans were more and more inclined to universalize the philosophical principles of law. This produced magnificent writers of jurisprudence, but it also encouraged superpositivist trends which tended to produce rules of constitutional law so "pure" that their relationship to social and political reality grew increasingly remote. Thus, in the upheaval preceding the advent of Nazism, democratic legal philosophers found their theories inapplicable to the seemingly obvious political problems at hand. Later many judges and lawyers saw no incompatibility in remaining at their posts as long as the legal framework was left standing, even though hollowed out by the Nazis with the substitution of their own arbitrary decrees.

THE JUDICIARY

German judges are very different from their American and British peers not only in their legal philosophy, but also in their training, their professional standing, and the role they play in the decision-making process. In contrast to the Anglo-Saxon countries where judgeships are usually awarded to mature lawyers after successful careers in private practice, German judges get their practical training solely within the judicial administration. At the conclusion of their studies, German law students decide whether to go into the regular civil service, private practice, or the judiciary. If they decide for the latter, they must be prepared to go through a prolonged period of preparatory service, examinations, and probationary service, similar to that expected for the highest grades of the civil service and stretching over a period of seven to eight years. Then, in their thirties, they are given lifetime appointments. They start at the bottom of the judicial hierarchy as local judges with salaries of about $6,000 a year, and they can hope for eventual promotion to the highest regular judicial appointments on the High Federal Court, whose members are paid about $16,000.

Partly because of the very large numbers of judges required to staff the many different kinds of German courts (there are more than five hundred judges in the city of Hamburg alone), the average German judge does not share the exalted position of his British colleague. He is, at all but the highest levels, very much like a civil servant, dependent upon the Justice Ministry for promotion within the hierarchy, and imbued with a spirit and tradition very much akin to that of the regular civil service. He has been characterized as seeking to clothe himself in anonymity, to hide his person behind his office, to insist that it is the "court" and not the "judge" which proclaims the verdict. Influenced by the traditional teaching that the judge should minimize his own role in the judicial process, he seeks conscientiously to apply the written law and does this with exacting objectivity. He "administers" the law; he does not "proclaim" or "find" it. However, in contrast to the Weimar period when many judges allowed their reactionary biases to distort equitable legislation, the administration of justice in the Federal Republic has left little ground for fundamental criticism, although not all courts have punished high ranking Nazis with sufficient severity.

GERMAN COURT STRUCTURE

The West German court system differs from the American most significantly, in that (1) the regular courts are paralleled by an array of specialized and administrative courts; (2) questions of constitutional law are decided by still another series of courts; and (3) although there are both Land and federal courts, these are integrated into a single hierarchy. The Land court systems include the lower courts and the middle echelon courts of appeal, while federal courts stand at the apex of both the regular and the various administrative and special court systems. Thus the regular courts have four levels, of which three are built into the Land system and the highest is on the federal level. At the lowest level, there is the district court (*Amtsgericht*) which has jurisdiction over the less important criminal and civil cases. The next highest court, the *Landgericht,* has original jurisdiction over more significant cases and acts in an appellate capacity for district court cases. The *Oberlandesgericht,* the highest regular court within the Land judiciary, is made up of separate senates for civil and criminal cases and has only an appellate jurisdiction. Finally, the highest court of the regular court system is the High Federal Court (*Bundesgerichtshof*) at Karlsruhe, where almost one hundred judges adjudicate nonconstitutional problems arising from the lower courts in all the Laender, seeking to preserve a uniform pattern of decision-making throughout the Federal Republic's regular court system. In addition to exercising wide appellate jurisdiction, the High Federal Court, whose members are named jointly by federal and Land authorities, exercises original jurisdiction in cases involving treason.

In addition to the regular courts and the constitutional courts (discussed below), there are the special courts to deal exclusively with controversies relating to administrative decisions, labor-management problems, and other specific areas. Most important are the *administrative courts.* These handle all manner of questions arising out of decisions made by administrative organs on both the Land and federal levels. An individual who feels he was not properly treated by an administrative action can ask the court to review whether the regulations were properly applied in his case. Similarly, civil servants who feel that their claims to promotion, tenure, and pensions have been ignored may ask these courts to review the decisions of their superiors. Basically, the administrative courts are supposed to serve as a check on the bureaucracy, but since much German rule-making is based on administrative decree rather than legislation, the administrative courts hear many controversies that would go before regular courts in other countries. Other special courts include the *labor courts,* which deal with questions related to collective bargaining agreements, working conditions, and the prerogatives of labor and management; the *social security courts,* which deal with cases arising out of the administration of welfare legislation; and the *finance courts,* which deal mainly with problems of tax law administration. All of these special court systems parallel the regular courts; they have lower courts on the Land level with final appeal centered in a federal administrative court, federal labor court, etc.

THE GROWTH OF JUDICIAL REVIEW

While the regular and special courts are all based on foundations established before 1933, the federal Constitutional Court with its sweeping powers of judicial review is only as old as the Basic Law, and its equivalents on the Land level are also postwar innovations. In view of their traditional respect for legalistic forms of decision-making, it is surprising that the Germans did not create a judicial organ analogous to the United States Supreme Court long ago. But until 1933 a number of factors impeded such a development. Some German lawyers and legal scholars, imbued with the continental code law tradition, believed a court to interpret the constitution unnecessary; they thought a trained regular judiciary administering a skillfully wrought body of constitutional and code law would be able to settle all conflicts. Others tended to deny that constitutional law had any special position, arguing that both constitution and statute were manifestations of the will of the same legislative power.[3] Finally, democrats of the Weimar period were inclined to regard the judiciary as a reactionary clan, not only in Germany but the world over. This impression was reinforced by their study of the role in American politics of the conservative United States Supreme Court around the turn of the century. The drafter of the Weimar Constitution had said that his plans for introducing judicial review in 1919 had been opposed by the Social Democrats mainly because they were horrified by the "notorious practice of the U.S. Supreme Court."[4]

By 1949, the perspective of German democrats had changed

[3] G. Dietze, "Judicial Review in Europe," *Michigan Law Review,* LV (1957), 564.
[4] *Ibid.,* p. 557.

considerably. For one thing, they now saw from the record of the New Deal Supreme Court that progressive judges could deal with social problems in the spirit of the times. But even more important was the imprint left by European experience. In Germany, and in other code law countries like Italy and Austria that had also had totalitarian or authoritarian regimes, the old legalist belief that good laws would by themselves assure good government was seriously undermined. Recalling that Hitler had come to power without seriously violating the letter of the law, Germans now were more willing to experiment with techniques that would make the constitution, the law, and the courts into more effective guardians of democratic systems. The old positivist belief separating the realm of law from the realm of politics had to be abandoned, together with the idea that sound law was virtually self-executing. Finally, it was necessary to accept the need for institutions which could (1) effectively supervise the judiciary's interpretation of constitutional norms; (2) interpret the constitution flexibly and yet in line with the liberal democratic spirit which produced it; and (3) possess the power to enforce a consistent reading of the constitution on the other branches of government. If the list of functions had ended here, then the powers of judicial review later vested in the Constitutional Court would have been no wider than those exercised by the United States Supreme Court. But the politicians who had observed the agonies of the Weimar system also felt the need for a power which could prevent deadlocks between the various governmental organs by arbitrating their claims to jurisdiction, which could exercise great discretion in preventing anticonstitutional forces from using constitutional rights to overthrow the system, and which could grant quick and effective relief to individuals whose constitutional rights were infringed. All of these powers came to be concentrated in the federal Constitutional Court.

THE CONSTITUTIONAL COURT

THE SELECTION OF JUDGES

Effective power to name the judges of the Constitutional Court rests in two committees, one composed of Bundestag and the other of Bundesrat members. These committees alternate in filling the openings which occur because of retirement or expiring terms. Party strength in the first Bundestag of 1949–53 was pretty evenly divided between CDU and SPD and so, consequently, were the political backgrounds of the first appointees. Then during the years of CDU dominance, Bundestag appointees were drawn predominantly from adherents of that party. The SPD held a stronger position in the Bundesrat, which is reflected in the Bundesrat's appointees. For the most part, the two major parties have alternated the appointments with a Bundestag-appointed Christian Democrat, a Bundesrat-appointed Social Democrat, a Bundestag-appointed Christian Democrat, a Bundesrat-appointed Social Democrat, and so on. Of some forty appointees up to 1969, only five have not been clearly identified with one of the two parties.

Since several dozen committee members as well as officials in the Ministry of Justice have a hand in the selection process, it becomes quite complex. The candidates who tend to win out are capable jurists with strong personal ties to influential party and judicial leaders. One Bundesrat-appointed Social Democratic candidate was the wife of an incumbent judge, the former student of a powerful CDU Land minister-president, and a protégée of a powerful SPD minister-president. She was selected in preference to another judge whose seven-year term had expired. Personnel politics become even more intense when the appointment involves the president and vice-president of the court. The requirement that all except the lifetime judges come up periodically for reappointment has drawn some criticism. A former vice-president suggested that reappointments be abolished altogether, and that nonrenewable appointments for periods of twelve years be made instead;[5] this rule was implemented in 1970. And another critic, who believes that the election of judges for specified terms has proved unsatisfactory, proposed that all appointments be made for life, as in the United States.[6]

[5] Heinz Laufer, *Verfassungsgerichtbarkeit und politischer Prozess* (Tuebingen, 1968), p. 219.

[6] *Ibid.*, p. 252.

THE TWO SENATES

The Constitutional Court is effectively divided into two senates of eight (previously twelve) members each. The personnel of these senates has differed in interesting ways (see Table 9–1). The First Senate has had more Social Democrats on it, and was for this reason referred to as the "Red Senate" during the Adenauer era. It also has contained a somewhat higher proportion of career judges. The judges on the Second Senate, who have less arduous work loads and are invited to speak more widely, have a longer record of continuous reelection and service. Significantly, no less than five judges in the Second Senate spent the Nazi period as exiles in the United States and Britain, and their experience abroad has been reflected in some crucial decisions affecting the constitution.[7]

TABLE 9–1: POLITICAL AND PROFESSIONAL BACKGROUNDS OF CONSTITUTIONAL COURT JUDGES, 1951–68

	APPOINTED TO	
	First Senate (N = 21)	Second Senate (N = 18)
PARTY IDENTIFICATION		
CDU/CSU	7	10
SPD	11	6
FDP	1	0
Unknown	2	2
PREVIOUS OCCUPATION		
Judge	10	7
Civil servant	5	5
Legislator	3	2
Professor	3	3
Lawyer	0	1

SOURCE: Donald P. Kommers, "The Federal Constitutional Court in the West German Political System," in Joel B. Grossman and Joseph Tanenhaus, eds., *Frontiers of Judicial Research* (New York, 1969), p. 92.

[7] Donald P. Kommers, "The Federal Constitutional Court in the West German Political System," in Joel B. Grossman and Joseph Tanenhaus, eds., *Frontiers of Judicial Research* (New York, 1969), p. 110.

FUNCTIONS OF THE COURT

The multiple functions of the Constitutional Court, plus factors arising from its role within a code law system, make even a sum-

---

CONSTITUTIONAL COURT

Article 92

Judicial authority shall be invested in the judges; it shall be exercised by the Federal Constitutional Court, by the Supreme Federal Court, by the Federal courts provided for in this Basic Law and by the courts of the Laender.

Article 93:

The Federal Constitutional Court shall decide:

1. on the interpretation of this Basic Law in the event of disputes concerning the extent of the rights and duties of Federal organs or of other participants endowed with independent rights by this Basic Law or by the Standing Orders (Rules of Procedure) of a Federal organ;

2. in cases of differences of opinion or doubts on the formal and material compatibility of Federal law or Land law with this Basic Law, or on the compatibility of Land law with other Federal law, at the request of the Federal Government, of a Land Government or of one-third of the members of the Bundestag;

3. in case of differences of opinion on the rights and duties of the Federation and the Laender, particularly in the execution of Federal law by the Laender, and in the exercise of Federal supervision;

4. on other public law disputes between the Federation and the Laender, between different Laender or within a Land, unless recourse to another court exists;

Article 100

(1) If a court considers a law unconstitutional, the validity of which is relevant to its decision, proceedings must be stayed and, if a violation of a Land Constitution is involved, the decision of the Land court competent for constitutional disputes shall be obtained and, if a violation of this Basic Law is involved, the decision of the Federal Constitutional Court shall be obtained. This shall also apply if the violation of this Basic Law by Land law or the incompatibility of a Land law with a Federal law is involved.

mary description of its jurisdiction complex. Perhaps one might start with its powers related to *judicial review of legislation*. Here the Germans distinguish between the court's exercise of "concrete" and "abstract" review jurisdiction. "Concrete" review occurs when the court is asked to rule on constitutional questions arising as aspects of an actual controversy being adjudicated in lower courts. Applicants for concrete judicial review of legislation are regular lower courts, which *must* submit problems of constitutionality encountered in the process of adjudication. Applicants for "abstract" judicial review may include organs of federal and Land governments contesting the constitutionality of legislation or the constitutional interpretations of other agencies even without reference to a particular case. In addition, any individual may complain if he believes that enacted legislation (as distinct from the way in which laws are administered) directly infringes on his constitutional rights.[8]

A few examples may illustrate how these powers are used. A case involving abstract review of legislation was initiated in 1957 by the Socialist Land government of Hessen, which charged that a federal law allowing contributions to political parties to be written off as tax deductions was unconstitutional because it violated the constitutionally guaranteed equality of political parties. Applying sociological jurisprudence, the court found, on the basis of scholarly and empirical evidence, that some parties received much larger contributions than others from business groups favored by these provisions. It reasoned that enforcement of the provisions would indeed cause those parties close to business interests to be unduly favored and declared the applicable provisions of the tax laws to be unconstitutional because they violated the constitution's equality clause.[9] In another case, the Land government of Baden in 1951 challenged federal legislation that was to merge several southwest German Laender into the new Land of Baden-Wuerttemberg. Baden argued that the Basic Law so fortified the position of the Laender that they could not be abolished without the majority approval of all relevant sectional

---

[8] Ernst Friesenhahn, "Verfassungsgerichtbarkeit," in *Handwoerterbuch der Sozialwissenschaften*, XXIX (Stuttgart, 1960), 83–91.

[9] *Entscheidungen des Bundesverfassungsgerichts*, VIII (Tuebingen, 1952–60), 51 ff.

groups. But the court ruled that territorial reorganization could be carried out, even against the will of a majority of the population in one affected unit.[10] In another case, the 1956 Federal Electoral Law was challenged by a small political party on the grounds that allowing only parties that received 5 per cent of the total vote to occupy Bundestag seats violated the equality principle. However, in this and similar cases, the court held that such provisions were justified because splinter parties prevented an "orderly handling of affairs," and the legislature could legitimately discriminate against them in this manner.[11]

A second distinct function of the court arises out of its constitutional power to *decide disputes concerning the extent of the rights and duties of the federal and Land organs, as well as parties functioning within them.* Many cases coming to the German court under this heading would probably be dismissed as "political cases" in the United States, but the German Constitutional Court must accept them and is drawn directly into the area of partisan political conflict. Thus in 1958 when the Socialists were fighting against atomic rearmament, the federal government came to the court to prevent the Socialist-dominated Land government of Hamburg from holding a popular referendum on the question. Siding with the Adenauer government, the court ruled that the Hamburg action was unconstitutional since matters relating to defense and foreign policy were exclusively the business of the federal government.[12]

But perhaps the most important decision shoring up Laender powers was handed down by the court in 1961 in the television case. The issues in this case were quite similar to those in the famous American case of *McCulloch* v. *Maryland,* but it was decided the other way. The case arose out of an effort by the federal government to break the Laender's control of radio and television by instituting a federal network on a nationwide basis. Chancellor Adenauer singlehandedly chartered the network in 1960, with instructions to begin operations the next year. Attack-

[10] Gerhard Leibholz, "The Federal Constitutional Court in Germany and the 'Southwest' Case," *APSR,* XLVI (1952), 723–31.
[11] Taylor Cole, "The West German Federal Constitutional Court: An Evaluation after Six Years," *JP,* XX (February, 1958), 294.
[12] *Entscheidungen des Bundesverfassungsgerichts,* VIII, 124 ff.

ing this attempt to expand the federal government's functions by a *fait accompli*, the Socialist-led Laender carried the case to the Constitutional Court, and the court decided against the Chancellor. It ruled that through his action the federal government had violated the constitution in manifold ways, most importantly by ignoring the provisions of Article 30, which specified that state functions not assigned to its jurisdiction remained automatically within the jurisdiction of the Laender.[13]

A third broad function of the Constitutional Court concerns its powers to *decide on petitions charging infringements of the constitutionally guaranteed basic rights of individuals*. These relate to the substantive and procedural guarantees of the Bill of Rights (ARTS. 1–19), whose provisions are "binding as directly valid law on legislation, administration and judiciary" (ART. 1). To encourage Germans to view the Constitution as a close and living guarantor of civil rights, the German legislature has provided that citizens who feel their rights violated by actions (such as acts of legislation) against which there is no alternative route of appeal may complain directly to the Constitutional Court. Such an action involves neither court costs nor even the participation of legal counsel—an ideal situation in which Hans Everyman can bring his woes to the attention of the country's highest tribunal!

The legislators might have foreseen that in a country as legalist as Germany such generous provisions would bring the Court a flood of complaints. Petitions have come in at the rate of over five hundred a year, making about 80 per cent of the business brought before the Court. Many complaints have been of a nuisance variety. Petitions have contended that police regulations relating to the closing of bars constituted infringements of the right of assembly, while prostitutes have argued that regulations against "loitering" conflicted with guarantees relating to the right to freedom of occupation and the right to choose one's place of work.[14] Serious complaints have also come in, and these account for about half of all the Constitutional Court decisions.

In still another role, the court has the power to *deprive groups and individuals of normal constitutional rights if they engage in*

---

[13] *Entscheidungen des Bundesverfassungsgerichts*, XII, 205 ff.
[14] Cole, "The West German Federal Constitutional Court," p. 288.

*enumerated kinds of antidemocratic and anticonstitutional be-
havior.* The court performed this role of constitutional police-
judge in two cases involving the outlawing of antidemocratic
parties. The first of these arose as a consequence of the initial
success achieved by extreme nationalist, neo-Nazi groups in the
period immediately after the Allies' licensing requirements for
the founding of political parties were dropped.

The second case, involving the Communist party, was submitted by the government at the same time, but the decision did
not come for over four years. One difficulty in this case was that
the relevant Basic Law clause clearly applied to neo-Nazi parties,
but its application to a party like the Communists was not self-
evident. Communist delegates had helped write the Basic Law,
and Communist ministers had served in West German Land
governments as late as 1948. But with the increasing tension
between the East and West German regimes, the court found
itself "unable to avoid rendering a decision in the face of continuing pressure from a government with its eye on both internal
and foreign policies." Basing its decision on extensive materials
seized in successive raids on Communist party headquarters, the
court decided that the Communists' campaign could, in the total
perspective, be interpreted in only one way: "It is the result of a
planned program of agitation which seeks to expose the constitutional system of the Federal Republic to slight and contempt . . .
and to shake the people's confidence in the values it has created."
In its decision of August, 1956, the court thus added the Communists to the list of banned parties.[15]

DISAGREEMENT AMONG JUDGES

German Constitutional Court judges engage in many public activities which American and British judges would do at their
peril, such as writing articles on current questions of legal interpretation. But, until recently, there was one important rule of
silence on the Constitutional Court: the judges could not reveal

---

[15] Edward McWhinney, "The German Federal Constitutional Court and
the Communist Party Decision," *Indiana Law Journal*, XXXII (1957),
295–312.

how they voted on a particular case. Indeed, the court gave no published indication whether a decision was reached unanimously or by a closely divided vote. This reticence was dictated by the German assumption that the law is anonymous and impersonal— a fiction that became rather frayed in two bitterly contested cases which brought the divisions among the judges into the open.

One of these cases concerned a complaint of unconstitutionality by *Der Spiegel* magazine against the federal government, arising from the now-infamous attempt by ex-Defense Minister Strauss to suppress the magazine on trumped-up treason charges. By the time the First Senate reached a decision on this case in 1966, it could no longer hide its deep division; it was split four and four, pretty much on the basis of party identification. In that instance, the court published the arguments of both groups of judges. Some time later the Second Senate revealed internal division in deciding whether the Party Finance Law, providing subsidies to political parties, was constitutional in its original form.

Gerhard Leibholz, the distinguished judge who had written most of the senate's earlier decisions affecting political parties, came under sharp attack for publicizing some of his well-known opinions at a meeting of public law specialists. One of the smaller parties seeking to upset the previous line of decisions entered a motion to disqualify Judge Leibholz, and the other judges acceded to the motion. Consequently the Party Finance Law was ruled unconstitutional. In this instance the political pressure was so great that the supposedly sacrosanct vote became a matter of public knowledge. Since reports would leak out in any event, especially in highly political cases, why not publish the positions as well as the dissenting opinions of individual judges? In the past all that dissenters dared do was to write a private dissent to circulate among their court colleagues. But in recent years, "judges jealous of their views and conscious of their skills find the respective submergence and dilution of both in collective opinions increasingly intolerable. These tensions are clearly evident in the Second Senate's recent adoption . . . of the practice of recording the simple vote in a case or specifying that a case has been decided unanimously. This is a monumental departure from German tradition."[16] In 1970 the federal government finally proposed an amendment making it permissible for a judge to publish his deviating minority opinion.

THE COURT AND THE POLITICAL SYSTEM

Whenever a court is set up as a third branch of government, some citizens will question its right to overrule the political decisions of constitutional organs elected by the people, except as a last resort in special circumstances. There is likely to be disagreement between those who argue on behalf of a policy of "judicial restraint" and others who expound a doctrine of "judicial dynamism."

Some German constitutional law experts soon began to fear that the court was using its powers too freely. In discussing its 1954 decisions one law professor took the court sharply to task for allowing itself to express opinions about historical developments under the Nazi regime.

> The great judicial art of moderation, the traditional judicial wisdom of saying only what is necessary for the decision of a particular case, seems not to stand in particularly high regard in our highest court. Rather, there is a tendency toward elaboration and pedagogic explanation which is not suitable. . . . It is never the task of a court, not even of a constitutional court, to enunciate historical lessons which are not pertinent to the case, or which are at least not necessary. . . . The Constitutional Court should remain what it was created: our highest court, the protector of the Constitution. But it should not regard itself as *Praeceptor Germaniae!*[17]

However, commenting that interest group pressure frequently causes law to be more "ad-hoc commands in favor of a certain group than a well-balanced rule promoting the common weal," a member of the court has written that it is "quite natural" that the judiciary should be called upon to exert a countervailing

---

[16] Kommers, "The Federal Constitutional Court," pp. 85–86.

[17] Otto Bachof, "Beamte und Soldaten," *Oeffentliche Verwaltung,* VII (1954), 226.

effect on behalf of "the individual and the whole community."[18] This argument might seem quite alien to an Englishman, but it is familiar and reasonable to an American. Germans, like Americans—although for different reasons—favor the idea of an arbiter who can curb irresponsibility on the part of the political power holders in the executive and the legislature.

The other power holders in the federal government have not always given the court due recognition in protocol. Thus at the annual receptions of the federal President, the head of the Constitutional Court has been placed together with the heads of other federal courts. Since such measures of recognition count in Bonn as they do in Moscow, this slight rankles. The court's strongest support comes from the judges themselves, particularly the prolific writers among their number who publish many articles defending its positions. But whether or not the court is genuinely respected in Bonn, the important thing is, as Kommers notes, that "no decision of the Court has been openly defied as yet by the political regime. No decisions have generated widespread defiance, promoting the strident denunciations that often greet the decisions of the U.S. Supreme Court in sensitive areas."[19] Another ardent champion of the court, Heinz Laufer, concludes that it has succeeded in filling "the abstract formulation" regarding the "free and democratic order" with contents "befitting the best of democratic traditions." He praises the court for having made "decisive contributions" toward the "removal of the ideological and institutional rubble of the National Socialist regime."[20] Laufer credits its flexible interpretation of constitutional norms with easing the governmental process while preventing the abuse of power.

BIBLIOGRAPHY

Baade, H. W., "Social Science Evidence and the Federal Constitutional Court of West Germany," *JP*, XXIII (1961), 421–61.

[18] H. G. Rupp, "Judicial Review in the Federal Republic of Germany," *American Journal of Comparative Law*, IX (1960), 46.
[19] Kommers, "The Federal Constitutional Court," p. 131.
[20] Laufer, *Verfassungsgerichtbarkeit*, p. 585.

240   THE FEDERAL REPUBLIC

Becker, Theodore L., *Comparative Judicial Politics* (New York, 1970).

Dietze, G., "America and Europe, Decline and Emergence of Judicial Review," *Virginia Law Review,* XLIV (1958), 1233 ff.

Entscheidungen des Bundesverfassungsgerichts (Tuebingen, 1952– to date).

Feld, W., "German Administrative Courts," *Tulane Law Review,* XXXVI (1962), 495 ff.

Holm, Hugo J., "Trends in the Jurisprudence of the German Federal Constitution," *American Journal of Comparative Law,* XVI (1968), 570–79.

Kirchheimer, Otto, *Political Justice: The Use of Legal Procedure for Political Ends* (Princeton, 1961).

Kommers, Donald P., "The Federal Constitutional Courts in the West German Political System," in Joel B. Grossman and Joseph Tanenhaus, eds., *Frontiers of Judicial Research* (New York, 1969).

Laufer, Heinz, *Verfassungsgerichtbarkeit und politischer Prozess* (Tuebingen, 1968).

Loewenstein, Karl, "Justice," in E. H. Litchfield, ed., *Governing Postwar Germany* (Ithaca, 1953), pp. 236–62.

Markovits, Inge S., "Civil Law in East Germany: Its Development and Relation to Soviet Legal History and Ideology," *Yale Law Review,* LXXVIII (November, 1968), 1–5.

McWhinney, Edward, *Constitutionalism in Germany and the Federal Constitutional Court* (Leyden, 1962).

Nadelmann, K. H., "Non-Disclosure of Dissents in Constitutional Courts: Italy and West Germany," *American Journal of Comparative Law,* XIII (1964), 268 ff.

Rheinstein, Max, "Approach to German Law," *Indiana Law Journal,* XXXVI (1959), 546 ff.

Rupp, H. G., "Judicial Review in the Federal Republic of Germany," *Amer. Jl. of Comp. Law,* IX (1960), 29 ff.

Schmid, Richard, *Justiz in der Bundesrepublik* (Pfullingen, 1967).

Weyrauch, Walter O., *The Personality of Lawyers: A Comparative Study of Subjective Factors in Law, Based on Interviews with German Lawyers* (New Haven, 1964).

PART THREE

CONFLICTS AMONG THE SEVERAL GERMANIES

10

The New Left, Educational Policies, and the Socialization Turmoil

During the summer of 1970, the twenty-fifth anniversary of the conclusion of World War II was noted with particular attention in the universities of the former Axis powers. The universities were among the few public institutions in those countries that survived the war with relatively unimpaired prestige. Disillusioned with generals, officials, and tycoons, the students listened all the more respectfully to their professors, though their deference was sometimes adulterated by cynicism. Twenty-five years later this relationship had changed beyond recognition. In Japan, student radicals were subjecting their professors to mass bargaining sessions, sometimes lasting over one hundred hours, in order to "burn out their consciousness of prestige." Student occupation of university buildings had become a routine occurrence there as well as in many Italian and German universities. In Germany, aggressive student demonstrators denounced their professors as "*Fachidioten,*" and they managed to undermine the authority systems of universities in a variety of ingenious ways. Though parallels were occurring throughout the Western world, generational alienation and revolt seemed to be most bitter and enduring in these three countries.

Once they recognized that the rebellion against the universities was part of a larger revolt against authority, observers were hard put to explain the differences between developments in Germany and elsewhere. Some agreed with sociologist Erwin Scheuch, who labeled the German student protesters "Anabaptists of the Welfare State" and accused them of surpassing American, French, and British students in their intolerance toward deviating points of view.[1] More sympathetic observers noted that in Germany, family, church, school, university, and other authority patterns which impinged upon the young were more closely tied to the defense of established prerogatives. In order to establish their absurdity, the youth had to go to greater extremes than in other Western countries. As elsewhere, "the key words of the contemporary revolt of youth are 'participation' and 'self-determination.' . . . Authority and domination structures which were previously legitimated through traditional concepts of social discipline or technical efficiency . . . are no longer uncritically accepted."[2]

In the historical homeland of ideologies, the revolting German youth resorted more readily to intellectual armories of an earlier day which they could turn against the pragmatic philosophies that had gained increasing predominance during the prosperous postwar period. Intellectually and culturally, the German New Left has been characterized more by its turning away from the optimism and self-assurance the middle-aged generation had developed during Germany's successful climb out of the rubble. Juergen Habermas may be near the truth in describing the student revolt as "the first bourgeois revolt against the principles of a bourgeois society which has functioned almost successfully by its own standards."[3] In turning away from latter-day German Babbittry, German youth of varying political persuasions have rediscovered the rich lodes of native *Kulturpessimismus*. As one observer wrote in 1969, "Today cultural pessimism constitutes a connecting link between the New Left, ultraconservative groups and the NPD."[4]

---

[1] Erwin K. Scheuch, "Soziologische Aspekte der Unruhe unter den Studenten," *Aus Politik und Zeitgeschichte* (September 4, 1968), pp. 15, 20.

[2] Walter Euchner, "Marxistische Positionen und linke Studentenopposition in der Bundesrepublik," *Aus Politik und Zeitgeschichte* (September 6, 1968), p. 53.

[3] Juergen Habermas, *Protestbewegung und Hochschulreform* (Frankfurt, 1969), p. 175.

[4] Giselher Schmidt, "Die Weltanschauung der Neuen Linken," *Aus Politik und Zeitgeschichte* (August 8, 1968), p. 21.

THE "ANTI-P EFFECTS"

Politically, the critical thrust of radical German youth has focused on some key political concepts and institutions which are closely related and which start with the letter "P."

Pluralist society is the most frequently employed slogan in the conceptual treasury of educated middle-aged postwar Germans. Following American precedent, the term took on positive associations during the postwar period because of its utility as a countermodel to the totalitarian system.[5] Radical critics have suggested that it be consigned to the intellectual junk-heap, because it has served mainly as window dressing to disguise the monopolistic positions of the real power holders and the continuing antagonistic character of class-based societies.

Parliamentarianism is viewed by radical German critics as a transformation mechanism through which the bourgeois constitutional state reduces social antagonism to more "digestible" pluralist elements. Parliamentarianism is viewed as an indispensable appendage of capitalism, particularly in welfare state situations where the state has assumed extensive redistribution functions. The representative techniques of parliamentary systems are seen not as a means of getting citizens to participate but as a technique for keeping the majority of the citizens away from the state's centers of power.[6]

Party democracy became an equally discredited concept among the New Left; they believed that party elites had become so preoccupied with institutionalizing their power positions that they had reduced the possibilities of criticism and meaningful debate within, as well as between, the parties. Within the parties, especially the SPD, the membership was held to "consume and silently obey" the "lonely decisions" of the party leadership, to

[5] Gert Schaefer, "Leitlinien stabilitaetskonformen Verhaltens," in Gert Schaefer and Carl Nedelman, eds., *Der CDU-Staat* (Munich, 1967), p. 242.

[6] Johannes Agnoli and Peter Brueckner, *Die Transformation der Demokratie* (Frankfurt, 1968), p. 25. Kurt L. Shell, in "Extraparliamentary Opposition in Postwar Germany" (*Comparative Politics*, II [July, 1970], 659), also emphasizes that growth of the APO should be seen as marked by the "reception of socialist antiliberal theory" and its "concretization in analyses of the FRG in the context of Western postwar industrial capitalism."

avoid hurting the party's image through public criticism. And the supposedly competitive party leaderships were held to pull their punches even when fulfilling an opposition role because they no longer dared to criticize each others' misdeeds, since the state-financed "party consortium" had led to an even tighter inter-lacing of their interests.[7]

THE ANTI-ANTI-C EFFECT

An intense reaction against anti-Communism caused a tremen-dous wave of skepticism and hostility among students toward important symbolic concepts and institutions. Its pervasiveness in the Federal Republic probably arises from the fact that it is the only Western country which possesses a significant frontier with a Communist state and which has had to compete with the claims of a Communist regime. During the Adenauer period, these factors contributed to the crystallization of a particularly pro-nounced and highly developed spirit of anti-Communist messia-nism. Adenauer expressed this well in an interview with Pope Pius XII in 1960: "I believe that God has set the German people a special task in the present stormy period, that of standing as guardian for the West against the powerful influences which affect us from the East."[8]

No group in German society reacted more strongly to the *Weltanschauung* based on this sort of sentiment than the German youth who came to political awareness after Adenauer's demise. The intense hostility toward the Soviet Union and the Communist countries declined steadily during the 1960's. When, in 1968, a sample of students were asked to name those countries they con-sidered dictatorships, only 23 per cent identified the Soviet Union, whereas 72 per cent named Franco's Spain. In this way, negative models and stereotypes were transferred from the left to the right side of the ideological spectrum. Ties to the Communist move-ment no longer disqualified ideas and individuals automatically. In 1953, Adenauer helped win the election by accusing—falsely —some Social Democrats of maintaining contacts with East Ger-

[7] Rolf Seliger, *Die ausserparlamentarische Opposition* (Munich, 1968), p. 41.
[8] Gustav W. Heinemann, *Verfehlte Deutschlandpolitik: Irrefuehrung und Selbsttaeuschung* (Frankfurt, 1966), p. 157.

many; in 1969, many political figures had good contacts of this sort, but attempts to exploit this fact in the election campaign did not pay off.

Taboos against the acceptance of Marxist models and techniques of analysis were rapidly disappearing, and Marxist writers came to be more widely read. But West German journals and publishing houses with extensive Marxist literature showed little sign of needing or receiving nurture from established Communist organizations. For the most part anti-anti-Communism did not directly favor the growth of pro-Communist groups. Thus the Action for Democratic Progress (ADF) party did very poorly in the 1969 elections, much worse than a smaller neutralist party did in 1965 before the New Left hit its full stride. In general, the Communist Marxist leaders of the GDR and the eclectic Marxist rebels in West Germany took remarkably little notice of each other.

OLDER CRITICS AND THE NEW LEFT

The tendency of German youth to escalate their demands may be explained by their position in society, as well as by the relative scarcity of like-minded radicals from other generations who might be able to restrain them. As in other developed societies with high longevity patterns, school-age youth in Germany in the 1960's constituted only about 20 per cent of the total population. By contrast, in many Asian and African countries similar age groups comprised 50 per cent or more of the population, and the mean age—thirty-five in Germany—was often less than twenty. Other Western countries with similar demographic structures, such as the United States, have long contained strong youth-centered elements in their general culture which tended to give resonance to ideas fashionable among the young. Germany veered toward a youth-centered culture during the Nazi period but reverted sharply to an age-centered status system in the Adenauer era.

When German youth in the late 1960's began to adopt radically different ideals from their elders, they found some sympathizers among the generation of their grandfathers but very few in that of their fathers. A similarity does exist between the political criticisms from the group born after 1945 and from the intellectuals and writers born before 1910. But the intervening generations were very short on radical spirits—except for literary intellectuals —who could empathize with the radical youth. Those of the more advanced middle-aged generation had had their fling at "Anti-P Effects," cultural pessimism, and youthful ebullience during the 1930's, but subsequent experience had cured them of any lingering inclinations of that sort (with the exception of a relatively small number who tended to drift into organizations like the NPD). Finally, the age group born in the 1930's had unusual opportunities to ride the expanding prosperity wave of the 1950's: they had the skills and energies to work up to, or close to, the top of professional ladders, and like their peers in other countries they looked askance at the bearded nonconsumers of the New Left.

After dismissing most postwar German social and political philosophies as "pro-P" apologetics, the New Left looked to older traditions for roots to nurture their critical analyses. They found and devoured Marx, Engels, and Rosa Luxemburg. Their inheritance of the Marxian tradition was particularly influenced by several important mentors who intertwined Marxian dialectic with Freudian and other schools of psychological and sociological analysis. Most prominent among these were Herbert Marcuse, Theodor Adorno, and other members of the Frankfurt Institute of Social Research. It was particularly through these interpreters that the New Left established its rapport with the earlier intellectual giants of German critical philosophy, including Marx and Hegel. The vocabulary they adopted in this process effectively undermined their subsequent plans to convey their radical enthusiasm to the workers, who found it all quite incomprehensible. In their more specific criticism of "Bonn democracy," the younger radicals were also able to relate to dissenting non-Marxian positions like those of philosopher Karl Jaspers.

Jaspers' philippic, *Wohin Treibt die Bundesrepublik?*, popularized negative evaluations of the institution-building accomplishments of the preceding two decades. Although he regarded the Basic Law as technically "a fine piece of work," he charged that "its dominant idea is distrust of the people. It lacks all feeling for the nature of great politics, for the uncertainty of freedom in the storms of history. . . . In 1945 our political and moral task was to found a new state. We have not performed it to this

day. . . . It was the Allies, not the German people, who authorized some Germans to establish the Federal Republic. A plebiscite
of ignorant men held in political darkness is no authorization."[9]
Jaspers also bitterly attacked the "system of oligarchy of parties"
as perpetuating "contempt for the people. It means a tendency
to keep things from the people, to prefer them stupid and ignorant of the oligarchy's goals. . . . The people can be offered
stirring phrases, trite generalities. . . . They can be left permanently passive in their habits, their emotions, their untested
accidental views."[10]

Jaspers' position was closest to that of the New Left when he
placed a positive value on the creation of distrust. "Our state
structure rests upon fear and distrust of the people, but the
people in turn do not sufficiently or effectively show the distrust
of parties, governments and politicians which they ought to feel
at this time. Once again the subject mentality seems to be asserting itself, trusting the government to do right. This is the
responsibility and the guilt of every one of our people. It was our
undoing before 1914, and before 1933." He outlined a sinister
and simple sequence of "development" possibilities for Germany.
"The Federal Republic would produce its own peculiar and presumably indirect type of military dictatorship. This would probably mean the definitive consolidation of the oligarchy of parties,
which the military, in exchange for the fulfillment of its every
wish, would uphold in fact."[11]

Jaspers was vigorously criticized by numerous reviewers,
among them the political scientist Kurt Sontheimer, who denied
that the Federal Republic was an oligarchy of parties or that it
was on the way to becoming a dictatorship. Sontheimer, the
author of a well-known book on antidemocratic thought in the
Weimar Republic, deplored Jaspers' attack on the parties as
merely another version of the antiparty effect which had undermined the legitimacy of the Weimar democracy. But Jaspers
refused to be identified with Armin Mohler, Ruediger Altmann,

[9] Karl Jaspers, *The Future of Germany* (Chicago, 1967), p. 57. This is an
adapted English version of Jaspers' book, with an introduction by
Hannah Arendt.
[10] *Ibid.,* p. 15.
[11] *Ibid.,* pp. 47–49.

and Winfried Martini, reactionary followers of the antidemocratic public law theorist Carl Schmitt. Unlike these critics, he wanted to further democratic freedoms by making Germans aware of the imperfections of their political mechanisms so that they could improve them. He admitted certain parallels to his posture in 1930. However, he posited a different causal relationship between the criticism of Weimar institutions and their downfall. "It was the other way around: Because this criticism was ignored both by the politicians and most voters, they permitted parliamentary conditions to get worse and worse, until finally everybody lost their head except the National Socialists."[12]

EXPERTISE AND THE
EDUCATIONAL SYSTEM

Who is regarded as an expert in various fields of knowledge is, of course, largely a function of the educational system, and it has long been a German characteristic to leave educational policy to education experts. There are few equivalents of parent-teacher associations, and local newspapers have devoted little space to school politics, which, for the most part, were laid down in the Land capital. This lack of critical interest is understandable in view of the generally favorable image that Germans held of their accomplishments in the fields of science and culture. Although difficult performance standards in the academic high schools kept most children from continuing beyond middle or vocational schools, this evoked little pressure from parents. Working-class families were content to have their children switch from school to the excellent apprentice programs run by industry, and there was limited emphasis on seeking upward social mobility via formal education. Teachers did not carry school questions to the public, partly because they had few serious grievances and enjoyed good status and reasonably good pay. In a number of Laender it had even been standard practice to give special grants to teachers going on exchange programs to the United States since it was felt that they could not maintain their standard of living on the salaries paid American teachers.

Then, in the 1960's, education suddenly became one of the

[12] Karl Jaspers, *Antwort: Zur Kritik meiner Schrift "Wohin treibt die Bundesrepublik?"* (Munich, 1967), p. 163.

most talked-about subjects and a hot political issue.[13] Although a similar development occurred in other European countries, the Germans were particularly hard hit by the realization that the rate at which they were producing many kinds of skilled personnel was low in comparison with other countries. Not only had German scientists won very few top awards like the Nobel prize in the postwar period, but many kinds of technical and scientific skills were in low supply. Critics pointed out that very little had been done to restore Germany's leading position in the social sciences, which had been violently interrupted under Hitler. The public became aware of something the specialist had long known —that Germany's scientific achievements were not up to its earlier standards. Concern also developed about the school system. Critics asked how a highly industrialized society could continue to be competitive in a technocratic age when the vast majority of its work force concluded their schooling at age fourteen. A study in 1964 showed that only 17.6 per cent of German youth in the 15–19 age bracket were engaged in full-time schooling—compared to 30.8 per cent in France, 32.3 per cent in Sweden, and 66.2 per cent in the United States—while the percentage of young people receiving at least ten years of education was said to be almost four times as high in East Germany. A minority expressed concern not only about the training of experts, but about education for citizenship. They charged that the introduction of civics courses in high school curricula was not only belated but ill-prepared, since teachers trained in traditional disciplines found it difficult to put the dynamics of social and political processes across to their students.[14]

THE SOCIAL SCIENCES
AND THE STUDENT REVOLT

Because the tendency to delegate responsibility to experts is so strong in the German political culture, German social scientists

[13] The growing importance of educational policy as a campaign issue is borne out by a measure of the comparative space taken up by party statements on the various policy areas in one 1969 brochure: education and science (26 pages), social policy (19 pages), economic policy (16 pages), foreign policy (14 pages).

[14] Thomas Ellwein, *Politische Verhaltenslehre* (Stuttgart, 1967).

have been placed in a highly interesting but often unenviable role by the manifold pressures of a changing society. Searching for specialists equipped to handle ideological protests and social change more peacefully than in the past, the authorities and the educated public turned to the social scientists for answers. But because many of their senior members had little experience in empirical research, these disciplines provided a limited arsenal of analytical techniques and even fewer tested answers. As in other countries, however, they accepted financial and other resources to set up more professorships, institutes, and research and teaching programs. This growth touched off internal conflicts and bitter attacks from the outside. Generalists like Jaspers, who were suspicious of social scientific techniques, aired their doubts widely. Within the universities, some scholars in other departments were jealous of the special favor shown their colleagues. Historians and law professors were particularly outspoken in their denigration of political scientists. The former were afraid that social and political science would replace history as a major subject in high schools, while the latter feared that university graduates with social science degrees might begin to replace law graduates in the civil service. But even as these established disciplines were denouncing the social scientists as aggressive and arrogant intruders, the social science professors found themselves increasingly attacked by their own students as servants of the establishment and defenders of the status quo.

Students majoring in the social sciences, particularly sociology, have been especially prominent challengers of the academic and societal establishments in most Western countries. Whether this is because the study of sociology turns students into radical or revolutionary thinkers, or because radical or revolutionary students are drawn to this subject, thinking it will equip them for their chosen roles, has not yet been answered convincingly. But in the German case, it is very likely that both of these socialization sequences occurred, and the several thousand student militants who supported Rudi Dutschke and Daniel Cohn-Bendit, both sociology students, and provided the local ideological leadership for the radical German student movement during the late 1960's were the result. During the 1960's, enrollment in social science departments increased much more rapidly than in other departments. In 1962 the largest German political science institute, the Otto-Suhr Institute in Berlin, had about two hundred students; by the end of the decade it had about one thousand. Enrollment in sociology courses throughout the Federal Republic increased by 400 to 500 per cent between 1960 and 1968. Most of these students were convinced that they knew what they were looking for, namely a "critical philosophy" and social science methodologies which would lay bare the inadequacies of existing social and political institutions. For a time at some universities—at Frankfurt, where critical sociology was taught by Marxist scholars like Theodor Adorno and Jurgen Habermas, and at Berlin and Marburg, where leading professors were consciously on the left—the students found their expectations fulfilled in lectures and seminars. Elsewhere, where the professors were oriented toward "stability" models or their narrower academic specialties, the students educated each other, mainly on the basis of Marxist literature. Thus the real locus of education was moved from the official seminars to informal student discussion groups, which then later developed into branches of the Socialist German Student Association (SDS).

Lacking much in the way of recent European tradition of empirical social science, the younger German social science professors built heavily on American trends, making names like Seymour Lipset and Talcott Parsons familiar ones for German college sophomores. The students quickly put their fledgling talents to work demolishing the sacred American texts. Thus, sociology student Stephan Leibfried used an attack on Lipset to buttress his general criticism of American universities. Hammering away at liberal pluralist theorists, Leibfried charged that Lipset sought to throttle student political activity and encouraged students to copy his model of compliance with the conformity-producing patterns of American "knowledge factories."[15]

The student demonstrators developed and refined techniques of partially breaking rules in order to show up the weak spots of the regime and expose the authoritarian reactions of the establishment. In this probing, they were encouraged by some radical

[15] Stephan Leibfried, *Die Angepasste Universitaet: Zur Situation der Hochschulen in der Bundesrepublik und den U.S.A.* (Frankfurt, 1968), p. 103.

professors who praised these initiatives as a means of weakening repressive structures and practices. But even sympathizers like Juergen Habermas objected when, in the aftermath of the attack on Rudi Dutschke and the Easter Demonstrations of 1968, portions of the SDS resorted to the large-scale use of force to take over universities and other institutions. He charged that the SDS leaders had lost contact with reality in confusing the symbolic new demonstration techniques with direct revolutionary struggle, and he maintained that "each and every one of the previously accepted indicators of a revolutionary situation is lacking."[16] To express their displeasure at this criticism, the extreme radicals occupied the Frankfurt Institute where Habermas teaches and demeaned and ridiculed Theodor Adorno, the senior Marxian professor there whose writings had introduced them to the "critical philosophy" in the first place.

Among those who took advantage of the troubled situation in German social science faculties was the federal minister of research in the Kiesinger cabinet, Gerhard Stoltenberg. A technological manager by orientation (he had briefly worked for Krupp), Stoltenberg became a spokesman for conservative groups by personally attacking the left-wing professors associated with the student left. He asserted that the social science students were radicalized by the lack of professional opportunities after graduation, but instead of remedying this situation, Stoltenberg proposed in a May, 1969, speech that public funds for expanding social science education and research be withheld. He wanted the funds to be invested in programs, such as those in the natural sciences and engineering, which would produce trained personnel of direct use to the economy.

When asked whether Germany should concentrate on turning out computer specialists or "critical social scientists," Stoltenberg opted for the computer specialists and won applause from many who shared his priority for keeping German industry competitive. Technically oriented scientists, however, expressed deep reservations about the simple-minded calculus. One of his critics was Karl Steinbuch, director of the institute of computer and com-

[16] Habermas, *Protestbewegung,* p. 197.

munication science at the University of Karlsruhe, who reviewed a book of the minister's speeches. He questioned the minister's fairness in accusing the students of following ideologies, while pretending that the principles of the established policy were "non-ideological and connected to the Absolute by a special umbilical cord." He confessed that after reading Stoltenberg's book he was "more disturbed than ever before: How can we ever hope to achieve a rational and peaceful solution of our social problems when the responsible politicians make so little effort to understand the problem of a suppressed minority."[17]

For some time it appeared that Stoltenberg's program for exiling critical social scientists to the fringes of academia might be implemented, despite the numerous young social scientists of various political colorations whom the German universities were turning out. German sociologists, in particular, felt obliged to take drastic action to avoid being caught in a crossfire between reaction at the top and revolutionary actionism from below. In April, 1969, the German Sociological Association, under the chairmanship of Ralf Dahrendorf, took the far-reaching step of advising against the creation of further sociology programs and recommending that universities abolish undergraduate sociology majors in favor of multidisciplinary social science degrees. The SPD/FDP election victory reduced the pressures somewhat, since progressive leaders in these parties were more optimistic about the long-term social utility of the bearded and arrogant social science students. Thus the program of some SPD education ministers to introduce political and social science as an obligatory high school area of concentration promised to create more openings for social science graduates at that level. But the Socialist leaders were apparently wary of getting too involved in the academic wars. The appointment of a nonparty federal research minister to succeed Stoltenberg was perhaps partly due to the realization that an independent could more safely be exposed to negative feedback in this area than an established party politician.

---

[17] *Der Spiegel,* April 15, 1969. See also Berndt Franke and Thomas Neumann, eds., *Antworten auf Stoltenberg: Zur Wissenschaftspolitik in der Bundesrepublik* (Frankfurt, 1968).

THE BATTLE FOR THE UNIVERSITIES

When he took office as federal minister of research in October, 1969, Professor Ernst Leussink's ability to resolve the crises of German universities was not overestimated by knowledgeable observers. As chairman of a very influential body in German education, the *Bildungsrat* (Educational Council), Leussink had acquired an intimate knowledge of the many competing interest groups and bureaucracies which had fought over alternative reform plans in the preceding ten years. But knowledge was only partially supported by political power. Although the revised finance laws had increased the federal government's role in university expansion, the universities still remained primarily under the jurisdiction of the Land ministers and parliaments. And most of the Laender had delayed action for years because they were unable to reconcile competing claims. Baden-Wuerttemberg finally forced through a new university law, but it was denounced by students and junior faculty for its failure to break up the full professors' monopoly of power.

The battle over the German universities was increasingly complicated as two major, and numerous minor, interest groups pressed for fundamental reform of the antiquated university structures. Had it not been for the period of reaction to Nazism, Germany might have led other European countries in reshaping its nineteenth-century elite universities to the demands of twentieth-century mass education. After 1945, university autonomy became a sacred object precisely because the Nazis had tried to break it down, and the concept of autonomy covered most of the professorial and other privileges which impeded the growth of a university structure that could effectively provide both basic research and the teaching of hundreds of thousands of students.

After 1945, universities expanded. Tuebingen University grew from a faculty of 80 professors and 80 assistants in 1931 to 230 professors and 750 assistants in 1967, but growth was not accompanied by reform. Professors still ran their own institutes rather than joining with their colleagues in departments. Student programs were quite unregulated, and the teaching and examining process was haphazard. In this context management specialists began discussing the need for fundamental reform, especially through study committees made up of organization experts from industry and leading professors. Their deliberations produced a number of models designed primarily to rationalize the education and degree-granting process, essentially by making German procedures more like the American system. Eventually, recommendations sent to the Education Council called for separation of undergraduate and graduate education, the limitation of student enrollment norms, specified testing times and requirements, and so on.

But in 1964, advice also came from another quarter. In a well-researched volume, *Universität in der Demokratie,* the SDS joined the onslaught on the nineteenth-century "Humboldt model," which had degenerated into an oligarchy of chairholders and a monocracy of institute directors. However, the SDS perspective was different from that of the administrative modernizers. It called for "one-third parity representation" for students, junior faculty, and professors in the powerful faculty senates and other university bodies, as well as for the "collegiality principle" in departments and institutes. Increasingly, the SDS and its student sympathizers resisted the rationalization measures, which they claimed would turn German universities into chrome-and-cement copies of American degree factories. They objected to the priority given to the education of specialists, as well as the disincentives that were to be introduced for the generalist who wanted to roam from subject to subject at his own pace.

In 1965, the German Rectors Conference voted 23–4 to follow the advice of the rationalizers and place a limit on the time a student could work toward a particular degree. The Education Council endorsed this change and urged abandonment of the "assumption of maturity which German universities had followed by allowing even freshmen complete freedom in selecting their study programs," and suggested prescribed and recommended course sequences. This action was bitterly attacked by sociologists like Habermas, who helped establish the critical counterposition that most students, in and outside of the left, subsequently adopted. Habermas deplored the tightened regulations, which could discourage students from following interests outside their initially selected major. Though he admitted that the existing unstructured situation caused most student difficulty, he claimed that the disorientation and frustrations of the student in such an atmosphere could lead to a salutary posing of new problems and also dissolve dogmatically established associations.[19] This position, which is inherently suspicious of disciplinary and other boundaries on knowledge, places great value on *Reflexion,* a learning process that undermines and changes established categories. The process became a cornerstone of the critical, neo-Marxist philosophy that attracted many students, and in the name of which they increasingly abused their specialist professors as *Fachidioten.*

NEW UNIVERSITY STRUCTURES

By 1970 the contours of a new German university model were beginning to appear. At its formal apex stood a university president elected by a university electoral body in which professors, junior academic "assistants," and students each held one-third of the electoral power. As the assistants made common cause with Leftist-led students, assistant candidates in their thirties easily defeated senior professors, first at Berlin, next at Hamburg, then at other universities. Venerable and omnipotent faculty senates were abolished and replaced by departmental structures in which most important course and research-related decisions were made by bodies in which student and assistant representatives had significant representation. Thus the great power previously held by full professors was greatly reduced, to the point where some of them charged infringement of their constitutional rights. Many other professors, especially the liberal ones, found that the amount of time taken up by endless discussions on policies left them no time for research pursuits anyway.

The most general outcome of this transformation was a great reduction in the status differences that had previously been so marked. Assistants not only saw their colleagues chosen for top administrative positions but also benefited from a change in status and nomenclature which incorporated them into the faculty structure by giving them the title of Assistant Professor on the American model. German students who previously had sat mute at the feet of professorial lecturers now were given greater opportunity

[19] Habermas, *Protestbewegung,* p. 105.

to participate actively in class discussions. To what extent their representatives should have the power to veto teaching and research plans of professors remained a moot point. At universities like Hamburg it became general policy for outside research contracts to be subject to the approval or rejection of institute or departmental councils, where students and assistants had considerable power. In this instance, the university constitution provided that a professor's freedom to conduct his own research should be interpreted to mean that he was entitled to claim space and limited research personnel for small research projects, but that larger ones required the endorsement of institute councils.

Social Democratic Land governments took the lead in passing new university laws that provided the basis for the reorganization, and this led in many cases to the selection of social scientists to key policy-making positions. In Lower Saxony a radical political scientist, Peter von Oertzen, was appointed Minister of Culture. In Hessen the sociologist Ludwig von Friedeburg, a colleague of Habermas' in the Institute for Social Research, was also appointed Minister of Culture, and pushed through legislation distasteful to most of his fellow professors. This elevation to administrative office of a member of the Frankfurt School culminated its critical influence, for with Habermas' departure from Frankfurt the "School" essentially disbanded.

Reaction to these changes among the majority of German professors was of course mixed. A considerable number of well-known ones resigned their positions at the embattled German universities in order to accept appointments abroad or to join research institutes without university connections. Their decisions reflected a prevalent fear that the universities would become so preoccupied with teaching and altercation that little scope for research activity would remain.

The fear of this development caused a number of professors to direct a complaint to the Constitutional Court, due to be adjudicated in 1971, on the grounds that the new university laws unconstitutionally circumscribed their right to freedom of research as guaranteed by Article 5 of the Basic Law. Another group of professors met in Bonn in June, 1970, to found a Federation for Freedom of Scientific Inquiry, which was intended to serve as an instrument of solidarity and counterattack against the radical reformers. The group's initiators were political scientists who were alumni of the Freiburg institute that, during the Adenauer period, had been headed by the doyen of conservative German social science, Arnold Bergstraesser. They were joined by other academics who had concentrated on the study of the rise of Nazism, such as the historian Erich Nolte, and who perceived awful similarities between the two periods. The polarization thus induced threatened to accentuate a situation in which "progressive" professors would receive appointments in universities in SPD-controlled Laender, while "conservatives" would be drawn to universities in Laender where the CDU/CSU influenced appointments.

MOBILIZING THE TEEN-AGERS

Once in high gear at the universities, the politicization of youth quickly spread downward to the high schools, where the blue flower of rebellion was nurtured by the many frustrations of German adolescents. At this level, structure and facilities are not the major problems, and an American student at a German high school would notice fewer academic differences than a transfer student at a university. Rather, the German schools, which operate according to rules laid down by the Laender, have found it difficult to meet the social needs of pupils.

In particular, the schools have not filled the increasing gap between the contemporary adolescent and his family. They have also remained aloof from social reality and, in the view of critics, continued to perceive themselves "as an authoritarian and remote complement to the necessarily *lebensfremd* family education in the home."[20] As a result, teachers and parents are denounced as repressive with equal acerbity and chagrin in such teen-age "rebel" magazines as *Underground,* which has found a ready market since its foundation in 1968. One continuing section is devoted to reports, sent in by readers, of teachers' misbehavior and maltreatment of students. Comic strips deal with tough "teenyboppers" who plant bombs to do away with teachers they

[20] Klaus Horn, "Zur Formierung der Innerlichkeit," in Schaefer and Nedelman, *Der CDU-Staat,* p. 197.

TABLE 10–1:   ADOLESCENT MODELS: CHANGE IN PREFERENCES
BETWEEN THE SEVENTH AND ELEVENTH GRADES (IN PER CENT)

Personality Whose Signed Autograph Most Desired	Seventh Grade %	Eighth Grade %	Ninth Grade %	Tenth Grade %	Eleventh Grade %
John F. Kennedy	30.5	32.4	39.6	32.1	40.4
Franz Beckenbauer	20.3	17.8	8.5	2.7	0.7
The Beatles	20.1	11.5	10.0	7.6	2.0
Albert Schweitzer	9.1	6.7	6.7	10.3	8.9
Mao Tse-tung and Adolf Hitler	4.0	9.6	12.0	15.8	27.4
All others*	16.1	23.0	23.2	31.5	20.6
TOTAL	100	100	100	100	100

* The others named were Brigitte Bardot, James Bond, Soraya, Udo Juergens, Rudi Altig, and Wernher von Braun.

particularly dislike but shrug their shoulders when the whole school blows up.

PUPILS AND TEACHERS

An empirical study of pupils' attitudes toward teachers found that the "principle of partner-like collaboration and mutual recognition" was very underdeveloped. The pupils saw the school mainly as "socially isolated space" with little relevance to their nonschool and leisure activities. Pupils were found to adjust to the pedagogical style of the teacher, since they recognized his role as a transmitter of knowledge and the need for a well-founded preparation for later job training. But the teachers were unable to come up to the social-emotional expectations of the pupils.

This study revealed some very suggestive data about adolescent hero-figures, and the way their popularity changed with age. John F. Kennedy was the single figure whose autograph was most desired by pupils from the seventh through eleventh grades. Albert Schweitzer was another figure admired by the adult world who maintained his attraction for a significant minority in all age groups. But the popularity of these two figures was slightly exceeded among the seventh-graders by the Beatles and a leading

TABLE 10–2:   TOLERATION LEVELS AMONG TEEN-AGERS

| | PERCENTAGE OF RESPONDENTS IN | | |
CHARACTERISTIC	Ninth Grade	Tenth Grade	Thirteenth Grade
High toleration of atheism	44	67	85
High toleration of "GDR recognition"	49	65	87
High toleration of "antidemocratism"	20	27	44
FREQUENCY OF DISCUSSION OF STUDENT UNREST			
Often	9	13	32
Sometimes	50	56	54
Never	41	31	14

SOURCE: "Correlates of Dissent Toleration among West German Youths," a paper reporting on the research of Hans N. Weiler, Stanford University.

German sports star. In the eleventh grade, however, the attraction of these popular culture idols had almost disappeared. What appeared instead as the heroes of these teen-agers were sinister political figures known to be taboo in the adult world. Thus, by the eleventh grade, more than a quarter of the pupils said they most desired autographs from Mao Tse-tung or Adolf Hitler. The authors interpreted this as a protest against adult inhibitions and linked it to the NPD's successful appeal to portions of the youth.[21]

However, a more recent and systematic study of high school students' political attitudes by Hans N. Weiler seems to show that toleration for all kinds of views that clash with adult norms increases markedly during these years. He found that whereas fifteen-year-olds were split about evenly as to how tolerant they were in regard to those who advocated atheism or recognition of the GDR, nine out of ten nineteen-year-olds in the last year of high school tended to be highly tolerant of such dissenters. The

[21] Thilo Castner, *Schueler im Autoritaetskonflikt* (Neuwied, 1969), p. 97.

percentage of those who were tolerant of dissenters from democratic values also increased, though the absolute levels were lower. This investigation showed that the frequency of discussion of student unrest and related controversies also increased markedly in the course of these high school years, with 86 per cent of the nineteen-year-olds reporting occasional or frequent discussion of the topic.

Since 1967, left-wing agitation among high school students has been largely coordinated by the Action Center for Independent and Socialist Students (AUSS), which was founded under the guidance of Helmut Reiche, a former SDS chairman and author of *Sexuality and Class Struggle.* Following the line that for "suppressed and apolitical pupils discussions about sexual problems would be more effective triggers of protest and demonstrations than the Vietnam war," the AUSS organized sex discussions in schools, which, when forbidden by principals, led to student attacks on the legitimacy of school authority. Reiche acknowledged frankly that in this instance the Springer press had been correct when it headlined the organization's tactic as "Catching Mice with Sex."[22] Sexual frustrations among older high school students may well be particularly strong in Germany, since studies have shown that advanced high school and university students often have their first sexual experiences as much as five or six years later than young people of lower educational (and social) levels.

---

[22] Hans-Juergen Haug and Hubert Maessen, *Was wollen die Schueler: Politik im Klassenzimmer* (Frankfurt, 1969), p. 78. Naturally these developments made school news in local German papers very interesting. One member of the older generation has carefully collected the relevant clippings to illustrate the infamy of the youthful rebels. See Kuno Barth, *Die Revolutionierung der Schueler, Hintergruende, Ziele, Abwehr* (Mannheim, 1969), especially pp. 146–48 for a typical description of how some radical students of Adorno brought sexual enlightenment to the small town of Homburg.

BIBLIOGRAPHY

Agnoli, Johannes, and Peter Brueckner, *Die Transformation der Demokratie* (Frankfurt, 1968).

Bermann, Uwe, Rudi Dutschke, Wolfgang Lefevre, and Bernd Rabehl, *Rebellion der Studenten; oder die neue Opposition* (Hamburg, 1968).

Castner, Thilo, *Schueler im Autoritaetskonflikt* (Neuwied, 1969).

Euchner, Walter, "Zum Demokratieverständnis der Neuen Linken," *Aus Politik und Zeitgeschichte* (August 9, 1969), pp. 3–17.

Franke, Berndt, and Thomas Neumann, *Antworten auf Stoltenberg* (Frankfurt, 1968).

Glaser, Hermann, and Karl Heinz Stahl, eds., *Opposition in der Bundesrepublik: Ein Tagungsbericht* (Freiburg, 1968).

Habermas, Juergen, *Protestbewegung und Hochschulreform* (Frankfurt, 1969).

Haug, Hans-Juergen, and Hubert Maessen, *Was wollen die Schueler? Politik im Klassenzimmer* (Frankfurt, 1969).

Hitzer, Friedrich, and Reinhard Optiz, *Alternativen der Opposition* (Cologne, 1969).

Jaspers, Karl, *The Future of Germany* (Chicago, 1967).

———, *Antwort: Zur Kritik meiner Schrift "Wohin treibt die Bundesrepublik"* (Munich, 1967).

Leibfried, Stephan, *Die Angepasste Universitaet: Zur Situation der Hochschulen in der Bundesrepublik und den USA* (Frankfurt, 1968).

Merritt, Richard L., "The Student Protest Movement in West Berlin," *Comparative Politics*, I (1969), 516–33.

Richert, Ernst, *Die radikale Linke* (Berlin, 1969).

Robinsohn, Saul, and Caspar Kuhlman, "Two Decades of Non-Reform in West German Education," *Comparative Education Review*, XI (1967), 311–30.

Scheuerl, Hans, *Die Gliederung des deutschen Schulwesens* (Stuttgart, 1968).

Schulz, Gerhard, ed., *Was wird aus der Universitaet: Standpunkte zur Hochschulreform* (Tuebingen, 1969).

Seeliger, Rolf, *Die ausserparlamentarische Opposition* (Munich, 1968).

Shell, Kurt L., "Extraparliamentary Opposition in Postwar Germany," *Comparative Politics*, II (July, 1970), 653–80.

Sontheimer, Kurt, "Student Opposition in Western Germany," *Government and Opposition*, III, 1 (Winter, 1968), 49–67.

Winkler, Hans-Joachim, ed., *Das Establishment anwortet der APO* (Opladen, 1968).

11

Socialism in the GDR: A Rival Sibling Achieves Maturity

In November, 1969, shortly after the German Democratic Republic had celebrated its twentieth anniversary, a West German Chancellor for the first time officially acknowledged the existence of "two states" on German soil. Although this acknowledgment by Willy Brandt fell short of diplomatic recognition of the East German state, it did mark the end of the intransigent policy of nonacknowledgment pursued by all of his Christian Democratic predecessors in the Bonn Chancellery. Previously, Bonn had sought to dismiss the smaller, Communist-led rival with such designations as "Soviet-Occupied Zone" (SBZ), *"Spalterstaat"* (Separatists' State), or "so-called German Democratic Republic." Brandt's moves toward acceptance of the Oder-Neisse line also promised to eliminate Bonn's practice of referring to the GDR as "Central Germany," a term which implied continued claims on the Polish-occupied territories. It thus became clear that in the 1970's West Germans would have to get used to the fact that East Germany bordered the Federal Republic on its west and Poland on its east, and that the GDR constituted a state with as good a claim to legitimacy as its neighbors.

A STATE WINS LEGITIMATION

When it was created in 1949, the German Democratic Republic (GDR), like the other East European Communist-dominated states, considered itself a "People's Democracy" at an intermediary stage of development toward a genuinely socialist state on the Marxist-Leninist model. The East German Communists claimed legitimacy for their incomplete proletarian dictatorship by virtue of the numerical and political dominance of workers and peasants. After the elimination of "class enemies" and "reactionaries" and the pushing forward of collectivization, the Communists declared, in 1952, that they were beginning to lay the groundwork for a "Socialist" order and later, in 1958, that this groundwork had been completed. In 1968, a new constitution proclaimed the Socialist state as achieved, and posited that "the social system of Socialism is continuously being perfected."[1]

The GDR has been hailed as the first state in German history in which the working class possessed power. "For the first time in the history of the German people the talents and capacities of the broad masses can develop freely. There has developed a powerful increase in the awareness, initiative, activity and work-discipline of the workers, farmers and other productive citizens."[2] In the 1968 constitution, the GDR identifies itself as "a socialist state of German nation[ality] . . . under the leadership of the working class and its Marxist-Leninist party."

The GDR's twentieth anniversary, celebrated on October 7, 1969, was marked with much more grandiloquence than was the anniversary of the Federal Republic some months earlier. The Ministry of Trade arranged for a special "holiday sale" at which high-quality clothes were sold at bargain prices. The military publishing house issued a 380-page book of lyrics that celebrated the state's virtues under the title "Thou, Our Love," while on billboards everywhere a pretty girl toasted herself with the exclamation, "I am twenty."

In a sense the hoopla was justified; reaching the age of twenty was much more of an achievement for the GDR than for the Federal Republic. For much of its first decade, its chances of surviving seemed slim. It had inherited a smaller industrial base than the FRG, and a greater proportion of that was taken away by the Russians as reparations. Then, in 1953, came the workers' revolt, which had to be put down by Russian tanks. Throughout

---

[1] Michael Bothe, "The 1968 Constitution of East Germany," *American Journal of Comparative Law*, XVII, 2 (1969), 268–91.

[2] From 1957 GDR law relating to local government.

the 1950's, the GDR lost many of its best workers to the West, a process that did not slow down until the Berlin Wall was closed in August, 1961. Only after the mass exodus to the West was stopped by police-state methods could the GDR begin to consolidate its political and economic systems.

It was during the 1960's that Walter Ulbricht, the GDR's dominant leader, brought his state up to the level of archrival Adenauer's West Germany in terms of political stabilization and economic growth. Particularly outstanding were the economic achievements, which, as they had done earlier in the West, helped to make the system politically acceptable to its own citizens. Between 1950 and 1969, the GDR managed to increase production by almost 500 per cent, becoming the world's eighth largest industrial power. Within the Communist bloc, the GDR ranked second in industrial production after the Soviet Union, and it outstripped all other Socialist countries in per capita national income, as the comparative figures in Table 11–1 show.

TABLE 11–1:   PER CAPITA INCOME IN THE GDR AND OTHER SOCIALIST COUNTRIES (INDEX: POLISH PCI = 100)

	1950	1965
Romania	48	82
Bulgaria	53	83
Soviet Union	82	115
Poland	100	100
Hungary	104	100
East Germany	115	165
Czechoslovakia	151	144

SOURCE: Stanley Zemelka, "The Problems of Specialization in Comecon," *East Europe*, XVIII, 5 (May, 1969), 11.

Because of their achievements in the mid-1960's, the East Germans were envied and admired throughout the Socialist bloc. Communist propaganda claimed that the *real* "Economic Miracle" had occurred not in Erhard's Federal Republic but in Ulbricht's GDR. East Germany began to draw many foreign "guest" workers. Just as West Germany had tackled its labor shortage by importing workers from Italy and Spain, East Germany began to bring in large numbers of workers from industrially under-developed countries like Hungary. By late 1968, some 10,000 Hungarians were working in East Germany, and the number was supposed to increase to 16,000 by 1972.[3] But partly because of the constant denigration of East Germany by Bonn information agencies, these achievements were scarcely noticed in the Federal Republic. A West German public opinion survey in 1966 revealed that half the West German population was unaware that the GDR produced any automobiles, while an equal proportion believed quite mistakenly that bicycles and baby carriages were still rationed "in the East." Most Federal Republicans continued to regard GDR inhabitants as "poor cousins," who required charity parcels from the West in order to survive. This attitude came to be resented even by East Germans who were indifferent to Communism but identified with the social system in which they had invested so much labor. Thus both the regime's economic achievement and reaction against unwarranted propaganda from the West gradually engendered a higher level of acceptance, and even support, of an initially despised political regime. The data in Table 11–2, based on an analysis of relatively frank conversations that American author Hans Apel conducted on successive visits to the GDR, seem to bear out a gradual decline of opposition and ambivalent feelings among East Germans during the 1960's.

Table 11–2:   Support and Opposition to the East German Regime, 1962–66

Posture toward Regime	1962 %	1964 %	1966 %
Loyal	37	51	71
Opponent	28	23	14
Ambivalent—"goes along"	35	26	15

source: Interpretative analysis based upon some 650 interviews conducted in East Germany by Hans Apel. Arthur M. Hanhardt, Jr., *The German Democratic Republic* (Baltimore, 1968), p. 124.

[3] Sandor Kiss, "Hungary's Gastarbeiter in East Germany," *East Europe,* XVIII, 10 (October, 1969), 8.

In the course of the 1960's, large sections of the population have become reconciled to the regime and integrated into the society, less through the instrumentality of explicitly political organizations like the parties than through the medium of the workplace. By granting not only fringe benefits but better working conditions and higher pay rates, the regime has developed in most workers a loyalty at least to the plant or work group within which they utilize their skills. "The pressure that led to the provision of fairer working conditions has had a deideologizing effect. One likes to perform a good day's work, both for its own sake and because of the bonus involved, rather than 'in honor of Ulbricht's birthday' or because of 'Friendship toward the Soviet Union.' "[4] Those who now feel "apolitical," according to Richert, see no acceptable solution to the problem of unification, or, especially since August, 1961, any personal opportunity to opt for another alternative. "Since then a new tendency has developed, for which one finds support both in Universities like those of East Berlin, Jena and Dresden as well as in the large factories in Magdeburg and Leipzig. This tendency expresses itself in a striving toward a pragmatic kind of 'people's democracy' of the Polish, Hungarian or possibly even Yugoslav type."[5] The reorientation of potential opponents into pragmatic reformers of the regime has permitted the latter to reduce its reliance on force and on frenetic mobilization drives. Should, therefore, the East German regime still be classified as totalitarian? In an attempt to answer this question, sociologists attached to the West Berlin Institute of Political Science completed a series of detailed studies of segments of East German society, which were published in 1964. The editor of the volume concluded that the regime was in the process of transmuting itself from a totalitarian into an authoritarian type.[6]

[4] Ernst Richert, *Das zweite Deutschland* (Guetersloh, 1964), p. 238.
[5] *Ibid.*
[6] Peter C. Ludz, ed., *Studien und Materialien zur Soziologie der DDR* (Opladen, 1964).

THE GDR'S "STATE PARTY": THE SED

The SED (Sozialistische Einheitspartei Deutschlands), which the 1968 constitution speaks of as entrusted with the leadership of the state, was created in 1946 by the merger of the Communist and Social Democratic parties of the Soviet Occupation zone and East Berlin. Toward the end of 1945, the Communists and their Soviet sponsors realized they stood little chance of winning in the forthcoming free elections. This awareness led them to issue a call for the putting forward of joint Communist-Social Democratic candidates and, subsequently, the suggestion for a complete merger of the two parties. This proposal was bitterly opposed by the Social Democratic leaders in the other zone, and overwhelmingly defeated in a referendum among SPD members in West Berlin. However, some SPD leaders in East Berlin and the Soviet zone reacted favorably; some went along out of convictions based on their Nazi period experiences, some because of pressure from the Soviet Occupation officials. After prolonged struggles, the two party leadership groups implemented the merger in April, 1946, and the SED emerged under the joint chairmanship of Socialist Otto Grotewohl and Wilhelm Pieck, chairman of the Soviet-zone Communist party.

Starting in 1948, the SED quickly transformed itself, as well as the political structure of the Soviet zone, along lines closely resembling Communist practice elsewhere. It gave up the idea of becoming a mass party and sought instead to transform itself into a highly disciplined, efficient mechanism, responding easily to direction from above and capable of controlling both state and economy. Many party members who had joined out of opportunism but lacked the qualities of "good Communists" were purged. New members were accepted only after undergoing prolonged periods of candidacy. The need to change the SED into a "cadre party" was underscored by the adoption, in the 1949–50 Two-Year Plan, of the principle of the fully planned economy. The consolidation and development of a vast economic bureaucracy to coordinate and administer the planning mechanism called for large numbers of reliable, trained administrators, which only the SED could supply. Ideological purity was emphasized. Those Communists who had earlier advocated a distinctly German road to socialism were forced to recant their heretical views, while Ulbricht and other Soviet-trained leaders emphasized the need for unhesitating acceptance of orthodox Leninist-Stalinist doctrine.

At the same time, the SED established itself as the fountainhead of political truth. In 1950, in discussing the resolutions of the SED party conference for the benefit of civil servants, Ulbricht dealt with the suggestion that these were after all *only* the resolutions of a party. "That is true. But it happens to be the conference of a party which is the spearhead of the German people, the only party which follows a progressive scientific doctrine. . . . Its resolutions constitute a document of the highest significance . . . with which all democratic forces must concern themselves."[7] And well they might, for no parties, trade unions, or women's organizations could afford to take positions differing from those of the SED. All such groups were now united in an organization called the "National Front," where the policy of the SED was imposed on the rest. In 1949, free competitive elections were discontinued; instead, the National Front set up unified lists that were submitted to the voters without an alternative choice. All the parties and other kinds of organizations were allotted specific quotas within the list, but the SED's own candidates and SED members running on trade union and other "mass organization" tickets were preponderant. The two middle-class parties—the CDU and LDP—were augmented by the licensing of two additional middle-class parties—the National Democratic party (NDPD) and the German Peasants' party (DBD). Run by tested pro-Communists, these new parties proceeded to rival the two older parties in their efforts to "guide" the nonworking-class, non-Socialist part of the electorate.

The fact that these smaller parties have been encouraged to remain in existence has produced a curious paradox: since 1965 there have been a larger number of parties represented in the parliament of the "one-party" GDR than in the "multiparty" Federal Republic. Their persistence is especially curious because the bourgeois and petty-bourgeois elements they were originally created to "represent" no longer exist in the official GDR ideology, since almost all private property in agriculture and small

[7] Walter Ulbricht (9).

business has been eliminated. Certainly the small number of self-employed artisans and retailers do not justify the maintenance of these parties, which are not even likely to be useful in developing contacts with groups in West Germany. Presumably their utility lies in providing educational and feedback mechanisms for those ex-bourgeois strata which the SED cannot reach. In 1959 a leading Communist remarked that the "multiparty system" was justified as long as "the reeducation of the entire population in the spirit of Communism has not been completely carried through."[8] Thus these curious structures continue to serve as "extra-Socialist Ombudsmen" for the ideologically backward components of a society which has become accustomed to a relatively painless system of "consultative authoritarianism."

The fact that the GDR leadership found a flourishing economy the most efficient technique for strengthening its political legitimacy also implied significant adjustment in the structure and functions of the SED. If the economic planners and experts responsible for the economic success were to have the necessary authority, they needed status and autonomy vis-à-vis the old-line Communist functionaries who had been dominating the party apparatus. Ludz believes this led in the 1960's to the evolution of a loosely organized "counterelite" of experts and intellectuals with a joint interest in limiting the powers of the "strategic elite," those holding the orthodox power positions in the party secretariat.[9] The attempt to accommodate the rival leadership groups eventually loosened up the top levels of the party organization. And the need to lessen the gulf separating the party from the bulk of the population dictated a parallel strategy on the party's lower levels. If the workers were to become even more dedicated and efficient, they had to be convinced that the party's officials merited their trust. All this placed greater demands on party officials and made a full-time career in the party bureaucracy somewhat less attractive to ambitious young men with alternative opportunities in the government administration or in state enterprises.[10] How-

[8] Rodrich Kulbach and Helmut Weber, *Parteien im Blocksystem der DDR* (Guetersloh, 1969), p. 34.

[9] Peter C. Ludz, *Parteielite im Wandel* (Cologne, 1968).

[10] *Ibid.*, p. 258.

ever, these other careers also entailed SED membership and activity.

Meanwhile, more young and more well-educated people were brought into the party and moved up its complex hierarchy of offices. The average age of the party's mass membership of 1.7 million was considerably lower in the late 1960's than it had been earlier. In 1966, the 31–40 age group constituted 25.1 per cent of the membership, compared to 18.7 per cent in 1950. Between 1961 and 1966, the proportion of party members described as intellectuals increased from 8.7 per cent to 12.3 per cent, while that of less-educated "employees" declined markedly.[11] Within two years, the number of university and technical school graduates in the party doubled (130,000 in 1964). In subsequent years, the proportion of graduates approached 75 per cent in the staff of the party central committee, 50 per cent in the staffs of the party regional secretariats, and 25–30 per cent in the staffs of local party secretaries.[12] Because well-educated, hardworking SED members can rise very quickly in many branches of party and state activity, many East German officials are considerably younger than their West German equivalents. In 1967, the average age of the GDR Council of Ministers was less than forty-five years, almost ten years younger than that of the West German cabinet at that time.

There is much to say for Ludz's thesis that the younger technological-managerial leaders who climbed rapidly to high positions in the mid-1960's constituted something of a "counterelite." They certainly succeeded in breaking down many previous taboos very quickly. Western theories and models that related to East German problems could be discussed openly and without continuous reference to the earlier clichés of blanket condemnation. This freer atmosphere derived from the introduction of econometric and other techniques which broadened the conceptual repertoire of party discussions. At the local levels the previously all-powerful first party secretaries found their influence checked by new commissions that insisted on a more rational evaluation of social and technical problems. But Richert is probably correct

[11] *Ibid.,* p. 147.
[12] *Ibid.,* p. 149.

in cautioning against extrapolating long-term consequences from this trend. He points out that the top East German managers are too well disciplined to openly challenge the supremacy of the more orthodox party apparatus.[13] Certainly their initiatives never approached the provocative nature of Czech economists like Ota Sik, who prepared the way for Dubcek's ill-fated "thaw" of spring, 1968. The snowballing challenge to Communist orthodoxy that was started by experts and intellectuals in Czechoslovakia probably influenced Ulbricht to hold the East German technologists by a tighter rein. "Convinced that in Czechoslovakia the 'counter-revolution' went hand-in-hand with the rise of 'counter-elites,' " Ulbricht probably became "more than ever concerned about the party's monopoly of power. Indeed, in the SED's major domestic pronouncement of the period immediately following the Soviet invasion of Czechoslovakia . . . one point has been hammered home: if the party's primacy is not to be lost, it must be vigorously asserted."[14]

CONSULTATIVE AUTHORITARIANISM

One of the peculiarities of most Communist regimes is that they generally seek to create the appearance of diversified decision-making, not only by bestowing great constitutional powers on the legislature but also by providing for a plural executive and head of state. In this, they differ both from totalitarian regimes of the right and from most Western political systems. Thus in West Germany, both the functions of the head of state and those of the head of the political executive are centered in individuals. In East Germany, however, both of the major executive organs— the Council of State, which functions as the nominal head of state, and the Council of Ministers, which is in charge of the actual political and administrative work—operate on the collegial principle, at least outwardly.

Paradoxically, this tendency to emphasize collegial structure has increased as the power has been centralized in the hands of

[13] Ernst Richert, *Die DDR Elite, oder unsere Partner von Morgen* (Hamburg, 1968).
[14] Melvin Croan, "Czechoslovakia, Ulbricht and the German Problem," *Problems of Communism,* XVIII (January, 1969), 2.

one man. Originally there was an individual head of state, the President of the Republic. In 1949, Wilhelm Pieck, the "ex-Communist" cochairman of the SED, assumed this position, while Otto Grotewohl, his "ex-Socialist" colleague, became minister-president and chairman of the Council of Ministers. Ulbricht at that time was only a vice-chairman of the Council of Ministers. But, increasingly, Ulbricht used his control over the SED party organization to win power at the expense of the other leaders. It soon became evident that the vice-chairman of the Council of Ministers had much more influence than the chairman himself. Then, when Wilhelm Pieck died in 1960, the position of the presidency was replaced by a twenty-four-man Council of State, similar to the U.S.S.R.'s Presidium of the Supreme Soviet. In having himself elected president of this body, Ulbricht outdid even Stalin by simultaneously holding the positions of head of state, vice-chairman of the Council of Ministers, and general secretary of the SED.

The Council of Ministers had been the most important executive body in the state machinery, but in the course of the 1960's the Council of State took over more and more of its responsibilities. Thus there developed a model of a two-pronged state directorate composed of two medium-sized groups of state-and-party leaders. As modernization of the economy assumed high priority, the Council of Ministers devoted itself increasingly to the top-level supervision of the economy. In December, 1965, it outlined its main responsibilities as the development of science and technology so as to secure the greatest possible growth rate in national income; the determination of the optimal structuring of the component industries of the economy; the development of international economic relations and integration processes; and the realization of a uniform socialist educational system, and of a high material and cultural standard of living for the population.[15]

Meanwhile, the Council of State took over more and more of the directly political supervisory functions. Under Ulbricht's chairmanship it began to coordinate the policies laid down by the Council of Ministers with those of other administrative, legisla-

[15] Ludz, *Parteielite im Wandel,* p. 237.

tive, and judicial branches of the government in order to ensure the "unity of state leadership." Its broad responsibilities are partly evidenced by the fact that the 1968 constitution devotes twelve articles to its powers and jurisdictions, and only three to the Council of Ministers, in recent years headed by Premier Willi Stoph.

The Council of State usually has about ten members, the Council of Ministers about forty, and almost all of these officials are simultaneously members of a top-level SED party organ. Outstanding students of GDR politics, such as Peter Christian Ludz, have devoted intensive study to the complex pattern of overlapping memberships and responsibilities because periods of liberalization tend to coincide with changes in institutional arrangements between these state and party bodies. Thus the development of greater responsiveness and decentralization of functional autonomy has generally been accompanied by (a) the granting of more initiative and autonomy to the state organs (Councils of Ministry and Planning Commission) vis-à-vis the top party organs; (b) within the state institutions, greater autonomy for the economy-oriented Council of Ministers vis-à-vis the Council of State; and (c) within the party, more influence for the Central Committee vis-à-vis the Politburo. During periods of retrenchment and "refreezing," the tendencies have been reversed by a reassertion of centralized direction by the top party leaders.

AUTONOMY OF GOVERNMENT APPARATUS

In his detailed study of institutional and career patterns during the early 1960's, Ludz identified "tendencies making for the greater independence of the governmental vis-à-vis the party apparatus."[16] During this period more of the ambitious, highly qualified young entrants chose to begin their careers in the government rather than the party. Thus the greater emphasis on economic goals reversed the previous trend of appointing tried party functionaries to key administrative positions. At one point, there was even a marked decline in the percentage of ministers who were simultaneously members of the party central committee. Later on, more of the experts and intellectuals who had proved

[16] *Ibid.,* p. 257.

themselves in government service were given comparable party positions. Following the reorientation of party priorities at the 1963 SED Congress, and in other similar periods, the high-level specialists asserted greater autonomy and self-consciousness vis-à-vis the "old-line party functionaries," whose specialty in the 1950's had been techniques of control rather than of growth and innovation.

THE NEED TO SUBORDINATE ECONOMIC GOALS

East German living standards might be even farther ahead of the other Socialist countries had not the party leadership felt it necessary to trade economic advantage for political support. Suggestions of international conflict in this area were evident after the signing of the Soviet-East German friendship treaty of June, 1964, which guaranteed the viability of the East German system. The treaty called for a tightening of trade relations, at a time when the economic reforms initiated by the Planning Commission and the Council of Ministers were beginning to show remarkable results. An East German delegation led by Ulbricht went to Moscow in September, 1965, to work out the details of an economic exchange agreement that was to lead to DM 60 billion in trade over a five-year period. To guarantee continued Soviet political support, Ulbricht and the Council of State were willing to accept the highly unfavorable terms of the trade agreement. But economic experts like Erich Apel, leader of the Planning Commission and a member of the Council of Ministers, were bitter about the agreement, deeming the economic price too high. An hour before he was to sign the agreement Apel committed suicide.[17] Although this event has never been thoroughly explained, it seems to be an instance where goals dear to the economic reformers had to be sacrificed. Later, in 1968, when the Soviet Union supported East Germany against an exposed flank resulting from Dubcek's departure from orthodoxy in Czechoslovakia, Ulbricht may have congratulated himself on his earlier decision.

[17] Arthur M. Hanhardt, Jr., *The German Democratic Republic* (Baltimore, 1968), p. 99. For a different version, see Richert, *Die DDR Elite*, p. 62.

THE SED CENTRAL COMMITTEE

In the 1950's, the SED Central Committee, usually composed of about 150 members and candidate members, was primarily an acclamating body for decisions worked out in the Politburo. But in line with the trend toward a more responsive party, the Central Committee has taken on new functions and become an important coordinating, transforming, and consultative body. Its deliberations now focus less on questions of ideology and more on the technical and social aspects of specific policy areas. To increase the flow of objective expertise, an impressive group of social science institutes were founded or expanded under its auspices in the mid-1960's. These included an institute of public opinion research, one for social science research, and another for socialist economics. Sociologists and economists in these institutes prepared reports for Central Committee members, who themselves were being drawn increasingly from among academically trained experts and technicians. In earlier periods the "strategic elites" who ran the party Politburo and Secretariat expected and received little criticism on policy drafts sent to the Central Committee. But changes in personnel and information-bases have transformed the Central Committee into an important coordinating and consulting organ that adjusts high-level plans to the demands and needs of a highly industrialized society.

THE VOLKSKAMMER

The body gaining least in the power shuffle was the East German legislature, the *Volkskammer*, composed of some 500 delegates representing the small parties, the SED, trade unions, and other mass organizations. The 1968 constitution makes the legislature look like the most important political body in the GDR. But this significance is superficial; in practice the Volkskammer has transferred almost all of its powers to the Council of State and other executive bodies. Its sole remaining function is that of acclamation, and it meets only on symbolic occasions. The most significant aspect of the Volkskammer is its membership profile, which provides almost a photographic image of the social structure of the East German population as seen through Communist lenses. According to official statements, the social structure is predominantly working-class, with workers and employees (the categories are defined very broadly) making up 78 per cent of the population. After the 1958 elections, 74 per cent of the delegates in the People's Chamber had working-class or employee backgrounds, and smaller social groups were represented proportionately. The makeup of the legislature also changed as a greater proportion of the means of production was socialized. Whereas private farmers and artisans had played a significant role earlier, by 1958 seventy members of agricultural and artisan collectives predominated over only five remaining representatives of private farmers and artisans.

The data presented in Table 11–3, based on an analysis of the personal backgrounds of members of the West and East German legislatures in the period 1958–63, show that the East German legislators more closely resemble the demographic and social composition of their constituencies. While there was a tendency toward a disproportionate number of middle-aged and older men in both legislatures, the East German legislature contained a higher proportion of women (24 per cent against 9 per cent) and also more legislators under forty-five (30 per cent against 25 per cent). Because it is the recruitment base of the dominant SED, the East German legislators came predominantly from the lower —and largest—strata of the population with little formal education. Whereas only 16 per cent of the Bundestag members on whom data were available came from the two lower strata, 56 per cent of the Volkskammer deputies were in this category. As for formal education, 60 per cent of the East German deputies had not gone beyond elementary school and only 15 per cent had attended university, whereas the West German proportions were almost reverse.

In its capacity as legislator, the People's Chamber has been limited mainly to giving passive approval to bills brought in from the outside, although frequently it is not even called upon to do that. When it comes to making new rules, the East German executive much prefers to introduce them as administrative ordinances rather than as law via the legislative route. Despite the enormous changes in all aspects of East German life, the People's Chamber has passed as few as ten new laws some years, and the overall average is not much higher.

TABLE 11–3: RECRUITMENT PATTERNS IN THE BUNDESTAG AND THE EAST GERMAN VOLKSKAMMER, 1958–63

	Bundestag %	Volkskammer %
AGE (YEAR OF BIRTH)		
1876–1895	8	7
1896–1915	66	53
1916–1925	20	25
1926–	5	14
No data	1	—
	100	100
EDUCATION		
Elementary school	22	60
High school	25	24
University	50	15
No data	3	1
	100	100
SEX		
Male	91	76
Female	9	24
	100	100
FATHER'S SOCIAL STRATUM		
Upper middle	15	8
Lower middle	20	34
Upper lower	4	11
Lower lower	3	45
No data	57	3
	100	100

NOTE: This analysis was based on the biographical information of the 544 deputies who were members of the Bundestag in 1961–63 and of the 474 deputies who belonged to the Volkskammer in 1958–60.

SOURCE: Wolf Mersch, "Volksvertreter in West und Ost," in Wolfgang Zapf, ed., *Beitraege zur Analyse der deutschen Oberschicht* (Munich, 1965), pp. 33–35.

Almost all of the bills considered in the legislature originate with the executive, since neither the People's Chamber nor any of its parties—not even the SED—utilize their constitutional power to introduce bills. In the People's Chamber about half the bills considered are passed without any discussion at all, and all are accepted by unanimous vote. The most important function of the members of the legislature is not to represent the people to the state but to represent the state to the people. As one German writer put it: "In the deputy, the people have right at their front door a 'hunk of state' with whom they can talk . . . and who has official authority to extend help in case of need."

The regime's anxiety to maintain contact with the people, both for ideological reasons and to forestall possible trouble, can be seen in the very large number of persons holding elected positions on the national, district, and local levels. It has been estimated that there are no less than 100,000 elected representatives, or about one for every hundred adult citizens. The local legislative organs have little opportunity to make policy, but they and the local councils have an important function as auxiliary organs for the executive, helping to realize the objectives of the economic plans, especially in view of the attempt, since the late 1950's, to avoid overcentralization of the administration. The regional and local councils maintain auxiliary commissions, and these in turn have teams of local citizens who serve as advisers on certain local problems. Thus the rigid bureaucracy of full-time state and party functionaries is supplemented, and to an extent checked, by a large army of part-time volunteers.

DIRECTING THE SOCIALIST ECONOMY

In adapting the planned economy models imported from the U.S.S.R., the GDR found it necessary to reorganize its economic institutions much more frequently than its political ones. Since the vast bulk of economic enterprise had been collectivized by the mid-1960's, private ownership of the means of production was pretty much confined to small-scale artisans. Industry consisted primarily of state enterprises (86 per cent) or production collectives (14 per cent), and by 1964 these two property forms were also predominant in commerce (34 per cent and 43 per cent) and in agriculture (16 per cent and 74 per cent). But because the planning mechanisms could not adequately relate productive capacities to the demands of domestic and foreign markets, the GDR in 1963 became one of the first Socialist countries to follow the Soviet Union in adopting "Liberman-type" reforms to decentralize the direction of the economic system.

The mid-1960's constituted a kind of reorganization period for East Germany's economy, as well as for those of other Socialist countries. During this period, the long-term foreign trade agreements of the East European countries under COMECON, the Communist-bloc trade organization, were temporarily de-emphasized. National economic planners were encouraged to mix resources in different ways to produce goods which would find new markets, including those in the West. The paths chosen by reformers to break out of the confines of national and bloc plans and quota systems were manifold. The outcome in East Germany was less dramatic than elsewhere, because East Berlin never attempted to open as large an "economic window to the West" as the Czechs later did. However, in production terms the East German reforms were among the most successful, as the national income figures cited earlier indicate.

The New Economic System, which Ulbricht launched in January, 1963, sought to restore a balance between rejuvenated planning methods and the increasingly complex needs of the economy. Central planning authorities were deprived of supervisory responsibility over management, and many of their previous powers were transferred to about one hundred different industry associations. These associations were made up of all the enterprises in any one branch of industry. Each association had a general director chosen from within the industry who was endowed with considerable autonomy.[18] The associations were to act as clearinghouses to facilitate the implementation of directives from the central planning authority and reconcile them with the financial, personnel, and raw material needs, as well as the production preferences, of the component enterprises. Since the associations were urged to give priority to the introduction of new technologies and to encourage new cost-accounting prac-

---

[18] Warren S. Grimes, "The Changing Structure of East German Industrial Enterprises," *American Journal of Comparative Law*, XVII, 1 (1969), 61–76.

tices that would enable goods to be sold without reliance on previous state subsidies, a new and high value came to be placed on the skills of management. Enterprise profits, rather than raw production efforts, were to become indicators of achievement.

In social terms, the new policy constituted a concession to reality because it acknowledged the manifold popular dissatisfactions of workers and consumers which had been stifled by propaganda campaigns suggesting that dissatisfied citizens were potentially disloyal citizens. For the first time, social conflicts rooted in regulations affecting conditions of work, living standards, and consumption were considered legitimate. The economic theorists urged the identification (and removal) of "contradictions between the basic interests of society and the personal material interests of the individual in everyday life."[19] Sociologists demanded that the "homo oeconomicus" model of the consuming masses be abandoned and the highly differentiated interests and proclivities of various groups be recognized. They asked the orthodox Marxists to acknowledge that economic decisions were not based solely on economic factors because the working individual was not an economic constant.[20]

Two important factors in the successful revamping of East German economic processes were the state's high investments in education and its adoption of cybernetic models using increased brainpower for system improvement. As indicated in Chapter 2, the GDR invested much more in various forms of technical and advanced education than the Federal Republic. It spent almost three times as much per capita on adult education and educated four times as many students proportionately at advanced technical schools. Even at the university level the ratio of students to total population has been about 50 per cent higher. In the 1960's, the GDR's policy began to pay off as more highly skilled technicians and research workers became available for its industry.

To transform educated men into creative elements in a planned

---

[19] Erich Apel and Gunter Mittag, *Planmaessige Wirtschaftsfuehrung und oekonomische Hebel* (Berlin, 1964), p. 55.

[20] Karl Braunreuther, "Oekonomie und Soziologie aus der Sicht eines Leiters soziologischer Untersuchungen," in *Soziologie und Wirklichkeit: Beitrage zum VI Weltkongress fuer Soziologie* (Berlin, 1966), pp. 38, 41.

economy, East German social theorists attempted to replace out-dated models based on orthodox Marxist concepts of dialectical and historical materialism. East German old-timers found it difficult to understand the behavioral concepts that the younger theorists considered essential for restructuring Communist ideas of social planning. The young men turned to cybernetics as the new method, and by applying its concepts to the planning pro-grams, they sought to substitute self-regulation for command as the guiding principle of the Socialist socio-economic system.

Theorists like Uwe-Jens Heuer have developed cybernetics and system theory to make them seem relevant to the problems of Socialist planners. Thus in a discussion of "Accident" and "Neces-sity," Heuer argues that unforeseen accidents are not necessarily unwelcome disturbances. "Creativity, whether it takes the form of invention, innovation or economic experiment, or the daring opening of new markets, may in the individual case be the fruit of accident. The capacity of sub-systems to cope with disturbances autonomously is to demonstrate their capacity to deal creatively with the environment."[21] Heuer urges the society and economy to seek new "dynamics of movement" and advocates an "open society." To generate such organizational forms Heuer would utilize the experiences of Western social systems, arguing that "the critical absorption of bourgeois experiences would contribute to-ward the strengthening of our competitive economic position."[22]

TOWARD CONVERGENCE?

Some Western observers believe that the momentum toward a con-vergence of Marxist and Western methods of social and economic analysis was a phenomenon of the mid-1960's. They point out that SED leaders started curbing the reformers as early as 1966 and took pains to replace the New Economic System with the Economic System of Socialism in April, 1968. Those who are pessimistic about the Cold War maintain that an abrupt halt to the socio-economic thaw in East Germany was as inevitable as

[21] Uwe-Jens Heuer, *Demokratie und Recht im neuen oekonomischen System der Planung und Leitung der Volkswirtschaft* (Berlin, 1965), p. 106.
[22] *Ibid.*, p. 161.

the fate of the experimental Dubcek regime. They argue that orthodox Communist leaders in countries like the Soviet Union and the GDR have too much to lose to permit far-reaching liberties and experiments.[23]

Other observers differentiate between comprehensive models of modernization that were developed within the Socialist bloc. Ludz distinguishes the "national-conservative model" followed in the GDR from the "national-liberal model" used by Dubcek until 1968. He concedes that bureaucratic commitment to technological-scientific progress in the GDR did not bring in comparable liberal political tendencies. The present impetus will maintain the GDR's economic lead within the Communist bloc into the mid-1970's, Ludz believes, but, unless the younger leaders who succeed Ulbricht reverse course toward a more imaginative and broad-based program of liberalization, the GDR will enter a period of stagnation.[24]

The course taken by Ulbricht's successors will probably depend largely on the security and stability of the GDR. If they feel that the state's existence is threatened, as Ulbricht did in 1968, they will not in all likelihood relax controls within the system and will continue to harass deviant intellectuals who call for greater liberties. However, a consistently nonchallenging, conciliatory policy on the part of the Bonn government can help assuage those fears. The declarations of Willy Brandt's government in 1969 seemed to prepare the way for such a policy, and the East German newspapers' recognition that "the political landscape in Bonn has changed, which we regard as progress," seemed a positive initial response.

Should this rapprochement continue to dissolve the East German leaders' feelings of insecurity, the explorations of East German theorists and social scientists during the mid-1960's may serve as the groundwork for the gradual development of objective dialogue with the West as well as the East. And recognition of the considerable scientific, intellectual, and economic achievements of the East Germans could allay their resentment over

---

[23] Konstantin Pritzel, *Die Wirtschaftsintegration Mitteldeutschlands* (Cologne, 1969), p. 129–31.

[24] Hans Christian Ludz, "Die Zukunft der DDR," *Die Zeit,* October 21, 1969.

having been treated as second-class citizens in international relations outside of the Communist bloc.

BIBLIOGRAPHY

Albrecht, Guenter, ed., *Dokumente zur Staatsordnung der DDR* (Berlin, 1959).

Bothe, Michael, "The 1968 Constitution of East Germany," *American Journal of Comparative Law,* XVII, 2 (1969), 268–91.

Croan, Melvin, "Czechoslovakia, Ulbricht and the German Problem," *Problems of Communism,* XVIII (January, 1969), 1–7.

Doernberg, Stefan, *Kurze Geschichte der DDR,* 3d ed. (Berlin, 1968).

Foertsch, Eckart, *Die SED* (Stuttgart, 1969).

Grimes, Warren S., "The Changing Structure of East German Industrial Enterprises," *American Journal of Comparative Law,* XVII, 1 (1969), 61–76.

Hanhardt, Arthur M., Jr., *The German Democratic Republic* (Baltimore, 1968).

Ludz, Peter C., "Discovery and 'Recognition' of East Germany: Recent Literature on the GDR," *Comparative Politics,* II (July, 1970), 68–92.

————, *Parteielite im Wandel* (Cologne, 1968).

Nawrocki, Joachim, *Das geplante Wunder* (Hamburg, 1967).

Polak, Karl, *Die Demokratie der Arbeiter und Bauernmacht* (Berlin, 1957).

Richert, Ernst, *Die DDR Elite, oder unsere Partner von Morgen* (Hamburg, 1968).

————, *Macht ohne Mandat* (Cologne, 1958).

Smith, Jean Edward, *Germany Beyond the Wall* (Boston, 1969).

Stern, Carola, *Ulbricht: A Political Biography* (New York, 1965).

12

Toward a Resolution of the "German Problem"

Throughout the 1960's, the major West German party leaders gingerly experimented with ways to climb down from Adenauer's position of "only Bonn represents Germany." None dared go so far as to advocate the official recognition of the GDR, but few of them still stood by the Hallstein doctrine under which Bonn had automatically broken off diplomatic relations with any state that recognized East Germany. The SPD had a more relaxed attitude about the GDR than the CDU, and at times the small FDP seemed the most daring in its willingness to give up old positions. However, even within parties there were many nuances of policy. A Berlin political scientist believes that in the mid-1960's Willy Brandt, then mayor of West Berlin, "was the only leading West German politician who was decisively in favor of a policy of détente."[1] Unlike Foreign Minister Schroeder, he was in favor of developing contacts with the GDR as well as with the other Communist states.

ECLIPSING CONFRONTATION

The vast acres of yellowing documents on *Deutschlandpolitik* are difficult to map, but Karl Kaiser thinks that the landscape contains a Rubicon, which "was crossed during 1966, when pressure for reform produced significant changes in the policies of the SPD and FDP."[2] The SPD congress that year recommended pursuing

[1] Arnulf Baring, "Die westdeutsche Aussenpolitik in der 'Ara Adenauer'," *PVS*, IX, 1 (1968), 52.
[2] Karl Kaiser, *German Foreign Policy in Transition* (New York, 1968), p. 101.

contacts at all levels with East Germany; even if the two regimes did not recognize each other, they should stop threatening each other and coexist peacefully. Some months earlier the SED, acting on its own initiative, had addressed a letter to the SPD party conference proposing interparty contacts which might lead to the creation of an all-German body, meeting alternatively in East and West, to study concrete measures that would foster German unity. The SPD presidium replied to Ulbricht's offer, and to everyone's surprise their letter was printed in full in *Neues Deutschland,* the SED organ. Excitement ran high as the SED proposed that leaders of the two parties enunciate their positions publicly in visits to each other's cities. To lay the groundwork, the Bundestag had to pass special legislation allowing the Communists to enter the Federal Republic without being indicted. But after the law was passed, the East Germans called off the meeting. Though there were no concrete results, Kaiser notes that this exchange "broke the spell that had prevented direct dealings with the East German regime."[3] By the summer of 1967, Chancellor Kiesinger and East German Premier Stoph were exchanging official notes.

The informal alliance of West German "recognitionists" who agitated behind the scenes to reverse Bonn's sterile boycott policy vis-à-vis the GDR included members of various parties and diverse groups. One of the most prolific authors of imaginative "unthawing" proposals was Wilhelm Wolfgang Schuetz, director of the *Kuratorium Unteilbares Deutschland.* Some of his privately circulated memos on policy changes drew bitter attacks from the Springer press and the expellees' organizations. Initiatives also came from Protestant study groups that broke taboos by calling for policy changes toward both the GDR and Poland. Within the parties, sentiment for ending the nonrecognition policy was strongest within the FDP and SPD. Two Social Democrats were instrumental in bringing about a further departure in policy after the formation of the SPD-FDP government in 1969. One of these was Egon Bahr, Brandt's longtime adviser in Berlin, the Foreign Office, and later the Chancellery. Bahr had been mainly responsible for Brandt's détente policy during the mid-1960's, and by

[3] *Ibid.,* p. 105.

1970 he was very influential as state secretary in the Chancellery. The other important "mover and shaker" was Herbert Wehner, who carefully explored all possibilities for opening contacts with East Berlin and worked patiently toward a complete disavowal of the nonrecognition policy.

These advisers were instrumental in guiding Chancellor Brandt to take the crucial symbolic initiatives that led to a transformation of "the German problem" in the 1970's. Brandt's approach was to break up the "German problem" into component parts and negotiate concurrently about its various aspects with the East Germans, the Poles, and the Soviets. His readiness to admit that the GDR was likely to remain a "state of the East," just as the Federal Republic "would remain a state of the West," paved the way for his proposal for mutual nonaggression pacts. But when Ulbricht quickly responded by sending a treaty draft to Bonn, some problems were brought into the open. Ulbricht insisted that Bonn extend full diplomatic recognition under international law, whereas Brandt initially argued that he could never acknowledge the GDR as a "foreign" state and, besides, the common nationality of the two states should make a more limited agreement acceptable. He proposed that two states eventually exchange high commissioners rather than ambassadors. In urging negotiations between the two German governments, Brandt was strongly supported by public opinion; an INFAS survey in November, 1969, showed that 74 per cent of West Germans favored them and only 11 per cent were opposed.

In the debate that followed Chancellor Brandt's State of the Union message of January 14, 1970, the Social Democrats decisively rejected the restrictive conditions the CDU leaders sought to impose as the price for continued bipartisanship in Eastern policy. The Socialists contended that before an effective détente could be reached the GDR leaders needed reassuring, since twenty years of the CDU's policy had left them very insecure. Wehner even conceded that full diplomatic recognition might ultimately take place, and he asked for maximal maneuver room for the Brandt government in view of the CDU's history of failure and insincerity in this area. This debate was widely identified as a turning point in West Germany's policy toward the GDR and the reunification question. The tone was one of melancholy rather than rejoicing, but, as *Die Zeit* noted, "the departure was a final one, as an epoch of twenty years reached its end."

DROPPING THE "REUNIFICATION" SLOGAN

In order to persuade their potential negotiating partners in East Berlin, Warsaw, and Moscow of their willingness to revise West German preconceptions, the Social Democrats felt they should give up some extremely popular slogans. One of these was "Reunification," which for several decades had supposedly been the first goal of all West Germans. In 1966, German leaders like Helmut Schmidt realized that public opinion in the Western countries "at present is only mildly interested in Germany's reunification. [Western leaders] depend on a public opinion in which for a long time, to say the least, fear of the risks involved in changing the status quo in Europe has been greater than a desire to see Germany reunified. In other words, the policy of strength has definitely and unequivocally failed."[4]

Leaders elsewhere in Europe, realizing that a reunified Germany might be a more powerful economic force than France and Britain combined, had always retained some reservations about reunification. Finally, in the late 1960's, German elites stopped paying lip-service to the "reunification first" policy posture. In 1968, an elite survey contained the question: "How would you rank the political objectives or tasks facing German policy-makers in terms of their relative urgency?" Of the objectives mentioned, "German reunification" ranked *fifth* behind two domestic and two foreign policy goals—"political unification of Western Europe," "stable economic growth," "development of educational system," and "peaceful East-West cooperation."[5]

After the formation of his government in 1969, Chancellor Brandt told a *U.S. News and World Report* interviewer that he too had ceased to give priority to the reunification concept. He wondered whether the term had been a happy choice to start with, since it implied a return to boundaries that had existed under

---

[4] *Ibid*, p. 17.
[5] Lewis J. Edinger, "The German Federal Republic and NATO: Problems and Prospects," in Edwin Fedder, ed., *NATO in the 1970's* (forthcoming).

Bismarck or Hitler. The retirement of this standard West German patriotic slogan drew fire from hardliners, like the expellees and other opponents of "recognitionism." Among those who reacted bitterly was Alex Springer, Germany's leading press lord, who found Brandt's statement "monstrous." On Christmas Day, 1969, he broke off relations with Brandt's state secretary, Egon Bahr, explaining that he had not been able to send his usual holiday greetings because

> . . . Willy Brandt's dreams of "changed circumstances," and of cooperation instead of confrontation, are exactly that, namely dreams. Reality is otherwise. East of the Wall and east of the Elbe they will read this intellectual wish-dream to mean: "The SPD-Chancellor has given up on re-unifica-tion." Because nothing happened in 25 years? History can move slowly. . . . After reading this interview I can only say: The Chancellor has laid an evil present under the Christmas tree, one whose consequences cannot yet be envisioned.[6]

After this, the Springer papers utilized every opportunity to harry the government, and in so doing strengthened their alliance with Franz Josef Strauss, who remarked: "Brandt is not selling Germany out, he's giving it away!"

OLYMPIC POLICY—
A PARADIGM

When millions of foreign visitors throng to Munich to watch the Olympics in 1972, a small number may bother to make a side trip to the Olympic Stadium in Berlin, where Adolf Hitler pre-sided over the Olympic Games of 1936. The Berlin stadium will probably still be housing Occupation troops, as it has since the end of World War II, but the look back into recent history will be worthwhile. For the stadium serves as a reminder of Germany's changed, and sharply reduced, position in world affairs. Some of the proud cities of Hitler's Germany, like Breslau and Koenigs-berg, now are listed as the hometowns of Polish and Russian ath-letes. In 1936, as the Germans won first place on point scores,

[6] *Der Spiegel,* January 26, 1970.

Hitler was preparing to incorporate yet other German-speaking areas—such as Austria and the Sudetenland—into his *Grossdeutsche Reich*. But in 1972, with German athletes represented by two different teams, each with its own distinct anthem and flag, Germans are not likely to be top contenders for team honors.

Had he lived to watch the 1972 games, Konrad Adenauer would have been deeply chagrined to hear the East German anthem being played in Munich. He had believed that West Germany's alliance with the United States and the other NATO powers would eventually bring about German reunification on Bonn's terms. But Adenauer's "policy of strength" did not achieve its goal.

THE OLYMPIC ROAD TO MUNICH

Bringing the Olympics to Munich was a considerable achievement for West Germany, but one which required the sacrifice of claims that had been strongly entrenched in Bonn's foreign policy. For years, the rival West and East German claims have preoccupied the sessions of the International Olympic Committee, as well as those of other international associations. Throughout the Adenauer period, Bonn declared that it was the only legitimate German state entitled to send teams to the games. For years the committee respected its wishes and refused the GDR's request to send its own team. At the 1964 Tokyo games, East and West German contingents entered as what from the outside was supposed to look like a single team. In 1965, the East Germans renewed their demands, strongly reenforced by the other Communist countries, and in a tumultuous meeting in October, 1965, the International Olympic Committee finally admitted the East German Olympic Committee as a full member. This paved the way for separate "German" and "East German" teams to enter the 1968 Olympic games in Grenoble and Mexico City, although they were scheduled to enter the stadium together singing the hymn from Beethoven's Ninth Symphony, which celebrates the impending brotherhood of all mankind. This compromise was sweetened somewhat for the West Germans because their team would continue to be recognized as the "German" one without a qualifying adjective, while others were pleased that twice as many German athletes could now be entered. Ironically, the city where this decision was hammered out was Madrid, where thirty years earlier German "teams" had fought against each other in the Spanish Civil War.

At the 1968 summer Olympics, the West and East German teams won twenty-five points apiece, tying with Japan for fourth place. Had they formed a single team they would have come in third behind the United States and the Soviet Union. Galling to some West German sports fans was the fact that the smaller GDR had not only tied the Federal Republic in point scores, but had walked away with nine gold medals while the West Germans had won only five. West German sports officials argued that this was to be expected, since their teams received nowhere near the amount of state support given their East German rivals. They also complained that for years much of their time and energy had been absorbed in negotiating points of Cold War protocol raised by conflicting positions of their own government and that of the International Olympic Committee (see "The Olympics Hassle," below). In a post-Olympic survey, a third of the population declared themselves dissatisfied with the outcome. Two-thirds of the respondents with only an elementary education felt that West Germany should do everything possible to surpass the East Germans the next time. But, significantly, among those with advanced education, two-thirds felt that no such special effort should be made. Looking ahead to the 1972 Olympics in its home town, the Munich *Sueddeutsche Zeitung* speculated how foreign visitors would react to a possible protocol conflict between the West and East German teams: "At the Munich Olympics they could be confronted head-on with the bewildering German question. Is it likely that again a David and Goliath effect would be achieved? In that case, who would be the David?"[7] Meanwhile the Kiesinger government moved cautiously away from the earlier position that West German teams would boycott all events at which GDR emblems were displayed. Prior to Mexico City it had announced that it would accept the playing of the GDR anthem at sporting events abroad, and would even tolerate Soviet zone emblems on sport jerseys worn at sports events in the Federal Republic. But a decision that the GDR anthem and flag could be played and dis-

[7] *Sueddeutsche Zeitung,* January 28, 1969.

THE OLYMPICS HASSLE

1956

West and East German Olympic committees agree that the all-German team should wear the same emblem, five Olympic rings superimposed upon the black-red-gold colors of the German flag. They also agree that the victory of a German athlete should be celebrated by playing neither the West German nor East German anthem, but with a selection from Beethoven's Ninth Symphony.

OCTOBER, 1959

GDR creates its own state flag through superimposition of a hammer and circle on the black-red-gold colors. A month later GDR fencers boycott an international meet in Hamburg when permission is refused to hoist the GDR flag.

NOVEMBER, 1959

Adenauer cabinet refuses to accept new "all-German" Olympic flag design suggested by International Olympic Committee. West German Olympic committee accepts flag compromise, but announces it will not permit hoisting of East German flag on West German territory.

JULY, 1960

Chancellor Adenauer tells West German sports delegation that he is against all-German teams, because they serve to disguise the division of Germany from the eyes of the world.

MARCH, 1961

West German Olympic officials emerge from prolonged negotiations with top cabinet ministers: East German emblems can be worn on West German soil only in international play-offs; on the other hand, West German teams can attend play-offs elsewhere if East German flag is hoisted "among the massed flags."

JUNE, 1961

Chancellor Adenauer tells sports press that athletes are "Germans first, and athletes second."

DECEMBER, 1962

After West German teams had to miss several important European play-offs on East German soil, Bonn Foreign Office issues proclamation saying that if it is not possible to prevent the hoisting of the East German flag, it "is, if need be, acceptable to overlook its appearance among a mass of flags."

1964

Joint German team appears in Tokyo Olympic Games.

SPRING, 1965

East Germans, continuing to press for their own Olympic teams, refuse to join West Germans in regional preliminaries.

OCTOBER, 1965

International Olympic Committee extends full recognition to East German Olympic committee, and accepts separate German teams with their own flags, emblems, etc.

1968

Separate East and West German teams compete at Mexico City and Grenoble.

AUGUST, 1969

Kiesinger cabinet decides that East German anthem may be played in West Germany and at 1972 Munich Olympics.

---

played on West German territory was not forthcoming for several years. Finally, at one of its last meetings prior to the 1969 elections, the Kiesinger cabinet swallowed its reservations and announced that the GDR hymn and flag would henceforth be permitted at all sports events in the Federal Republic.

BERLIN AND INTRA-GERMAN DIALECTICS

ESCALATION AND EXTERNALIZATION

What interest do other nations have in helping the two German states end their twenty-five-year-old policy of hostile confrontation? According to Karl Kaiser, one inducement should be the removal of a potential instrument for escalating international conflicts. International issues or disagreements, once entangled in the dialectics of intra-German relations, "assume a different character in the domestic context—usually a more threatening one, since each regime suffers from its own version of a deep sense of insecurity; and since the structures of both polities have been shaped decisively by a specific international constellation that is now undergoing a transformation, both regimes have become hypersensitive to the 'domestic,' intra-German consequences of changes in the environment . . . any problem, once fed into the workings of intra-German dialectics, becomes magnified."[8] Thus, just because the GDR signed the Nuclear Nonproliferation Treaty, the Federal Republic withheld its signature for a long time, blocking progress toward world arms control.

[8] Kaiser, *German Foreign Policy in Transition,* p. 28.

Kaiser argues that perpetuation of a divided Germany also serves to "externalize domestic problems. Since it is on German soil that the two opposing systems meet, overlap, and, so to speak, interpenetrate, a wide range of domestic problems in the two polities immediately concern the international environment."[9] Thus questions of local administration in Berlin, the rise of right-wing parties in West Germany, and the method of electing West German officials have often in the past precipitated hot East-West exchanges, which have sent the diplomats of dozens of nations scurrying around with fire extinguishers. A particularly dramatic incident of this kind occurred in April, 1969, when the West German Bundesversammlung was preparing to meet to elect a successor to Federal President Luebke. The meeting had been scheduled in West Berlin, which elicited threats from the GDR and the Soviets that there might be blockades of the city's access routes. There were numerous meetings between Chancellor Kiesinger and the Soviet ambassador, but apparently the GDR would not make the requested concessions in exchange for relocating the meeting. Then, just a few days before the meeting, the Soviet's bargaining position was weakened by the outbreak of hostilities with Communist China on an island in the Ussuri River in Siberia. The West Berlin meeting proceeded on schedule, resulting in the election of Gustav Heinemann as President of the Federal Republic. Several months later, when President Heinemann celebrated his birthday, he received a bouquet of fifty red roses from Soviet President Podgorny. No similar gesture emanated from the GDR.

THE STATUS OF WEST BERLIN

When and if the Federal Republic and the GDR agree to stabilize their relationship, they will have to follow up their agreement with a special codicil regarding the status of West Berlin. For the two governments have held contradictory positions on Berlin's place on the German political map. The East Germans contend that East Berlin is their capital and an integral part of the GDR, whereas West Berlin is a third German political entity, which Bonn cannot claim to represent. The West Germans, on the other hand, argue that West Berlin has almost all the characteristics of

[9] *Ibid.*, p. 30.

a Land of the Federal Republic, but that ultimate responsibility for both West and East Berlin still rests with the four Occupying Powers. These positions have not changed substantially during the decade since Ulbricht built the Berlin Wall in August, 1961.

The story of Berlin's special status begins with the wartime agreements of 1944 and 1945, when the victorious Allies agreed to divide Germany into four Occupation zones, but to run Berlin jointly, allocating a sector of the city to each of the four major powers for administration. Then in June, 1948, the Soviets imposed a blockade on all land traffic into West Berlin in retaliation for the introduction there of the new West German currency. In November, the city council and administration split into separate parts. During the airlift the West Berliners displayed great courage and endurance, and it was their toughness which finally forced the Soviets to back down and cancel the blockade after eleven months.[10] After that the new German Democratic Republic officially declared East Berlin to be its capital, while West Berlin concentrated on economic revival. Eventually the abnormal relationship was accepted as normal, and throughout most of the 1950's life in the divided city continued with many minor, but few major, upsets. A series of strong Social Democratic leaders— Ernst Reuter, Otto Suhr, and Willy Brandt—provided excellent leadership in the position of Governing Mayor of West Berlin. There was little official contact between the two administrations, but those who wanted to could usually travel freely throughout Berlin. While many streets led to dead ends at the sector border, the main thoroughfares were kept open, and the subway and elevated trains continued to run.

The Berlin situation was changed radically on the night of August 13, 1961, when the Communists erected a physical wall to seal off hermetically the two parts of the city. Until that date, Berlin, though divided, had been something of a "clamp that held the parts of Germany together." Relatives from East and West could meet there with comparative ease, and West Berlin was a showcase where in one year visitors from East Berlin and East Germany had bought 9 million theater, movie, and concert tickets.

---

[10] W. P. Davison, *The Berlin Blockade: A Study in Cold-War Politics* (Princeton, 1958).

All that was ended when the Communists stopped virtually all German crossings at the few check points where traffic could still move across the sector borders. Along the twenty-six-mile wall of prefabricated cement slabs topped by barbed wire and frequently reinforced by secondary obstacles, East German soldiers and police patrol ceaselessly. Many of their countrymen have still found means of escape, but many others have died in unsuccessful attempts.

The Berlin wall was primarily Ulbricht's answer to the mass exodus of the GDR's population. Meanwhile the status of West Berlin, which the Federal Republic subsidizes heavily,[11] remains a subject of acute controversy.

THE FRG AND EASTERN EUROPE

The problem of normalizing diplomatic relations with the countries of Eastern Europe has been accorded top priority by politically aware West Germans. After the formation of the Grand Coalition, it was realized that the latent hostilities carried over from the war must be dispelled before a long-term solution of the German problem could be attempted. Following this pattern, the West Germans have even set diplomatic trends recently. Thus the exchange of visits by West German and Rumanian leaders in 1969 set a pattern which was followed by President Nixon, whose visit to Bucharest in August, 1969, was the first by an American President to a Communist country since 1945.

Bonn's new policy toward Eastern Europe made rapid progress in regard to those countries where no unsettled border questions complicated negotiations. But first it was necessary to reconsider the Hallstein doctrine, requiring the Federal Republic to forgo diplomatic relations with any state that recognized the GDR. It was argued that since as "Soviet satellites" the East European countries had been forced into granting recognition to the GDR, they should be exempt from the doctrine.

On this basis, Chancellor Kiesinger in December, 1966, announced the government's intention of "improving relations with

[11] Charles Robson, ed., *Berlin: Pivot of German Destiny* (Chapel Hill, 1960), pp. 134–55.

our eastern neighbors in cultural and political life and, wherever possible in the circumstances, establishing diplomatic relations as well." A month later Foreign Minister Willy Brandt and his Rumanian counterpart, Curneliu Manescu, agreed to establish diplomatic relations and exchange ambassadors. The Rumanians broke away from their previous position that no Socialist country should establish relations with Bonn unless the latter recognized the GDR; but, of course, Rumania did not renounce its relations with East Berlin. Rumania and West Germany agreed to disagree in public on the question of which German government represented the German people. The Rumanian government stated that it "deems it necessary to reiterate its legal viewpoint that there are two German states and that this is one of the fundamental realities with which Europe was confronted as a consequence of the Second World War and further development of things." Later, when he visited Bucharest, Brandt went even further toward recognition of the GDR when he said:

> We also agree that, with regard to the problems of European security, the existing relations have to be accepted as a point of departure, and all states regardless of their size have to fulfill equally important tasks in creating a European peace order. This also applies to the two political systems which at present exist on German soil.[12]

Subsequently, consular relations were established with Czechoslovakia, and diplomatic relations were reestablished with Yugoslavia. With regard to Poland, the Christian Democrats' refusal to recognize the permanent nature of the Oder-Neisse line was a stumbling block for a long time. And then the Soviet invasion of Czechoslovakia in August, 1968, threatened to reverse the whole momentum of Brandt's Eastern policy. But Chancellor Kiesinger restrained the numerous rigid anti-Communists who sought this end, and the crisis was surmounted. Looking ahead to the 1970's, West German political elites have given top priority to the problem of improving relations with Eastern Europe. In early 1968, no less than 54 per cent of an elite sample felt that "adjusting relations with East European states" was the most im-

[12] Kaiser, *German Foreign Policy in Transition,* p. 118.

portant diplomatic objective. Since then, the question has been whether the West Germans favoring détente would be able to prevail over those who have tried to prevent Bonn from paying the necessary diplomatic price. The price—especially as far as Poland is concerned—would have to include official West German recognition of the Oder-Neisse line. Although by 1969 some German politicians, particularly in the SPD and the FDP, had declared their readiness to take this position, the powerful expellee associations and allied groups were fighting the trend every inch of the way. But, aside from the Czechoslovak intervention, Soviet behavior in the late 1960's seems to have "increasingly persuaded West German leaders that the Soviet Union is also becoming less bellicose and more reasonable in its relations with the Federal Republic."[13]

THE ALLIANCE SYSTEMS

In 1945 the victorious Allies seemed determined to prevent a revival of German military power, and they tried to wipe out all military organizations and to impress on the German people the close connection between German militarism and the disaster of 1945. But a demilitarized Germany was not in the cards. Within five years after Germany's unconditional surrender the very powers who had defeated and dissolved her armies were themselves encouraging the reestablishment of German military contingents. The constitutions of both the Federal Republic and the Democratic Republic contained provisions forbidding large-scale rearmament; they were soon amended.

After the near success of the Communist attempt to take over South Korea by force raised further doubts as to the ability of the democratic countries to meet localized Communist aggression, American and British spokesmen in 1950 began to call for the formation of West German contingents. To allay the well-founded skepticism regarding the political effects of the reestablishment of a German army, it was proposed that the German

[13] Edinger, "The German Federal Republic and NATO."

troops be placed under a European army made up of contingents from other European countries. The West German government strongly supported these plans, and after some discussion the French cabinet overcame its initial hesitation and agreed to the principles of the European Defense Community (EDC). However, successive French governments proved unable or unwilling to put through the plan, and in August, 1954, the treaty was defeated in the French National Assembly.[14] As an alternative it was agreed that Germany could join NATO, and that German armed forces, though organized on a national basis, would be placed under the supreme command of NATO. This formula was finally accepted by the French, the Germans, and all the other nations involved.

Building on the functional approach to European unification, the impetus of the six-nation Common Market, and the promise of closer political integration encompassed in the Rome Treaties, Germany, France, Italy, and the Benelux countries built up an infrastructure of increasing economic and political significance. However, crucial differences developed over the speed with which national political institutions were to be replaced by supranational ones, the power relationships to be aimed at, and the admission of new members. To ensure the predominance of French influence, de Gaulle built on Adenauer's well-known interest in solidifying German-French friendship. This "Bonn-Paris axis," symbolized in melodramatic tours and meetings of the two patrician leaders, alarmed their smaller neighbors, who welcomed Britain's decision to seek Common Market membership. From the beginning, critics of the Adenauer policy had argued that the Federal Republic's policy of alliance with the West was making German unification impossible. But the Chancellor always rejected this position, believing that a Western policy of strength would ultimately induce the Soviets to relinquish the GDR. This calculation proved to be mistaken, for the Communist willingness to bargain on German unification in fact decreased as the German military buildup and its integration into NATO were stepped up. Thus, when Adenauer retired in October, 1963, Bundestag President

[14] Daniel Lerner, ed., *France Defeats EDC* (New York, 1957).

Gerstenmaier could not carry his eulogistic comparison to Bismarck all the way. Unlike Bismarck, Adenauer could not, he said, "look back on the implementation of the unification of Germany, an achievement which has up to now been denied to you and ourselves."

THE MILITARY AND POLITICS

No West German soldiers were yet in uniform when five days after the Federal Republic's admission to NATO the states of the Communist bloc met in Warsaw and formed a counterpart pact, with reciprocal defense guarantees and a joint command for their combined military forces. Thus, the effective control exercised through the top-level Communist leaders was augmented by a supranational military organization similar to NATO, whose existence underlined the polarization of the two hostile blocs. A Soviet general was named to command the forces of the Warsaw Pact countries, and a staff organization was established in Moscow. The GDR had not yet given its "police" formations explicit military status, so although it became a member of the pact, no provision was made regarding its forces. In January, 1956, the East German People's Army was officially formed, and a few days later the Warsaw Pact countries announced the admission of East German contingents into the unified command. By 1959, an official East German source described the function of the armed services as "successfully fulfilling, at the side of the glorious Soviet army and of the other fraternal socialist armies, the duties assigned to us within the framework of the Warsaw Pact."[15] To tie the People's Army to German traditions, the new army uniforms closely resembled those of the Wehrmacht, despite the fact that the Communists had denounced the latter as an ally of fascism.

In the Federal Republic, the problem of reconciling old traditions and new roles also caused difficulty. Up to 1945, the ranks of the top-level German military men and those of genuine democrats had, for the most part, been quite distinct. "The German democrats had no military heroes in their tradition . . . and the

[15] Deutsches Institut fuer Zeitgeschichte, *Jahrbuch der Deutschen Demokratischen Republik, 1959* (Berlin, 1959), p. 86.

German military had no democrats among their ancestry."[16] The character of West Germany society and the rapid buildup that was necessary after the long delays over EDC made training a completely new military leadership impracticable, and officers who had grown up in the antidemocratic Reichswehr and in the service of the Nazi state had to be used. But to prevent the re-emergence of a reactionary officers' corps and a tyrannical military tradition, the West Germans took extraordinary precautions to sift out politically unreliable candidates and to keep a democratic check on the armed forces. When recruitment for the higher offices began, all candidates for positions with the rank of colonel or above were subjected to close individual scrutiny by a special committee set up by the Bundestag. Many candidates were weeded out on political grounds. Then, building on a Swedish model, the parliament created a parliamentary "Commissioner" whose job it would be to look into complaints from individual soldiers and to report to it periodically on the internal affairs of the military forces.

There is little evidence that the military romance has again cast a spell over the German imagination, and indeed the official public relations efforts to make military careers seem more attractive have not been too successful. Although resistance to draft calls has not been a great problem, recruiting permanent officers and noncommissioned soldiers has been difficult. In fact a majority of the West German officer corps is composed of natives of East Germany, which is in part a reflection of the fact that settled natives have preferred civilian careers. Nor has the magic of Bundeswehr uniforms impressed the general population. When asked in 1965 whether they thought a man looked better in civilian dress or in uniform, 72 per cent of a West German sample opted for civilian dress and only 13 per cent for the uniform. In the same survey, only 7 per cent of the males questioned said they actually like performing their military duty, while 43 per cent did it against their will and 42 per cent were ambivalent.

Observers of the German political scene have nevertheless been uneasy because the reform group inside the Bundeswehr which emphasized the development of democratic leadership and

---

[16] Emil Obermann, "Kraeftespiel um die Bundeswehr," *Neue Gesellschaft,* VI (1959), 96.

disciplinary traditions around the principle of "Innere Fuehrung" seems to be declining. Some writers believe that "the new spirit has struck roots in the Bundeswehr," and that "the old traditionalists who speak about the 'Innere Fuehrung' with contempt and ridicule are a shrinking group."[17] But there has been much, though inconclusive, evidence suggesting quite another trend. Most of the reform groups of generals have been transferred out of the ministry, while the program at the Bundeswehr "Internal Leadership" school has been watered down and its civilian teachers forced out. A civilian-military power struggle also developed over replacing the civilian head of the Defense Ministry's personnel section with a general; in 1965, after much debate in the cabinet, the military won. Perhaps these conflicts occurred because the officer corps was claiming the powers which would be theirs in most armies. But at times their hostility to outside suggestions and criticisms has provoked even those who could hardly be accused of antimilitary prejudice. In 1964 the parliamentary defense commissioner, who was not only a former CDU deputy but also an ex-admiral, issued a passionate indictment of the Bundeswehr for not accepting the concept of civilian control and for reviving a "state within a state" mentality.[18] He became the second commissioner to resign from this office, primarily because the army's lack of cooperation made his job impossible. His successor also got into a scrap with the Defense Ministry when it appeared that his civil servants were, at the behest of the ministry, undercutting the control and investigation functions of his office.

In 1970, fifteen years after the formation of the Bundeswehr, the problem of reconciling German military caste traditions with the values of a civilian-oriented democratic society was still not resolved. Baudissin's formula for creating a new military *esprit de*

[17] Eric Waldmann, *The Goose Step Is Verboten* (New York, 1964), p. 151. This study has been attacked by a knowledgeable German reviewer as "nothing more or less than propaganda for the Bundeswehr . . . in the guise of value-free scientific research." Wilfred von Bredow, "Die Bundesrepublik und ihre Streitkraefte," *PVS*, X, 3 (September, 1969), 428.

[18] H. P. Secher, "Controlling the New German Military Elite," *Proceedings of the American Philosophical Society*, CIX (April, 1965), 63–84.

corps was considered "dead."[19] But the military seemed to find no adequate substitute for the special status and public adoration they had enjoyed in earlier eras. This was partly due to the fact that almost all of the higher officer corps were Reichswehr veterans. Twelve thousand of these men had been called back to the colors in the 1950's, and in 1970 this group still constituted almost 40 per cent of the officer corps. But even the younger officers and noncoms with no prewar military indoctrination complained of society's lack of appreciation and fervently applauded reactionary advocates of a return to the "grand traditions" of earlier days. These included pathetic pronunciamentos by writers like H. G. von Studnitz, who yearned for the day when "Germans overcome their alienation to rediscover the soldier and again become aware of the significance of the military for nation and state."[20] In expressing the military's grievances, top generals have frequently made arrogant statements. Lieutenant General Albert Schnez, inspector of the Bundeswehr, claimed in a 1969 report that soldiering merited special dispensation as a "unique profession." He suggested organized action—such as letters to the editor and pressures on the television studios—to counter unfavorable references to the military in the mass media. He even went so far as to write that "only a root and branch reform of the Bundeswehr and society" could appreciably improve the effectiveness of the military. Such remarks pointed up the continuing difficulty of getting the German military to accept the fact that their institutions were only means, and not ends in themselves.

THE BRANDT GOVERNMENT'S OSTPOLITIK

"We are witnesses to a development without precedent in the twenty-year-old history of the German Federal Republic," a journalist for the Polish journal *Kultura* dramatically reported in March, 1970. "It concerns the Bonn's diplomatic activity in the capitals of the Socialist countries. Talks have begun in Moscow, Warsaw, and Berlin, the capital of the DDR." This lively reaction from Warsaw reaffirmed for Willy Brandt and the West German Foreign Office that their intensive preparatory activity

[19] Von Bredow, "Die Bundesrepublik und ihre Streitkraefte," p. 425.
[20] H. G. von Studnitz, *Rettet die Bundeswehr* (Frankfurt, 1967).

for an unfreezing in West German relations with the Communist bloc was indeed eliciting due recognition in the East European capitals. Within the next few months, this activity was to carry Brandt and West German Foreign Minister Walter Scheel across what in Adenauer's day had been regarded as an "iron curtain," in order to conduct personal negotiations or even to sign treaties with Communist leaders in East Germany, Moscow, and Warsaw.

What distinguished the diplomatic activity of 1970 from that which had preceded it was the evident willingness of the Brandt government to go further toward giving final recognition to the East European status quo than the CDU-led predecessor governments in Bonn had been. Because of this willingness, in the eyes of another Polish observer, "Willy Brandt and his party have a number of opportunities to inscribe themselves in European history by reducing the barriers of distrust which separate the Federal Republic from its near and more distant neighbors. The question of whether the Social Democrats will utilize these opportunities remains to be answered." Subsequent developments were to show that the Brandt government was indeed determined to persist in its course, even in the face of savage opposition from West German expellee and nationalist groups. *Because of the great impact of these negotiations, important excerpts from the more significant documents are reproduced in the Appendix, together with background analyses and comments that will help to place them in context.*

THE BRANDT-STOPH MEETINGS

As was to be expected, the most difficult of Bonn's negotiating partners were the fellow-Germans from East Berlin. The East Germans had in 1966 discussed exchange visits between East and West German politicians which then failed to come off. But in 1970 similar preparations actually led to unprecedented meetings between the two heads of government. Urged on by the other Communist bloc leaders, the East Germans agreed to direct meetings between Chairman Willi Stoph and Brandt, the first of which took place in March, 1970, in the East German city of Erfurt. It was followed two months later by a second meeting in the West German city of Kassel. Both were occasions of high drama, with considerable background accompaniment. Thus, in Erfurt the crowds broke through police lines to cheer Brandt, while in Kassel right-wingers tried and temporarily succeeded in lowering the East German flag.

Although the initial meeting at Erfurt proceeded with considerable cordiality, incompatibilities between the positions of the two governments came to the fore at the second meeting. Brandt's position that the two governments should enter into contractual relations that would "regularize the relations between the two States in Germany" was carefully chosen to imply a set of nonfinalized relationships that would leave the way open for the "sleeping Germany" to possibly recover its unified sovereignty. But Stoph refused to be satisfied by anything short of full diplomatic recognition under international law, which implied a degree of finality Brandt was under strong pressure not to accept. A second point of contention concerned the status of West Berlin. As its former mayor, Brandt was bound to demand full guarantees of its ties to the Federal Republic, which Stoph in turn was under strong hard-line pressure not to give in to. After this cool confrontation, contacts between the two governments were only resumed six months later, when progress in the negotiations with the Soviet Union and Poland hinged on solving the intra-German Gordian knots.

THE MOSCOW TREATY

The cornerstone of Bonn's new Eastern policy was officially put in place in August, 1970, when Brandt traveled to Moscow to sign the Soviet-West German treaty on the renunciation of the use of force, which had been the subject of prolonged negotiations conducted mainly by Egon Bahr. Through the treaty the signatories bound themselves "to respect without restriction the territorial integrity of all States in Europe within their present frontiers," and here specific mention was made of the Oder-Neisse line as well as the frontier between the FRG and the GDR. In return for this agreement, the Soviets renounced some legal bases, such as Articles 53 and 107 of the UN Charter, which they had earlier claimed gave them special powers to intervene in German politics, and recognized the legitimacy of West Germany's adherence to the Western alliance.

On balance the West Germans undoubtedly yielded more in the way of latent legal claims, particularly in regard to the recoverability of the Eastern territories and with respect to modes of implementing German unification. The signing of the treaty might have aroused still stronger protests among West German expellee groups had it not occurred at a time when most Germans were on vacation. But Brandt pointed out to his fellow countrymen in a dramatic television broadcast from Moscow that "nothing is lost by signing this treaty that was not lost a long time ago. We have the courage to open a fresh page in history." The treaty-signing ceremonies were attended by an unusually high proportion of the Soviet Communist leadership, and observers believed that the symbolic reconciliation document might also usher in a period of highly intensified Soviet-West German economic relationships.

After the intensive diplomacy of spring and summer, 1970, activity slowed down somewhat during the fall of 1970, when negotiations continued to proceed at parallel levels simultaneously, while the policy's opponents in Bonn unleashed bitter attacks on it. Thus, the status of Berlin was the subject of Four-Power negotiations, the slow progress of which delayed the government's submission of the treaty for Bundestag ratification. The draft treaty with Poland also proved thorny to work out in its details, but was finally signed in December, 1970. Through its provisions the millions of former East Prussians and Silesians were apprised that the only way they would ever return to their native areas might be as tourists.

In terms of domestic policy ties, it became apparent that the SPD and the FDP would be able to benefit from their accomplishment only if they could survive a sharp series of counterattacks and attempts to prevent the treaties from becoming ratified. These attacks were spearheaded in the first instance by the expellee organizations, the Springer press, and Franz Josef Strauss. The expellees went so far as to utilize governmental subsidies to implement their attacks on the integrity of the Brandt government. In the SPD, party discipline held up against the attack, but this did not prove true of the FDP. In October, 1970, three Bundestag deputies from the right wing of the party, including the former party chairman, Erich Mende, announced their resignation from the party. This development reduced the SPD/FDP majority in the Bundestag from twelve to only six votes. Thus, the fate of the Brandt government hung on a very narrow margin in the autumn of 1970. But then as previously it was helped by disunity in the CDU, which was badly split as to the positions it should take in regard to the Brandt government's Eastern policy. At first former Chancellor Kiesinger sought to lead the CDU into a frontal attack, but his rival, Rainer Barzel, prevailed in his advice for a wait-and-see policy. After the desertions from the FDP camp, all CDU/CSU leaders did their utmost to exploit the government's weakness. But a decisive challenge was delayed both by the difficulties in the way of overthrowing an incumbent Chancellor and by different calculations by the rival party leaders.

Brandt's foreign policy, however, certainly served well to reintroduce an element of polarization into Bonn politics. Those who had complained of the lack of real difference between government and opposition in the mid-1960's, and later of the effective loss of opposition during the period of the Grand Coalition, were once again witness to sharp and bitter Bundestag debates in the foreign-policy area. The patriotic and ideological symbols here utilized aroused a depth of feeling that had not been aroused by controversies over domestic issues for many years. Indeed, the style of confrontation was reminiscent of the period in the early 1950's when Kurt Schumacher had led the SPD in bitter opposition to the treaties Konrad Adenauer was negotiating with the West. At that time Adenauer was able to use the pressure from the domestic opposition in order to extract better conditions from Western negotiators. Supporters of Brandt were hoping that Moscow and its allies might similarly make concessions that would help sustain the SPD/FDP coalition, rather than see it fall victim to its political opponents.

BIBLIOGRAPHY

Adenauer, Konrad, "Germany: The New Partner," *Foreign Affairs*, XXXIII (1955), 177–83.
Albert, E. H., "The Brandt Doctrine of Two States in Germany," *International Affairs*, XLVI, 2 (April, 1970), 293–303.

Baring, Arnulf, *Aussenpolitik in Adenauer's Kanzlerdemokratie* (Munich, 1969).

Beyme, Klaus von, "The Ostpolitik in the West German 1969 Elections," *Government and Opposition*, V, 2 (Spring, 1970), 193–217.

Bluhm, Georg, *Die Oder-Neisse Linie in der deutschen Aussenpolitik* (Freiburg, 1963).

Croan, Melvin, "Czechoslovakia, Ulbricht, and the German Problem," *Problems of Communism*, XVIII (January–February, 1969), 1–7.

Curtis, Michael, *Western European Integration* (New York, 1965).

Davison, W. P., *The Berlin Blockade: A Study in Cold-War Politics* (Princeton, 1958).

Deutsch, Karl, and Lewis Edinger, *Germany Rejoins the Powers* (Stanford, 1959).

———, et al., *France, Germany and the Western Alliance* (New York, 1966).

Freund, Gerald, *Germany between Two Worlds* (New York, 1961).

Haas, Ernst B., *The Uniting of Europe: Political, Social and Economic Forces, 1950–1957* (Stanford, 1958).

Hartmann, Frederick H., *Germany between East and West: The Reunification Problem* (Englewood Cliffs, N.J., 1965).

Heinemann, Gustav W., *Verfehlte Deutschlandpolitik: Irrefuhrung und Selfsttäuschung* (Frankfurt, 1966).

Kaiser, Karl, *German Foreign Policy in Transition: Bonn between East and West* (London, 1968).

Meissner, Boris, ed., *Die deutsche Ostpolitik, 1961–1970* (Cologne, 1970).

Plischke, Elmer, "Integrating Berlin and the Federal Republic of Germany," *Journal of Politics*, XXVII (1965), 35–65.

———, "West German Foreign and Defense Policy," *Orbis*, XII, 4 (Winter, 1969), 1098–1136.

Prittie, Terence, *Germany Divided: The Legacy of the Nazi Era* (Boston, 1960).

Richardson, James L., *Germany and the Atlantic Alliance* (Cambridge, Mass., 1966).

Robson, Charles, ed., *Berlin: Pivot of German Destiny* (Chapel Hill, 1960).

Secher, H. P., "Controlling the New German Military Elite," *Proceedings of the American Philosophical Society*, CIX (April, 1965), 63–84.

Shell, Kurt L., *Bedrohung und Bewaehrung: Fuehrung und Bevoelkerung in der Berlin-Krise* (Cologne, 1965).

Smith, Bruce L. R., "The Goverance of Berlin," *International Conciliation* (1959), 171–230.

Thielen, Hans-Helmut, *Der Verfall der Ihneren Führung* (Frankfurt, 1970).

Waldmann, Eric, *The Goose Step is Verboten* (New York, 1964).

White, John, "West German Aid to Developing Countries," *International Affairs*, XVI (1965), 74–88.

Wiskemann, Elizabeth, *Germany's Eastern Neighbors* (London, 1956).

APPENDIX

Bonn, East Germany, and the Soviet Union: New Departures in 1970

THE FEDERAL REPUBLIC'S NATIONAL INTEREST

The situation we are confronted with is completely clear: the GDR is the institutionalized war booty of the USSR. This she will remain as long as the USSR is a Great Power, since no one can pay the ransom price. The GDR is just as firmly established in the world as the Federal Republic, even if we properly make a great distinction about the claims to legitimacy of either state. In point of fact, there have long existed two states of the German nation on the contemporary international scene, and at least since that point in the middle of the fifties when the Soviet Union abandoned the notion of neutralizing Germany after it could no longer be realized. No wonder West Germany's policy on Germany, failing to recognize this fact, quickly reached an impasse. The refusal to own up to this circumstance served for a time as a useful means of consolidating the character of the West German state proper. But later on, political isolation in the world threatened the Federal Republic in her cul-de-sac of Adenauer's German policy.

WALDEMAR BESSON,
Aussenpolitik,
XXI, 2 (1970).

THE RIGHT TO CHANGE ONE'S MIND

There can be no denying the existence of a contradiction between Willy Brandt's tenet of the "two German states" and past documents of Social Democratic policy that cannot be explained away by means of exegetical and apologetical reinterpretation.

It cannot be gainsaid that the present Chancellor takes great care to avoid the term "reunification" and no longer considers it to be an attainable goal of German politics. Yet for more than a decade the SPD postulated reunification as not only the prime but also the most urgent of goals.

In all honesty it must also be admitted that Christian Democrat Rainer Barzel put his finger on a delicate issue when, in the course of the January 1970 debate on the state of the nation, he bombarded the Chancellor with past statements of his own on, say, the Oder-Neisse frontier, that can hardly be reconciled with the policy lines of Federal Republic diplomacy in the form they have taken since the coalition of Social Democrats and Free Democrats came into office last September [1969].

This, however, gives rise to an issue deserving attention far over and above the specific context. Does a politician—and a political party, too, for that matter—not have the right to change his mind? Can he really be accused of lack of character or inconsistency when practical experience has taught him lessons of which he could not have been aware from the beginning? It is as true now as it has been in the past that the division of

Germany is unjust, that it was imposed on the people concerned against their will. . . . It is nonetheless equally true to
say that the GDR, founded on illegality and refusal to countenance justice, has consolidated itself both within and without
since the erection of the Berlin Wall in such a way as to
render it practically impossible to continue to regard it as a
negligible quantity. As far as can humanly be foreseen, circumstances are not even conceivable under which unification
with the Federal Republic might ever come within the scope
of reality.

FRITZ RENÉ ALLEMAN,
Der Monat,
April 1970.

TWO STATES IN A "SLEEPING GERMANY"

The Federal government distinguishes between full diplomatic recognition of the German Democratic Republic (GDR)
by the Federal Republic and full diplomatic recognition of the
GDR by third parties. It has ruled out recognition by the Federal Republic and is still trying to hinder recognition by third
parties. But it has held out the prospect of relaxing this blockade if inter-German talks lead to acceptable settlements. . . .

The starting point for the Federal government is the assumption that Germany still legally exists. "Germany" is thought of
as a unit containing two states. It has no institutions, its political power is *"sleeping,"* but it is "legally presupposed." Inter-
German settlements cannot therefore be "purely on the basis
of international law." They are of a "special nature," though
no less binding as a consequence. One of the political aims
behind this formula is the maintenance of the attainable minimum of institutionalized national unity under the given circumstances, such as making possible inter-German trade and
association of the GDR with the European Economic Community. . . .

Adhering to a "Sleeping Germany" is also necessary because in the German Treaty the Western powers have reserved
their rights concerning Berlin and "Germany as a whole"
embodied in the Potsdam Agreement. We cannot legally dis-
pose of any questions that deal with Germany as a whole.
Full diplomatic recognition of the GDR would mean that

"Germany as a whole" would legally cease to exist. The Federal Republic is therefore in no position to recognize the GDR on the basis of international law. Even if it wanted to, it would be impossible before the conclusion of a peace treaty.

MARTIN KRIELE,
*Frankfurter Allgemeine
Zeitung,* May 19, 1970.

BRANDT AND STOPH AT KASSEL*

Chairman Stoph: Mr. Chancellor, twenty-five years have gone by since the end of the Second World War and yet not even the present Government of the Federal Republic of Germany has shown itself clearly ready to recognize the defeat of Hitler fascism, to learn the lessons of history, and to throw overboard the ballast of the revenge-seeking policy initiated by the CDU/CSU in order to redress the consequences of the Second World War. The unavoidable necessity finally and unreservedly to recognize the frontiers in Europe—including the Oder-Neisse line—which came into being in Europe as a result of the Second World War, is still denied by the Government of the Federal Republic of Germany.

Still ringing in our ears is the slogan of "liberation of the Zone," which, moreover, was not enunciated only by the CDU politicians. Therefore, after twenty years of hostile policy on the part of the Federal Republic of Germany against the German Democratic Republic, words about harmonious relations and equality of status, fine assertions of peaceful intentions are not sufficient to arrive at normal relations. . . . Declarations of loyalty to the Atlantic Alliance result in an entire union of interests and responsibilities with the policy of the United States, which, particularly at present, is meeting with indignation and resistance in all parts of the world.

In this connection a word must also be said about West Berlin. In recent weeks the Government of the Federal Republic of Germany has in sharper form raised its illegal

*The second meeting between Chancellor Brandt and Chairman Stoph was held in the West German city of Kassel, May 21, 1970, following their earlier encounter in Erfurt.

claim to West Berlin. It is universally well known that the independent political entity, West Berlin, which is situated in the middle of the German Democratic Republic and on her territory, was not, and whatever happens never will be, a part of the Federal Republic of Germany. . . .

Chancellor Brandt: The relations between the Federal Republic of Germany and the German Democratic Republic are determined, as we see, by the situation of Germany and the Germans as a consequence of the Second World War and the subsequent development in the two States in Germany. On this basis, both States in Germany should agree to a contractual regularization of their mutual relations. . . .

We regard the conception of nation primarily, but not solely, as embracing the past. Nation, in our view, embraces more than common language and culture, and still more than political and social systems. Its foundation is the feeling of people of belonging to one another. And in this sense there is, in our opinion, a unity of the nation. Neither by you nor by us can the unity of the nation be destroyed.

Even if you describe the integration of the two States in, on the one hand, NATO and, on the other, the Warsaw Pact, as a deep divide, this could affect, at the most, the sphere of the State, but not, as we understand it, the continuance of the nation.

On the other hand, there is no one among us who disputes the fact that life in general in the two parts of the nation differs greatly in many spheres through political and social development. In spite of this, the Germans are bound together not only by the common language, the common history, a still-existing, persisting feeling of belonging to one another, but also by the common destiny of cleavage brought about by the Second World War and its consequences.

TREATY BETWEEN THE FEDERAL REPUBLIC AND THE UNION OF SOVIET SOCIALIST REPUBLICS (EXCERPTS)

Article 1

The Federal Republic of Germany and the Union of Soviet Socialist Republics consider it an important objective of their policies to maintain international peace and achieve détente.

They affirm their endeavor to further the normalization of the situation in Europe and the development of peaceful relations among all European States, and in so doing proceed from the actual situation existing in this region. . . .

Article 3

In accordance with the foregoing purposes and principles the Federal Republic of Germany and the Union of Soviet Socialist Republics share the realization that peace can only be maintained in Europe if nobody disturbs the present frontiers.

They undertake to respect without restriction the territorial integrity of all States in Europe within their present frontiers; they declare that they have no territorial claims against anybody nor will they assert such claims in the future; they regard today and shall in future regard the frontiers of all States in Europe as inviolable such as they are on the date of signature of the present Treaty, including the Oder-Neisse line which forms the western frontier of the People's Republic of Poland and the frontier between the Federal Republic of Germany and the German Democratic Republic.

Article 4

The present Treaty between the Federal Republic of Germany and the Union of Soviet Socialist Republics shall not affect any bilateral or multilateral treaties or arrangements previously concluded by them. . . .

BRANDT'S TELEVISION ADDRESS FROM MOSCOW

Dear fellow-citizens:

The signing of the treaty between the Soviet Union and the Federal Republic of Germany is an important moment in our postwar history.

Twenty-five years after the capitulation of the German Reich destroyed by Hitler and fifteen years after Konrad Adenauer established diplomatic relations here in Moscow, it is our aim to revise our relationship with the East—and indeed to revise ideas on the mutual renunciation of force, proceeding from the political situation existing in Europe. . . .

This treaty with the Soviet Union is a success of this country's postwar policy. It is a decisive step to improve our relations with the Soviet Union and our Eastern neighbors— a quarter of a century after the catastrophe that demanded unspeakable sacrifices from the peoples, in the East even more than in the West.

It is in the interest of the whole German people to improve relations with the Soviet Union, which is not only one of the great world powers but also bears her part of the special responsibility for Germany as a whole and for Berlin.

Nine years ago tomorrow the Wall was built. Today, I confidently hope, we have made a beginning to counter the cleavage, so that people no longer need to die on barbed wire, so that the division of our people can hopefully be overcome one day.

Europe ends neither at the Elbe nor on Poland's Eastern frontier. Russia is inextricably involved in European history, not only as an enemy and a danger but also as a partner— historically, politically, culturally, and economically.

Only when we in Western Europe look this partnership in the face and only when the peoples of Eastern Europe see this can we come to a settlement of interests.

Dear fellow-citizens, nothing is lost by signing this treaty that was not lost a long time ago. We have the courage to open a fresh page in history. This will be of benefit above all to the younger generation which has grown up in peace and without responsibility for the past but which must bear the consequences of the War as no one can escape the history of his people. . . .

Evaluation

OPENING THE DOOR

The treaty initialed by Walter Scheel and his delegation in Moscow was described by the Foreign Minister on his return to this country in these words: "A treaty which, without altering the fact that we are covered by the protection of an alliance and friendship with our partners in the West, now opens a door for us to Eastern Europe—a door which presents great new possibilities for us, the people of the Federal Republic."

Friends in the West and no enemies in the East—this is a situation which people in this country have rarely enjoyed.

Until now in times of war this country has kept morale high with slogans such as "more enemies, more honor." We have found ourselves more or less alone against all others. In times of peace we have all too often found ourselves in an Eastern camp confronting the West, or in a Western camp confronting the East.

The Moscow Treaty, on the other hand, is expressly aimed at promoting peace in Europe and serving the cause of detente. It is designed to provide the basis for a process of normalization between the two countries concerned in the treaty, and later perhaps normalization between West and East.

Die Zeit,
August 7, 1970.

NO GENUINE CONCESSIONS

Disregarding for a moment the verbal greenery, two facts prove to be of decisive importance: first, the undeniable acknowledgement of the status quo in Central Europe to the benefit of policies persistently pursued by the Soviet Union and second, the Berlin question, a solution to which is formally dependent on the Four Allies but in practice depends on the Soviet Union, in whose sphere of influence the city is located.

Debate on these two issues can only continue at home. As far as the Russians are concerned the treaty is signed, sealed, and delivered. They are in any case convinced that they have gone a long way toward meeting the German demands—and so is the Federal government in Bonn.

It is pointed out that the intervention clause has been eliminated and that the preamble, in particular, incorporates and formalizes the right of self-determination.

In view of the widespread feeling of euphoria it will not be easy to make it clear that no genuine concessions have been made. The Soviet Union is giving nothing away. It is merely satisfying a need for verbiage—formulas that will have no practical results other than what Moscow is prepared to countenance.

The concessions this country has made are of greater consequence because the power ratio, or rather the imbalance in power between the two sides, compels Bonn to adopt an extremely cautious approach.

Die Welt,
August 11, 1970.

A HISTORICAL MILESTONE

The signing of the Bonn-Moscow Treaty by the two heads of government is a historic act in relations between the two countries. Even though it is a far cry from the Rapallo treaty of spring 1922 and the Ribbentrop-Molotov pact of August 1939, it will prove of no less significance for Europe and the rest of the world.

What has changed is the balance of power between the two sides. In 1922 two weak countries agreed to help each other in overcoming the consequences of the First World War. In 1939 two powerful countries joined forces to annihilate Poland. Now one of the main victors and the loser of the Second World War have concluded a treaty designed to eliminate the poison of mistrust in international relations.

Hannoversche Presse,
August 12, 1970.

INDEX

Action Center for Independent and Socialist Students, 263
Action for Democratic Progress party, 129, 138 (*tab.*), 247
Adenauer, Konrad, 85, 124, 153, 160, 267, 318; anti-Communism of, 246–47, 287, 292, 294, 306; Chancellery powers and, 65, 70, 120–21, 130, 157, 158, 162, 164, 178, 181; Cologne and, 79, 81, 139, 203; Constitutional Court and, 231, 234; Laender and, 201, 202; Western alliance policies of, 155, 301–302, 309, 314
Adorno, Theodor, 248, 253, 254
agriculture, 5, 22, 50, 61 (*tab.*), 73, 199, 279; collectives (GDR) and, 41, 55–57, 266, 271, 281; election of 1969 (FRG) and, 129, 134, 136, 141–42, 143 (*tab.*), 144; interest groups (FRG) and, 41–42, 89, 90, 92, 167, 168, 169; Nazis and, 31
Agriculture Ministry (FRG), 153, 165
Alleman, Fritz René, 314–15
Allied Powers, 35, 209, 249, 391; civil service reform and, 211–13; Economic Council of, 67–68; Laender creation by, 72–73, 192; municipal government and, 204; Nazi trials and, 66, 110; party licensing by, 236; the press and, 98; Prussia and, 72, 191–92; surveillance by, 75; taxation and, 194; Western-Soviet rift, 36, 44, 68, 246; World War I and, 15

Altmann, Ruediger, 249
Anti-Cartel Law (FRG, 1957), 48
Apel, Erich, 277
Apel, Hans, 268
APO (Extra-Parliamentary Opposition), 78, 136, 137
armies (*see also* Reichswehr [Germany]), 61 (*tab.*), 71, 302; militarism and, 6, 11–12, 21, 26, 27, 28, 31–32, 33, 34, 89, 129, 216, 301, 303–305
artisans, 22, 90, 92, 168 (*tab.*), 279; anti-Semitism and, 14, 31
assembly, right of, 11, 16, 70, 235, 237
atomic warfare, 117, 118, 156, 234, 295
Aussenpolitik (periodical), 314
Austria, 7, 9, 27, 32, 36, 124, 214, 292; anti-Semitism in, 14; code law of, 229; Holy Roman Empire of, 4, 6, 8
Austro-Prussian War, 9
authoritarianism (*see also* National Socialist party), 106 (*tab.*), 154, 156; GDR and, 269, 270–71, 272, 274–81; law and, 225, 229; New Left view of, 243–44, 246, 248–49, 253, 257–63; of Prussia, 7–8, 9–13, 15; secrecy and, 97; Weimar Republic and, 15–17, 19, 21, 23–24, 25
automobiles, 49–50, 52, 220, 268

Baden-Wuerttemberg, FRG, 159, 183, 192, 204, 233–34, 256;

SA (*Sturmabteilung*), 28
Saar, the, 31, 183, 192; tax income, 197, 198 (*tab.*)
Scheel, Walter, 86, 161, 165, 306; quoted, 319
Scheuch, Erwin, quoted, 243–44
Schiller, J.C.F. von, 17
Schiller, Karl, 85, 128, 132, 162, 165, 218; currency revaluation and, 134, 140, 160
Schleswig-Holstein, FRG, 72, 146, 183, 192, 198 (*tab.*), 202; city government in, 204, 205
Schmidt, Helmut,161, 165, 290
Schmitt, Carl, 250
Schnez, Albert, quoted, 305
Schopenhauer, Arthur, 8
Schroeder, Gerhard, 159, 287
Schuetz, Wilhelm Wolfgang, 288
Schumacher, Kurt, 79, 82, 84, 178, 309
Schweitzer, Albert, 261 (*tab.*)
science, 13, 106 (*tab.*), 107, 251, 254; GDR and, 273–74, 275, 278, 282, 283–84, 285
Scientific Research Ministry (FRG), 165
SED, *see* Sozialistische Einheitspartei Deutschlands (SED)
sex (*see also* women), 263
Shonfield, Andrew, quoted, 217–18
Sik, Ota, 274
Silesia, 40, 42, 308
Social Democratic party (SPD), (*see also* Grand Coalition), 42, 46, 67, 69, 77, 78, 79, 80, 81–85, 92, 179; Bad Godesberg program of, 82–83, 91, 141; Cold War and, 287–88, 289, 290, 291, 297, 300, 306, 314; East German SED and, 82, 270; election of 1969 and, 127–48, 153, 155, 165, 170; Emergency Laws and, 74; the Empire and, 11, 14, 15; FDP coalition and, 85–86, 127–28, 138, 140, 159, 160–63, 201, 288, 308–309; Heinemann and, 153, 154, 155; judicial review and, 228, 230, 231, 234, 235; Landtag elections and, 202; mem-

Social Democratic party (SPD) (cont.)
bership of, 82, 94, 95–96, 119–20, 144, 168, 171; Moscow Treaty and, 308; New Left view of, 84, 245–46; planning and, 68, 83, 218, 222; subsidy issue and, 121–23; Weimar Republic and, 17, 20, 23, 25, 29, 30, 81
Socialism, *see* Marxism; Social Democratic party (SPD)
Socialist Reich party (SRP), 87, 236
social science, 248–55, 259–60; in the GDR, 278, 283–84, 285
social security, 14; courts, 228
Sontheimer, Kurt, 249
South Korea, 46, 65, 300
Soviet Union, 14, 17, 35, 36, 40, 48, 61 (*tab.*), 67; Brandt and, 289, 290, 305–306, 307–309, 318–19; FRG attitudes toward, 108, 246, 265, 296, 298, 300, 313–314, 319–21; GDR trade of, 54, 277; GDR worker revolt (1953), 266; income, 267 (*tab.*); invasion of Czechoslovakia (1968), 274, 285, 299, 300; land reform in, 55; Moscow Treaty (1970), 307–309, 313–21; New Economic System and, 59, 60, 282; Nuremberg Trials and, 66; Olympics and, 293; Warsaw Pact and, 302
Soviet Union Presidium, 275
Sozialistische Einheitspartei Deutschlands (SED), 82, 270–77, 279, 281, 288
Sozialistischer Deutscher Studentenbund (SDS), 95, 254, 257, 263
Sozialistischer Hochschul Bund (SHB), 95
Spain, 32, 48, 246, 267, 293
SPD, *see* Social Democratic Party (SPD)
speech, freedom of, 16, 70, 74, 100–101, 105 (*tab.*), 237; dissent and, 95, 113–16, 238–39
Spiegel, Der (periodical), 101, 116, 121–22, 155, 239